BATHROOM SONGS

Fig. 1. Hieronymus Bosch, *Ship of Fools* (1490–1500)

First published in 2017 by punctum books, Earth, Milky Way.
https://punctumbooks.com

ISBN-13: 978-1-947447-30-1 (print)
ISBN-13: 978-1-947447-31-8 (ePDF)

LCCN: 2017957440
Library of Congress Cataloging Data is available from the Library of Congress

Book design: Vincent W.J. van Gerven Oei
Cover image: Photograph of Eve Kosofsky Sedgwick with Buttons (Dayton, c. 1954) by Leon Kosofsky.

HIC SVNT MONSTRA

Bathroom Songs

Eve Kosofsky Sedgwick as a Poet

Edited by Jason Edwards

To our dear friend Hal —
who made it all possible —
who's always so kind.

Sarah McCarry,
What would we do without you?
How much less we'd know.

Contents

Acknowledgments

I am grateful to the History of Art department at the University of York and the Eve Kosofsky Sedgwick Foundation, for funding the conference that formed the origin of many of the chapters of this book. I want to thank Ben Madden, for talking Merrill with me, and much else. It has also been nothing but a pleasure to work with both Eileen Joy and Vincent W.J. van Gerven Oei at punctum books.

I shall be eternally in the debt of Hal A. Sedgwick and Sarah McCarry for giving me access to the Eve Kosofsky Sedgwick archive, and to Wabi-Sabi, its resident divinity, for keeping me company there. I will probably never get over Hal's generosity in suggesting that Sedgwick's uncollected poems be a part of this volume. My ridiculous love for Hal, Sarah, and all the contributors to this volume knows no bounds. Finally, to Eve, who I think about every day and whose life and work mean the world to me. As Shawn Colvin says of Joni Mitchell, "me wimp, you master". Master, I lay this succulent mouse at your door. I probably got almost everything wrong but I hope you didn't just hate this.

PART I

EVE KOSOFSKY
SEDGWICK
AS A POET

Bathroom Songs?
Eve Kosofsky Sedgwick as a Poet

Jason Edwards

An Important Writer of, and on, Poetry?

Waking in the morning, I remember first
I'm grown up. I have some money and a car
and anything I want, to cook and eat,
and (in the horrid, doggerel blank verse
in which I — no, not "think" — but breathe, and represent
continually to my own ear the place
of my unthinkingness) repeats, repeats
some vapid version of a Shakespeare phrase,
"Yet Edmund was beloved."
Waking alone, yet E- is beloved.
Also: "an important writer of
fiction and poetry,"
                              of *criticism*
and poetry, of course, it's meant to say,
but 'fiction', in this empty register,
scans, so "fiction" in my head it always is.

— Eve Kosofsky Sedgwick, 'The Warm Decembers'[1]

---

1   Eve Kosofsky Sedgwick, *Fat Art, Thin Art* (Durham: Duke University Press, 1994), 147.

Bathroom Songs represents the first study to consider the poetry of one of the most significant literary theorists of the late-twentieth and early-twenty-first centuries, Eve Kosofsky Sedgwick. Most renowned for her trilogy of ground-breaking, queer-theoretical texts — *Between Men: English Literature and Male Homosocial Desire* (1985), *Epistemology of the Closet* (1990), and *Tendencies* (1993) — Sedgwick was, from the outset, and always in her mind a poet. For example, as Hal A. Sedgwick documented, all of the entries on his wife's CV from 1967 to 1975 were prizes for poetry.[2] In 1977, Sedgwick submitted her first book of poems, *Traceable, Salient, Thirsty,* to various presses, containing key poems from the previous four years; but the volume, bafflingly, failed to find a publisher.

Undeterred, Sedgwick began work, the following year, on her most ambitious poem: 'The Warm Decembers' (1978–1986), a meta-Victorian novella that would find a home in *Fat Art, Thin Art* (1994), the only collection of poetry Sedgwick published during her lifetime. The volume was acclaimed as a "work of poetic distinction and indispensable human use" by fellow poet Allen Grossman, and as a "thrilling experience" by literary critic Maud Ellmann, who thought the poems proved Sedgwick one of the "truly innovative" poets of her generation. Richard Howard, meanwhile, located Sedgwick in a tradition of American critic-poets, whose critical and poetical interests were closely entwined.[3]

In 1999, Sedgwick published a second book of poetry, *A Dialogue on Love* — considered in this volume, in the context of queer therapy, in a deeply informed essay by Monica Pearl. The book represented a haibun memoir of Sedgwick's psychotherapy with Shannon Van Wey. Employing a seventeenth-century Japanese form, much loved by James Merrill, the volume wove together haiku and prose. The book was also a key companion volume, and partly an autobiographical guide, to *Fat Art, Thin Art.*

---

2   Hal. A Sedgwick, 'A Note on 'The 1001 Séances'', *GLQ* 17.4 (2011), 452–453.

3   All cited on the flyleaf to *Fat Art, Thin Art.*

Mindful of such details, *Bathroom Songs* develops, in four ways, our sense of what Hal Sedgwick characterized as his wife's "complex and changing relation" to poetry, especially her own.[4] Firstly, by providing, in this essay, an unusually 'fat' — indeed potentially 'obese' — introduction to Sedgwick's collected poetry and writings about poets; one taking advantage of her preference for corpulent aesthetics. The first part of the book then includes six alternately svelte and generously proportioned essays, on *Fat Art, Thin Art* and *A Dialogue on Love*. The second part of the book subsequently includes more than forty of Sedgwick's previously uncollected poems, ranging from the final narrative poem and lyrics she published before her death in 2009 to the earliest writings of her adolescence. These poems are prefaced and contextualized, in a seventh essay, within the context of Sedgwick's broader corpus.

Beyond *Novel Gazing*: Numerous Poems are Being Read and Written

In spite of her fame as a novel gazer, Sedgwick wrote repeatedly about the English, European, American, and East Asian poetic canons, penning eleven essays on poetry across her career.[5] These included 'The 1001 Seances', on Merrill (1975);[6] Walt 'Whitman's Transatlantic Context: Class, Gender, and Male Homosexual Style' (1983);[7] 'Swan in Love: The Example of Shakespeare's Sonnets' (1985);[8] Alfred Lord 'Tennyson's *Princess*: One

---

4   Sedgwick, 'A Note', 453.

5   For more on Sedgwick and the novel form, see Sedgwick, ed., *Novel Gazing: Queer Readings in Fiction* (Durham: Duke University Press, 1997).

6   Sedgwick, 'The 1001 Seances', *GLQ* 17.4 (2001), 457–517.

7   Sedgwick, 'Whitman's Transatlantic Context: Class, Gender and Male Homosexual Style', *Delta* 16 (1984), 111–124; reprinted as 'Coda: Towards the Twentieth Century: English Readers of Whitman', in *Between Men: English Literature and Male Homosocial Desire* (Columbia: Columbia University Press, 1985), 201–218.

8   Sedgwick, 'Swan in Love: The Example of Shakespeare's Sonnets' (1985); *Between Men*, 28–48.

Bride for Seven Brothers' (1985);[9] 'A Poem is Being Written' (1985), on her own poetic practice;[10] 'Writing, Gay Studies, and Affection' (1991), a memorial for poet Michael Lynch;[11] 'White Glasses' (1991), a second, more famous memorial for Lynch;[12] the afterword to *Gary in York Pocket: Stories and Notebooks of Gary Fisher* (1996), on queer-of-colour American poet, Gary Fisher;[13] 'Confusion of Tongues' (1996), a second essay on Whitman, co-authored with Michael Moon;[14] and 'Cavafy, Proust, and the Queer Little Gods' (2007).[15]

In the latter, Sedgwick described how important Cavafy's "antidepressant" poetry had been to her body and soul, and the "peculiar feelings of tenderness and intimacy" she felt for it "stored-up" and "half-remembered" for decades.[16] 'Confusion

---

9 Sedgwick, 'Tennyson's Princess: One Bride for Seven Brothers', *Between Men*, 118–133.

10 Sedgwick, 'A Poem is Being Written', Representations 17 (Winter 1987), 110–143; reprinted in *Tendencies* (Durham: Duke University Press, 1993), 177–214.

11 Sedgwick, 'Writing, Gay Studies and Affection', *Lesbian and Gay Studies Newsletter* 18 (November 1991), 8–13.

12 Sedgwick, 'White Glasses', *Yale Journal of Criticism* 5.3 (Fall 1992), 193–208, reprinted in *Tendencies*, 252–266. For more, see Monica Pearl, 'Eve Kosofsky Sedgwick's Melancholic 'White Glasses'', *Textual Practice* 17.1 (2003), 61–80.

13 Sedgwick, 'Afterword' to ed., *Gary in Your Pocket: Stories and Notebooks of Gary Fisher* (Durham: Duke University Press, 1996), 273–291. For more see Jose Esteban Munoz, 'Race, Sex and the Incommensurate: Gary Fisher with Eve Kosofsky Sedgwick', in Elahe Yekani, Eveline Killian and Beatrice Michaelis, eds., *Queer Futures: Reconsidering Ethics, Activism, and the Political* (Aldershot: Ashgate, 2013), 103–115; and Ellis Hanson, 'The Future's Eve: Reparative Readings After Sedgwick', *South Atlantic Quarterly* 110.1 (2011), 101–119.

14 Sedgwick and Michael Moon, 'Confusion of Tongues', in Betsy Erkkila and Jay Grossman, eds., *Breaking Bounds: Whitman and American Cultural Studies* (Oxford: Oxford University Press, 1996), 23–29.

15 Sedgwick, 'Cavafy, Proust and the Queer Little Gods', *The Weather in Proust* (ed. Jonathan Goldberg; Durham: Duke University Press, 2011), 42–69. Given its use of Randall Jarrell's 'Hope' as a prefatory poem, we might also think about 'Interlude: Pedagogic' (2003), as a piece in dialogue with Jarrell (*Touching Feeling: Affect, Pedagogy, Performativity* [Durham: Duke University Press, 2003], 27–34).

16 Sedgwick, *The Weather in Proust*, 42–43.

of Tongues', meanwhile, was published in the play-script style of Sedgwick and Moon's better-known 'Divinity' essay,[17] the essay's title deriving from a psychoanalytic article that represented a significant source for Sedgwick's narrative poems: Sándor Ferenczi's 'Confusion of Tongues Between Adults and the Child: The Language of Tenderness and of Passion' (1932).[18] Sedgwick and Moon's exchange begins with, and often features, their speaking *as* Whitman without quotation marks. In so doing, the essay consciously follows Louisa Whitman's epistolary poetics, her lack of "marks of punctuation, except for a rare close parenthesis"; a confusion of tongues that was one of Sedgwick's favourite poetic idioms, as we shall see, as a means of exploring the play of "intense identifications and dis-identifications" amongst poets, critics, and others.[19]

But poetry, generally, was central to Sedgwick's literary criticism and too-little-known work as both a poet and fibre artist, with genres of interest including haiku, lyric, and narrative poetry; soliloquies and dramatic monologues; prayers, hymns, and lullabies; grave, votary inscriptions and pseudo-inscriptions; pop and country songs as well as the blues; Bible and bedtime stories as well as bathroom songs; the fictional and factional, autobiographical, and literary critical; as well as the epistolary, novelistic and pornographic. Sedgwick's texts and textiles are also dappled with the voices of Virgil, Dante, and Chaucer; Wyatt, Shakespeare, Traherne, and Spenser; Gryphius and Milton, Marvel and Lovelace, Pope and Cowper; with Bashō, Ryoho, and Saikuku; Choko, Fusen, and Saiba; Roshu and Kyotara;

---

17 Michael Moon and Eve Kosofsky Sedgwick, 'Divinity: A Performance Piece, A Little Understood Emotion', *Tendencies*, 215–251.

18 Ferenczi, Sándor. 'Confusion of Tongues Between Adults and the Child' (1933), in Michael Balint, ed., *Final Contributions to the Problems and Methods of Psycho-Analysis* (London: Karnac, 1994), 156–167. The overlapping Ferenczian eroticism of children and adults finds an early articulation in the sonnet 'To a Swimmer', which compares the "wet forehead" and "straggling defiant hair" of a post-ejaculatory lover, to a fantasy of that same man as a "shivering schoolboy" just "out of the water" the day he won his school a race.

19 Moon and Sedgwick, 'Confusion of Tongues', 26.

with Shelley and Keats; Wordsworth and the Lake Poets; von Scheffel, Blake, and Byron; with Rossetti and Bronte; the Brownings and Hopkins; Baudelaire, Swinburne and Tennyson; with Longfellow, Whitman, and Dickinson; with Kipling, Wilde, T.E. Lawrence, and Cavafy; with Yeats and Pound, Stevens and Eliot; Cummings, Auden, Frost and Stein; with Cornford, Plath, Bishop and Sexton; Riche, Gluck and Lorde; Jarrold and Winters; Merrill, Lynch, Gunn, and Fisher; as well as Dr. Seuss and Untermeyer, and the lyrics of Folliott S. Pierpoint and Isaac Watts; Lorenz Hart, Yip Harburg, and George Gershwin; June Carter Cash and Loretta Lynn; Bessie Smith, Hank Williams, Woodie Guthrie, and Conway Twittey; with Dionne Warwick, Nina Simone, Carly Simon, and Sheena Easton.

Sedgwick's most notorious and influential account of poetry is, certainly, 'A Poem is Being Written': her mid-eighties meditation on her own poetry. "Part of the motivation behind" the essay, Sedgwick acknowledged, was a "fantasy that readers or hearers would be variously — in anger, identification, pleasure, envy, 'permission'" and "exclusion" be "stimulated to write accounts 'like' this one (whatever that means) of their own and share those".[20] (The six contributors to *Bathroom Songs* have taken Sedgwick at her word, the first person looms large in this collection).

'A Poem is Being Written' explored examples of Sedgwick's poetry within the context of her queer autobiography and, in so doing, provided a precedent for *A Dialogue on Love*. The essay also provided a provocative account of lyric and narrative poetry *tout court,* that changed the way many readers came to consider the foot, beat, and s/m erotics of meter; the straddling together and pushing apart of *enjambment*; and the cropped, immobilized tableau of the lyric and dilations of narrative verse. In addition, the essay printed a number of poems not included elsewhere in Sedgwick's corpus: the now lost 'Stillborn Child' (1951) that she had written aged eleven; parts of 'Lawrence Reads *La Morte d'Arthur* in the Desert' (1964), written at thirteen and

---

20 Sedgwick, *Tendencies*, 214.

included here in full for the first time; and a trio of poems from the mid-1970s, completed as she was finishing her Ph.D. at Yale: 'Lost Letter' (1974), 'The Palimpsest' (1974), and 'Everything Always Distracts' (1975), again printed here for the first time; as well as significant sections of 'The Warm Decembers', which she had been working on for the previous seven years.[21] 'The Palimpsest' was originally published, alongside another uncollected poem reprinted here, 'Explicit', in the Winter 1975 issue of *Epoch*.[22] At around the same moment, Sedgwick published three other poems, this time in *Poetry Miscellany*: 'An Essay on the Picture Plane', which she later included in *Fat Art, Thin Art*; as well as two more previously uncollected poems, collected here: 'When, in Minute Script' and 'Ring of Fire'.[23] Two years, earlier, in 1973, Sedgwick published another poem again collected here, 'A Death by Water', in the Fall 1973 issue of *Epoch*.[24]

This did not, however, represent Sedgwick's first foray as a published poet. During her undergraduate degree at Cornell (1967–1970), she published two poems in *Trojan Horse*, a student literary magazine. This was the first venue in which readers could access the later republished 'Ring of Fire' and an otherwise neglected poem, collected here for the first time: 'Siegfried Rex von Munthe, Soldier and Poet, Killed December, 1939, on the Graf Spee', which is one of a number of poems indicating Sedgwick's interest in German poetry and cultural history, as we shall see.[25]

---

21 Sedgwick's Yale Ph.D., with the addition of its final chapter, 'The Character in the Veil: Imagery of Surface in the Gothic Novel', would become her first monograph, *The Coherence of Gothic Conventions* (New York: Arno, 1985).

22 Sedgwick, 'Explicit' and 'The Palimpsest', *Epoch* 24.2 (Winter 1975), 112–113.

23 Sedgwick, 'Ring of Fire', 'An Essay on the Picture Plane', and 'When in Minute Script', *Poetry Miscellany* 5 (1975), 42–44.

24 Sedgwick, 'A Death by Water', *Epoch* 23.3 (Fall 1973), 78–79.

25 For more on Sedgwick's time at Cornell, see Linda B. Glaser, 'The College Years of Eve Kosofsky Sedgwick, A Founder of Queer Theory', http://as.cornell.edu/college-years-eve-kosofsky-sedgwick-founder-queer-theory. I am grateful to Stuart Taberner for his help with Sedgwick's German sources.

In addition to ongoing work on 'The Warm Decembers', Sedgwick continued to develop her poetic career across the two decades spanning the completion of her doctorate and the publication of *Between Men*. In the Winter of 1979, *Salmagundi* published 'Sexual Hum', a poem later collected in *Fat Art Thin Art*.[26] In March 1980, Sedgwick published, in *Diacritics*, 'Trace at 46', a second, novella-length narrative poem.[27] This was again collected in *Fat Art, Thin Art,* but a poem to which Sedgwick had drawn attention in *Between Men*, where she documented that, eight years earlier, she had been at work on a "narrative poem about a musicologist with a writer's block".[28]

Whilst at work on *Between Men,* Sedgwick sought to develop her poetic profile further. In Winter 1984, she published 'Sestina Lente', in the *Massachusetts Review,* another poem collected into *Fat Art, Thin Art*.[29] In 1986, she published 'Selections from *The Warm Decembers*' in the fall issue of *Raritan*.[30] At some point before 1994, Sedgwick also published, on her Duke University homepage, a now-lost online resource, 'Shame and Mourning: A Dossier', to "catalyse some thoughts" on the topics of shame, mourning, and pedagogy, in the context of AIDS and "other identity-implicating illnesses". This contained fifteen lyrics from what would be the first section of *Fat Art, Thin Art,* which was, then, still "forthcoming"; thus, the first appearance of 'Joy! He's himself today! He Knows Me!', 'Guys Who Were 35 Last Year Are 70 This', 'Grave, Never Offering Back The Face of My Dear', 'A Vigil', 'The Navajo Rug', 'The Use of Being Fat', 'For Years It Drove Me Crazy', 'Not Like The Clownish, Friendly Way You Talk', 'How Not To Be There', 'Mobility, Speech, Sight', 'A Scar, Just a Scar', 'Not', 'Nicht Mehr Leben', and 'Performative (Toronto)' and 'Performative (San Francisco)'.[31]

---

26 Sedgwick, 'Sexual Hum', *Salmagundi* (Winter 1979).

27 Sedgwick, 'Trace at 46', *Diacritics* 10.1 (March 1980), 3–20.

28 Sedgwick, Between Men, 161.

29 Sedgwick, 'Sestina Lente', *Massachusetts Review* 25.4 (Winter 1984).

30 Sedgwick, 'Selections from The Warm Decembers', *Raritan* 6.2 (Fall 1986).

31 Sedgwick, 'Shame and Mourning: A Dossier', http://www.duke/edu/sedgwic/WRITING/SHAME.htm.

Meanwhile, in 1994, the year that *Fat Art, Thin Art* finally came out, Sedgwick published two lyrics excepted from that volume. 'Our' was published on September 25, 1994 in the *Raleigh News and Observer,* while 'Penn Central: New Haven Line' was printed on October 2 in the *Los Angeles Review of Books,* presumably to advertise the publication of *Fat Art, Thin Art.*[32]

Sedgwick published just four more poems during her lifetime, all collected here. January 1996 saw the publication of the much-loved queer bedtime-story-cum-performance poem 'Pandas in Trees' in *Women and Performance: A Journal of Feminist Theory.*[33] A 'Performing Reparation' special issue of the same journal was also the place where Sedgwick published her last three poems in July 2006: the Virgilian/Cavafian 'Forsan et haec olim meinisse juvabit' ('Perhaps this, too, will be a pleasure to look back on one day'), to which we shall return, as well as 'Death', and 'Bathroom Song', the poem that gives this volume its title.[34]

Fat Art, Thin Art?

Sedgwick's first collection of poetry, *Fat Art, Thin Art,* featured three different genres of poems, each prepared for by one of Sedgwick's essays on poetry. Part I of the book, written during the therapy she subsequently described in *A Dialogue on Love,* is primarily comprised of a form peculiar to her: a kind of loosely-rhymed, thirteen-line, 'thin', sonnet-like/sonnet-light, or lost-sonnet form, whose titles, internal line breaks, or blank lines suggest or replace the ascetically missing fourteenth line. A sequence of three 'fatter' lyrics, concerned with Sedgwick's husband and big sister, incorporate a 'greedy' fifteenth line. Alternatively, the 'additional' line of 'Little kid at the airport practicing'

---

32 Sedgwick, 'Our', *Raleigh News and Observer* (September 25, 1994) and 'Penn Central: New Haven Line', *Los Angeles Times Book Review* (October 2, 1994).

33 Sedgwick, 'Pandas in Trees', *Women and Performance: A Journal of Feminist Theory* 8.2 (January 1996), 175–183.

34 Sedgwick, 'Three Poems', *Women and Performance* 16.2 (July 2006), 327–328.

may be a sign that Sedgwick is keen to signal that she is "clumsy with servitude", like the three-year old described in the poem, who, similarly, can't quite master form.[35] 'In dreams they're interchangeable', meanwhile, thematises, in both its sentences and form, a "mauled and mauling" poetic foot,[36] whilst the fifteenth line of 'Our' perhaps marks the emphatic presence, outside the predominant couple logic of the poem itself, of the theatrically included/excluded single person. Sedgwick had prepared her readers for these sonnet-like forms through her earlier essay on Shakespeare.[37]

Part II of *Fat Art, Thin Art* contained six earlier, pornographic lyrics of the kind Sedgwick prepared her readers for in 'A Poem is Being Written'. These included the part art-historical, part-literary-theoretical 'An Essay on the Picture Plane' (1973), considered in a poignant, autobiographical essay, in this volume, by Angus Brown; and part of a wider intertextual and interdisciplinary practice, across Sedgwick's work. For example, 'Penn Central: New Haven Line' (1972) contains an epigraph from Northrop Frye, which, like the 'Last Poem of Y*r W*nt*rs', collected here for the first time, suggests the intimate relationship between Sedgwick's lyrics and New Critical theories of close reading.[38] 'Everything Always Distracts' and 'Sexual Hum' (both 1975), meanwhile, employ a tercet stanza form, derived from Shelley via Swinburne, which finds an echo in Sedgwick's earlier ambitious desire to provide an ending for Shelley's 'The

---

35 Sedgwick, *Fat Art, Thin Art*, 31.

36 Sedgwick, *Fat Art, Thin Art*, 32.

37 In addition, the first section of *Fat Art, Thin Art* includes a number of even fatter and thinner lyrics: 'In dreams on which decades of marriage haven't' possesses 22 lines; 'A Vigil' contains 41 lines; whilst 'Crushed. Dilapidated' contains an appropriately compressed eight lines; and 'When I got so sick it never occurred to me' a diminished 7. Part I also includes a long, dedicatory poem, 'Who Fed This Muse?' considered, in this volume, in breathtaking essays by Kathryn R. Kent and Mary Baine Campbell.

38 For more on Sedgwick in the context of the close reading tradition, see Angus Connell Brown, *Between Lines: Close Reading, Quotation, and Critical Style from Practical Criticism to Queer Theory*, Ph.D. dissertation, Oxford University, 2014.

Triumph of Life' (1822), reprinted for the first time here.[39] Such poems reveal a career-long preference for various, three-line forms that Sedgwick would return to in the haiku-rich *A Dialogue on Love* and across her fibre art work.

The two groups of lyrics, which move backwards in queer time from the mid-1990s, in part one of *Fat Art, Thin Art,* to the mid-1970s, in part two, are woven together with a third genre, another Sedgwick specialty.[40] This is the novella-length narrative poem, in the form of both 'Trace at 46', in section II, and 'The Warm Decembers', in section III, which Sedgwick had again prepared her readers for in her essay on Tennyson's narrative poem, *The Princess* (1847). We turn to these narrative poems next, to explore the close inter-relationship, in Sedgwick's oeuvre, of poetry and theory.

'Trace at 46', or Sedgwick's Grammatological Poetics

In her afterword to 'The Warm Decembers', Sedgwick documented that one of her primary motivations had been to explore the ways in which the "most writerly writing" and "thinkerly thinking" were not "generically alien to each other".[41] Her two novella-length narrative poems, 'Trace at 46' and 'The Warm Decembers' are, perhaps, the place where the genres of poetry and theory rub up against each other most fruitfully. For example, it is evident, from its title alone, that there may a relationship between 'Trace at 46' and Jacques Derrida's meditation on the 'trace' in *De la grammatologie* (1967). Indeed, during the time that Sedgwick began working on 'Trace', in the mid-1970s,

---

39 For more on Swinburne's poetic fascination with s/m, see John Vincent's 'Flogging is Fundamental: Applications of Birch in Lesbia Brandon', in Sedgwick, ed., *Novel Gazing,* 269–298.

40 For more on queer temporality and travelling backwards in time, see Heather Love, *Feeling Backward: Loss and the Politics of Queer History* (Cambridge: Harvard University Press, 2009); and Jane Gallop, 'Sedgwick's Twisted Temporalities, Or Even Just Reading and Writing'. in E.L. McCallum and Mikko Tuhkanen, eds., *Queer Times, Queer Becomings* (Albany: State University of New York Press, 2011), 47–75.

41 Sedgwick, *Fat Art, Thin Art,* 160.

not only was the English translation of Derrida's *De la gram-matologie* published in 1976, but Derrida took up a post at Yale in 1975, the year in which Sedgwick was appointed to a year-long lectureship in New Haven, having already worked with a number of Yale School deconstructionists, strongly influenced by Derrida, including Paul De Man, Harold Bloom, Geoffrey Hartman, and J. Hillis Miller, who had chaired her doctoral committee.

Given the necessary brevity of this section, it is impossible to trace in full the complex relationship between these two texts, particularly given the emphatically 'writerly' writing of Der-rida and Sedgwick and that the word 'trace' appears more than 200 times in *Of Grammatology*. But a number of broad areas of overlap are worth emphasizing. Both texts are concerned with what Gayatri Chakravorty Spivak, in her translator's preface to the English edition of *Of Grammatology*, calls "the structure of knowing", and are interested in, but also challenge, what Spivak calls "the self-moving activity of cognition".[42] 'Trace' and Gram-matology also both want to think about what Derrida calls the *dissemination* of ideas, idioms, and textures, which open, in others, the possibility of different thoughts.[43] In Sedgwick's case, this is evident in the diffusion, across Trace's familial, social and sexual circles of his interest in water, silk, and costume jewel-lery; "walkiness", Gamelan music, and French composers Ga-briel Faure, and Claude Debussy; and similar osmoses across professional practices including poetry, psychoanalysis, literary criticism, anthropology, musical composition, and musicolo-gy.[44] Indeed, 'Trace' and *Of Grammatology* share a particular passion for musical and sonic traces. Trace himself is a musi-

---

42 Gayatri Chakravorty Spivak, 'Translater's Preface' to Jacques Derrida, *Of Grammatology* (trans. Gayatri Chakravorty Spivak; 1967; Baltimore: Johns Hopkins, 1976); ix–lxxxix; x.

43 Spivak, *Of Grammatology,* x–xii, xvii.

44 For example, Cissy acknowledges in detail "how clearly her recent produc-tiveness / has a filial bond to Trace"; whilst Flo's thighs are slightly chafed by "sensations of weedy underclothing in silk", a present from Trace (*Fat Art, Thin Art,* 62).

cologist whilst Cissy, one of his lovers, is a composer, and the poem's interest in translations from musicology to music, from anthropology to composition, and from Javanese to European music, all function as emblems of Derrida's broad interest in the "sonorous".[45]

In addition, 'Trace' shares Derrida's interest in what he calls the "fabric of the trace",[46] with Cissy trying to capture a "lure into texture, a texture not of contingency / or the lapse of other structure", but the

> ubiquity on every surface
> of every structure, waiting for the graze
> of any tangent of attention, to grow
> at once traceable, salient, thirsty[;][47]

the last three words giving the title to Sedgwick's rejected first book of poetry.

'Trace at 46', however, adds a more emphatically feminist-relational texture to the precise question of what it means to be in relation to a 'trace' and, in the poem, to a person named Trace, who is preoccupied, absent minded, and only more-or-less relationally and ethically motivated.[48] As such, the poem's eponymous hero represents a perverse anthropomorphisation of a Derridean trace, who is, similarly, both there and "not there"; both the thing people think they want and "not that"; and a person with a now more or less vestigial penis, whose body is filling in, "he supposes, / with femaleness", and so a witty emblem of the (tacitly Lacanian) "lack at the origin" of the Derridean trace.[49]

Indeed, the poem might be understood as a kind of queer, novella-length exploration of what Spivak calls the "trace-

---

45 Derrida, *Of Grammatology*, 65, 123.

46 Derrida, *Of Grammatology*, 65.

47 Sedgwick, *Fat Art, Thin Art*, 66.

48 For Derrida's discussion of the trace and its "immotivation" and "demotivation", see *Of Grammatology*, 51. For his discussion of its "presence-absence", see 71.

49 Sedgwick, *Fat Art, Thin Art*, 43; Spivak, *Of Grammatology*, xvii.

structure of expression", or what Derrida characterizes as "the concept" or "problematic of the trace";[50] especially as that intersects with the "structure of the relationship with the other" in Trace's strained relationships with his mother and lovers.[51] And I say *queer* because, in addition to Trace booty-calling his mother and addressing her as "Pussy", like Derrida, Sedgwick is interested in what he calls the "*a priori* space-time of the trace" in which "there is neither pure activity nor pure passivity",[52] a space that Sedgwick would later describe as "the middle ranges of agency".[53]

Finally, tracks, footprints, and furrows recur in both texts, with an anthropological passion for the lines made by various mammals across the landscape. For example, citing Claude Levi-Strauss, Derrida documents that "the furrow is the line, as the plough-man traces it", and reminds us that "writing is born with agriculture".[54] 'Trace' ends with a scene, supposedly derived from Javanese anthropology, and a sentence "furrowed — trenched, really" in the "rolling grass" visible only to the reader and "a high and distant viewer": a sentence revealing that a Trace-like male protagonist has been absent-mindedly raped, a "silver" snail-"trail" of semen disseminating from his rectum.[55] In addition, whilst Derrida focuses on a "crude trail", in Levi-Strauss, "whose 'track' is not easily distinguished from the bush", but a path that was "broken", "beaten" and "inscribed violently" in the "natural, savage [...] forest", and upon "wood as matter",[56] towards the end of 'Trace', we encounter a further faux-Javanese anthropological scene in which "two sibling mouse-deer" are "each nailed / by [their] hind paws halfway up one tree"; their

---

50 Derrida, *Of Grammatology*, 68, 70.

51 Derrida, *Of Grammatology*, 47

52 Derrida, *Of Grammatology*, 290.

53 For more, see *The Weather in Proust*, 89–93.

54 Spivak and Derrida, *Of Grammatology*, xv–xvi, 107–108, 287.

55 Sedgwick, *Fat Art, Thin Art*, 70–71.

56 Derrida, *Of Grammatology*, 107–108.

short, characteristic fur ruffled but
not broken, blood tugging against its own
viscosity to mark a trail from nostril or lips
to a stream that runs nearby from which these two tongues
                                    have supped.[57]

Sedgwick's long, *enjambed* sentence here both articulates the connectivity of the various *humanimal* traces, and emphatically breaks up the phrase as the deer are themselves rent apart, scenes of animal abjection explored in this volume, in the context of Sedgwick's 'The Warm Decembers', in Ben Westwood's ethically-important essay.

Bathroom Songs? Ferenczi and the Urethral Eroticism of 'The Warm Decembers'

                No woman knows where
her urethra is, but only some
hot floating place, at other times
imperceptible, somewhere between uterus and clitoris.
                                    — 'The Warm Decembers'[58]

The title of Sedgwick and Moon's 'Confusion of Tongues' essay on Whitman derived, as we have seen, from a 1932 article by Ferenczi. In 'A Poem is Being Written', Sedgwick pointed to the importance of the essay to 'Trace', documenting that she had been thinking of Ferenczi's contributions to the "controversy around the seduction theory" during the poem's composition, and deriving, from the analyst, a "lot of language".[59] She also documented that, eight years earlier, in 1977, she had been writing a narrative poem that "included a little literary joke: a fictional psychoanalyst in the poem was writing a fictional es-

---

57 Sedgwick, *Fat Art, Thin Art*, 69.
58 Sedgwick, *Fat Art, Thin Art*, 112.
59 Sedgwick, *Tendencies*, 198–199. The discussion of Ferenczi in the 'Confusion of Tongues' essay is on p. 27.

say for *Thalassa: A* (fictional) *Journal of Genitality,* on the then-fictional topic" of "Sustained Homosexual / Panic and Literary Productiveness" that featured "close readings from *Our Mutual Friend*". Sedgwick noted that, whilst it "didn't amount to much of a joke", it did "record the slightly incredulous beginnings" of her thinking about the "present project, and their inextricability from a reading of late Dickens".[60]

But if Sedgwick here emphasizes her poetry as the matrix of her later queer literary theory, the passage is significant in another way, particularly in its reference to *Thalassa*; in 'Trace' the name of the fictional journal, in reality the name of another Ferenczi text. *Thalassa: A Theory of Genitality* (1938) focused attention on what Ferenczi characterized as the "urethral individual" and on the "original urethrality" predating the sexual resonance of the genitals. Prioritizing "urethral [...] autoeroticism", Ferenczi characterized the "ejaculation of semen" as a "urethral phenomenon", and made clear that women could also gain "pleasure from emptying the bladder".[61] In 'Trace', Sedgwick clearly alluded to Ferenczi's text, when she had the wittily named Flo attend a "seaside conference organized / by the editors of *Thalassa: A Journal of Genitality*". Flo, herself, meanwhile, is a character who enjoys a "free-floating attention" that is characterized by "lapses / of meaning and wellings-up / of excess meaning", as well as "aggressive floodings", in the aqueous context of St Malo, in Brittany, with its "regular thalassic irrigation, then deletion, of rocks, causeways, / fortifications, outline".[62]

But Flo isn't the only character in Sedgwick's poetic novellas with thalassic interests. 'Trace' begins, as we have seen, with the eponymous central character "naked on the toilet", "brooding over himself / in his mother's bathroom".[63] To date, scholars have focused on Sedgwick's anality, and the poem that lends this volume its title, Sedgwick's last lyric, 'Bathroom Song', depicts just

60 Sedgwick, *Between Men,* 161.

61 Ferenczi, Sándor, *Thalassa: A Theory of Genitality* (1938; London: Karnac, 1989), 7, 11.

62 Ferenczi, *Thalassa*; Sedgwick, *Fat Art, Thin Art,* 60–61.

63 Sedgwick, *Fat Art, Thin Art,* 43.

that: with the poet sending her shit down the toilet, to Grandma and, tacitly, to grandpa, the aptly named Poopie,[64] as part of a meditation on dispensing with (parts of) the self, as death approaches. But, if focused on the more difficult task of "Letting go of Number Two", the poem is not oblivious to Number One. It acknowledges that, at an earlier age than she could defecate on cue, Sedgwick could "tinkle in the loo", even if she found shitting in the bathroom, rather than in her "potty" or "pyjama" a "wee bit more forbidding".[65] And Sedgwick's pun on "wee", a Scottish colloquialism meaning 'a little', reminds us of a related idiom in *A Dialogue on Love,* when Sedgwick revealed how she loved

> to be sealed with my
> favourite pronoun: the dear
> first person plural.

Indeed, it "never surprised" Sedgwick that *Oui* "in French, means yes", and, "even in adulthood", she was "addicted to the word". The chapter climaxes with a haiku on the subject of we/e that was, not so secretly, "a matter of pride" to Sedgwick:

> Promiscuous we!
> Me, plus anybody else.
> Permeable we![66]

The haiku, perhaps tangentially, but wittily, refers back to a seventeenth-century poem by Sedgwick's most prestigious predecessor in the form, Bashō, who, in *The Narrow Road to the Deep North,* documented that

> Bitten by flies and lice,
> I slept in a bed,

---

64 For more on Poopie, see Sedgwick, *A Dialogue on Love,* 209.

65 Sedgwick, *The Weather in Proust,* xv.

66 Sedgwick, *A Dialogue on Love,* 106.

A horse urinating all the time
Close to my pillow.[67]

With such texts in mind, *Between Men* is, perhaps, most notorious for insisting that "*Our Mutual Friend* is the only English
novel that everyone says is about excrement in order that they
may *forget* that it is about anality".[68] But Sedgwick's oeuvre may
be the only queer theoretical corpus that everyone *says* is about
anality because they have not spotted that it's also about *urethrality*.

For example, in 'The Warm Decembers', Sedgwick's alter ego,
Beatrix Protheroe, escaping from a boarding house owned by
her uncle, and, running through the fens, is forced to urinate
in public at night. Here, "over the finally cool", "never thirsty
enough clay", and having held her urine in throughout a long
day during which "the current of will" was "so little tolerant /
of control", Beatrix finally lets her urethral sphincter lapse, and
"the burning, banked-up piss" splits the "uneven ground", as the
sound reverberates around the surrounding "sloppy landscape".[69]
Beatrix's nocturnal piss is deeply humiliating. "Never respectable", she loses more respectability by the day, and "too shy (of
course) to urinate in the light", the painful sensation of her urine
is the sign of an oncoming, crazy-making, urinary tract infection, which finally causes her to black out, only to awake back
where she started: "undelirious" at home in Great Yarmouth.
This causes Sedgwick to ponder if any women in the nineteenth
century knew where their urethras were except as some "hot

---

67 Matsuo Bashō, *The Narrow Road to the Deep North and Other Travel Sketches*, ed. and trans. Nobuyuki Yuasa (London: Penguin, 1966), 120. See also
Bashō's account of a baby pissing (*Narrow Road*, 18). Sedgwick documents
that her friend Josh Wilner was reading Bashō whilst she was writing *Dialogue* and that the two discussed his haibun and haiku projects (*Dialogue*,
194).

68 Sedgwick, *Between Men*, 164.

69 Sedgwick, *Fat Art, Thin Art*, 110–111.

floating place, at other times / imperceptible", somewhere between "uterus and clitoris".[70]

Later in the poem, Sedgwick offers a second thalassic scene.
In a passage recalling the painful, earlier Ferenczian scene of a
child loving an adult, we are invited to imagine a

> child wetting its bed
> (and say the family's poor, the beds are shared,
> the washing's done in buckets and by hand,
> the drying sheet smothers the attic room)
> whose crazy father then decides:
> This is a child who 'must not' be given water.
> Or, that it's dangerous to let this child sleep,

the "parching child" waking to "violence or the expensive wet
that makes violence". Somehow, this child "survives / and finds,
somewhere, an art". Which is to say, that this child's road widens, and, somewhere, not quite over the rainbow, but certainly
away from Great Yarmouth and London, in Beatrix's case — and,
from Dayton Ohio and Washington D.C., in Sedgwick's — the
child finds poetry, a golden treasure in relation to which the author has a bladder-like "vacant, distended, paper-light globe /
called 'gratitude'", which "fills up the inner space / (gratitude as
it were for water and for sleep)".[71]

Taken together, these scenes recall one of Sedgwick's most
evocative pieces of fibre art: 'I borrow moonlight for this jour-

---

70 Sedgwick, *Fat Art, Thin Art*, 110–113. The passage recalls the moment, in
    Elizabeth Barrett Browning's *Aurora Leigh* (1856), when Marian Erle's simi-
    lar attempt to escape her own painful family situation results in her fainting,
    only to wake up the following morning, "ware / Of heavy tumbling motions,
    creaking wheels", and with the "cruel yellow morning" similarly "peck[ing]
    at her", except that, in spite of the "oozing" cruel yellow, it is Marian's *heart*,
    rather than her *bladder*, which, the night before had, "Kept swelling, swell-
    ing, till it swelled so big / It seemed to fill her body" and then "burst, / And
    overflowed the world, and swamped the light" (Book III, lines 1082–1105). I
    am grateful to Ben Westwood and Carolyn Williams for drawing my atten-
    tion to parallels with Barrett Browning.
71 Sedgwick, *Fat Art, Thin Art*, 147–148.

ney of one million miles', which combines the text of a Japanese death poem with the moonlight of Beatrix's moonlit flit, and the familiar, traumatizing, spreading yellow of urine across a child's bed-sheet. But Sedgwick's work includes paranoid and reparative thalassic scenes.

For example, *The Warm Decembers* documents the painful, interruptive scene of the "fire hose in the Alabama town" pissing all over the "glistening offal" of its black citizens protesting their civil rights, the "water's eye / washing itself away", and the "wrenching pulses" of "the current, / in a beheaded coil, wavering and swollen" able to "pull your legs from under you like / the running noose" of a lynching. But the poem is also responsive to the solitary, melancholy, but aesthetic and corporeal pleasures of pissing and of the body and landscape's water cycles.[72] Chapter 2 depicts the now grown-up Beatrix taking photographs of a twilight, equinoctial, December landscape where "mud silt in a slow river" is "alimenting some passage of countryside";[73] whilst the poem later conjures a landscape in which a "puddle of night in a hollow / of bright lawn, all day anxiously deforming" is

> eccentric toward the grassy lip at dawn,
> then shrinking southward and into the roots,
> and then, at noon, like mercury, dissembled
> to winking atoms, bridling in the afternoons
> one little knob, brimming from that
> up every grass to where the golden shield
> of the evening crushed it level — this plot
> of striving shadow, daily rolled around
> the grassy mouth, never could reach it over
> those shallow hummock lips; no, not by the breadth
> of one fine blade; never, until

---

72 Sedgwick, *Fat Art, Thin Art,* 110–111. The perhaps incongruous, interruptive scene makes more sense in the context of Sydney Poitier's 1973 film, *A Warm December,* a thus-far-unrecognised source for the poem, which tells of a recently widowed, comparatively young African-American man who falls in love with a terminally-ill young African woman.

73 Sedgwick, *Fat Art, Thin Art,* 95.

there leapt across the spread of grass and air
writ large, the earth's shadow, darkness, that had
no shadow, but washing downward embraced
the pool that leapt up into it.[74]

The poem's landscape is, of course, suggestively feminine and bodily. Fluids emerge from a urethral "little knob" and flow over "grassy", "hummock lips", filling and overflowing from a vulnerable, vaginal space — "no, not by the breadth" recalling the anguished, but resilient cry of the three little pigs threatened by the wolf at their door: "no, not by hairs on my chinny chin chin". But, if the threat of rape is never far from the women in the poem, the landscape scene also recalls a happier, queerer, all-male watering hole. That is the one depicted in the final, detumescent, post-coital lines of the famous bathing scene in chapter 12 of E.M. Forster's *A Room with a View* (1908), when "that evening and all that night the water ran away" and when, "On the morrow the pool had shrunk to its old size and lost its glory". Anticipating Sedgwick's description of Beatrix's "current of will so little tolerant / of control, will so local", Forster's pool had also formerly been a "call to the blood and to the relaxed will, / a passing benediction where influence did not pass, / a holiness, a spell, a momentary chalice for youth".[75]

Having now considered some of the key forms and themes of Sedgwick's first book of poetry, we turn, in the next section, to her second.

The Haiku Book, or, *A Dialogue,* with Merrill and Others, *on Love*

Five years after the publication of *Fat Art, Thin Art,* Sedgwick's second book of poetry debuted in 1999. *A Dialogue on Love* adopts a haibun form: the part-prose, part-haiku genre popularized, in melancholy and mournful travel narratives, by Bashō,

---

74 Sedgwick, *Fat Art, Thin Art,* 104.
75 E.M. Forster, *A Room with a View* (1908; London: Penguin, 2000).

and adopted by Merrill for his 1988 Japanese travelogue and
AIDS memoir, 'Prose of Departure'.[76] Sedgwick made her debt
to Merrill explicit. In *A Dialogue on Love,* she documented how
she had "long been haunted" by 'Prose of Departure', written
in an "unfamiliar form: prose interspersed with haiku". Only
"Spangled with haiku is more what it feels like", Sedgwick noted.
Merrill's "very sentences fraying

    into implosions
    of starlike density or
    radiance, then out

into a prose that's never quite not the poetry".[77] Before Merrill,
she confessed, she had "never really got haiku as a short form",
finding it "precious, insipid". But Merrill's haibun felt "so different", where "sweeping into and through" his "arias" were "silent
impasses" and "the fat, buttery condensations and inky dribbles
of the mind's laden brush"; a delicious description recalling the
repeated comparisons, in Bashō, of his haiku with traditional
Japanese forms of painting, which the poet practiced.[78]

Talking to Wilner about Merrill's haibun, Sedgwick thought
of it as a "possible form" for documenting her therapy. It was
a way to evoke her intimate, inter-subjective relation with Van
Wey that was more appropriate than the "bathetic" form of the
complaint or the "triumphalis[t]" genre of the "fixated" case
history, offering instead something combining the *novelistic,*
"where you needn't know in advance what the subject" would

76 For examples by Bashō, see *The Narrow Road*; for Merrill's 'Prose of Departure', see *Collected Poems* (New York: Knopf, 2002), 541–560.

77 Sedgwick, *A Dialogue on Love,* 194. The word "spangle" echoes Sedgwick's
'1001 Seances' essay which described how Ephraim's "small capitals […]
spangle the printed poem" (459). The word "spangle" also appears in *The
Book of Ephraim* in the discussion of Ellen's "spangled, spotlit twin" (cited
in Sedgwick, '1001 Seances', 469).

78 Sedgwick, *A Dialogue on Love,* 94. For illustrations of Bashō's combined
calligraphic, poetic, and painterly practice, see Makoto Ueda, ed., *Bashō
and his Interpreters: Selected Hokku with Commentary* (Stanford: Stanford
University Press, 1992), 58, 106, 148, 347, 401.

be; and the lyric, with its "melody" and "white space".[79] Indeed, *A Dialogue on Love* makes belatedly clear how important how the "narrative space of therapy" and its "transferential stuff" had been to Sedgwick's poetic project all along,[80] and especially to the novella poems, that had already featured free associations, accounts of dreams, Freudian slips, the practice of looking back at old family photographs, and deeply inter-subjective relationships, as we have seen, as well, in the case of the uncollected poem, 'Die Sommernacht hat mir's angetan', an addressee called 'Tim', a repeated interlocutor in Sedgwick's later memoir.[81]

Like many genres Sedgwick explored, the haibun aesthetic she adopted in *A Dialogue on Love* is mostly, but never entirely, systematic. Unlike Merrill, Sedgwick did not feel constrained to rhyme the first and third lines of her haiku. Thus, whilst she referred to *Dialogue* as her "POETRY BOOK" and "haiku book",[82] and although she was committed to the haiku form, she repeatedly bent it to her own ends. For instance, in Chapter 4, Sedgwick maintained the 17-syllable pattern of the traditional haiku, but dispensed with its three-line construction, employing a characteristic *enjambment* to split and pause the second line. Explaining to Van Wey how much she had been through, she noted that there was "only one phrase I want to hear":

'That's enough. You can
stop now.'
        Stop: living, that is.
And *enough*: hurting.[83]

---

79 Sedgwick, *A Dialogue on Love*, 194.

80 Sedgwick, *A Dialogue on Love*, 91.

81 For addresses to Tim, see *A Dialogue on Love*, 103, 118–120, 125–126. In giving this title to the poem, I follow the 1853 German original by Joseph Viktor von Scheffel. Sedgwick's handwritten manuscript has the slightly variant 'Die Sommer Nacht hat mir's angethan', whilst the title of the typed version is 'Die Sommer Nacht Hat Mir's Angethan'. I am grateful to Hal A. Sedgwick for establishing the precise composition history of the poem.

82 Sedgwick, *A Dialogue on Love*, 195, 198–199.

83 Sedgwick, *A Dialogue on Love*, 69.

Then, immediately afterwards, in the next section, whilst continuing to meditate on the same phrase, Sedgwick included a haiku-like, three-line form, but with each line representing a complete, multi-, but not necessarily 17-syllable, sentence:

At least, it means that in my native land.
Five miles across the border, phrasebooks say, it's different.
There, it's a way that parents calm their kids.[84]

Similar moments occur in Chapter 10, where Sedgwick emphasized the prose, rather than poetry-like form of her overall text, by inserting a paragraph tab-length break into the last stanza of her haiku sequence:

I tell Shannon — like
he couldn't guess — that Buddhism's
conscious love of

rest, death, nonbeing,
are more congenial to
me than the Western

heroic thrust for
individuation and
survival (which seems

plain phony to me).
    I like the explanation
Robert Thurman gives […].[85]

Across the gutter of the page, meanwhile, Sedgwick employed a second moment of pausing *enjambment* when, having just received the diagnosis that her cancer had metastasized, she described

---

84 Sedgwick, *A Dialogue on Love,* 169.
85 Sedgwick, *A Dialogue on Love,* 210.

Phones just outside the
Clinic door.
            Impermanence
Arrives so quickly![86]

Like a number of Sedgwick's works, and like Bashō's travel narratives, that frequently cite and allude to the haikus of past poets and present travelling companions,[87] *A Dialogue on Love* is
effectively co-authored, with Van Wey's notes increasingly taking centre stage, although unlike *Shame and its Sisters: A Silvan
Tomkins Reader* (1996), Sedgwick's co-author's name, does not
appear on the spine, just as Bashō's poetic interlocutors do not
appear on his.[88] Nevertheless, like many of Sedgwick's poems,
and especially the novella-length narratives, the book stands as
a testament to her relationality, and emphasises ideas of inter-
subjectivity;[89] an idea succinctly captured when Van Wey, ventriloquizing Sedgwick, documents that "THE NOTES ARE TOLD
MOSTLY FROM MY POINT OF VIEW".[90]

But, as in Bashō's account, a number of *poetic* forerunners
haunt and accompany Sedgwick on her therapeutic journey.
In addition to Merrill, we find Sedgwick translating Virgil,[91]
as she would do again in 'Forsan et haec olim meminisse juvabit'. Readers find Sedgwick recalling the hymns of Watts and
Pierpoint;[92] remembering, with sadness, Cornford's cruel 1910
poem, 'To a Fat Lady Seen from the Train';[93] and citing Wyatt's

86 Sedgwick, *A Dialogue on Love*, 209. For further examples, see *A Dialogue on
    Love*, 211, 217–218.
87 For example, see Bashō, *The Narrow Road*, 68–70, 81–84, 94–95, 101, 116,
    130, 138.
88 Sedgwick and Adam Frank, eds., *Shame and its Sisters: A Silvan Tomkins
    Reader* (Durham: Duke University Press, 1996).
89 In *A Dialogue on Love*, Sedgwick documented her desire to leave behind
    "A SENSE OF HER RELATIONALITY", even as she was afraid that reading Van
    Wey's notes risked ruining their actual relationship (198, 200).
90 Sedgwick, *A Dialogue on Love*, 200.
91 Sedgwick, *A Dialogue on Love*, 217–218.
92 Sedgwick, *A Dialogue on Love*, 16, 37.
93 Sedgwick, *A Dialogue on Love*, 193.

'I Find No Peace' (1557), in an indented, unrhymed, two-line couplet that again breaks with *Dialogue*'s haibun form. In addition, Sedgwick warns her shrink not to reduce her language to psychoanalytic clichés. Thinking, perhaps, about the Biblical Saul or T.E. Lawrence, speakers of two of her previously uncollected dramatic monologues, Sedgwick frets that she will "have to thirst" again in the "stony / desert of the self".[94]

But if Sedgwick engages closely with Bashō's haiku form, and with a wide variety of poets in her memoir, it is, perhaps, Merrill who she most channelled there.

1001 Seances or The Book of Merrill

Like *A Dialogue on Love,* Sedgwick's earliest written, and most recently published, essay on poetry, 'The 1001 Seances', primarily concerns Merrill. Published in 2011 in a memorial issue of *GLQ* devoted to Sedgwick, the essay dates from *c.* 1976–1977, the period in which she was hard at work on 'Trace', and examines Merrill's then-recently published narrative poem, *The Book of Ephraim* (1976). Like Sedgwick's later volume of poems, *Traceable, Salient, Thirsty,* the essay was, bafflingly, declined when it was submitted to the journal *Salmagundi* in June 1977, but, undeterred, Sedgwick sent the essay to Merrill himself, who politely acknowledged its receipt.

The essay, however, represented only the first gambit in what Hal A. Sedgwick described as his wife's sustained "interest in writing about Merrill over at least a twenty-year period from 1976–1996". [95] Like many of her essays on poetry, we might read 'The 1001 Seances' as a guide to the kind of poetry Sedgwick would write in the following decade. For example, there is a suggestive relationship between the 'lost' novel Merrill alludes to in *Book of Ephraim* and an uncollected Sedgwick poem collected here. The former concerns, in Sedgwick's words, "the fate of a

---

94 Sedgwick, *A Dialogue on Love,* 7.
95 For more on the biographical context of the poem, see Sedgwick, 'A Note', 452.

river and waterfall in the south-western landscape whose flow is to be interrupted by the building of a power damn",[96] whilst Sedgwick's 'Another Poem from the Creaking Bed', collected here, begins

> When the first white man rolled into Owens Valley
> Before Los Angeles needed the water, it was very green;
> and within even memory you drove by yourself
> in a truck over Westguard Pass from Bishop
> back to deep Springs.
> We can never, in the future, enter the valleys like that.

Another Merrill poem Sedgwick cites, to conclude the essay, 'From the Cupola', featuring "an intercalated novel", an "intercalated typographic differential", and "intrusions from the gods", similarly haunts one of her later, collected poems. The end of Merrill's poem describes how, in typing out his verse,

> My hands move. An intense,
> Slow-paced, erratic dance goes on below.
> I have received from whom I do not know
> These letters. Show me, light, if they make sense.[97]

Similarly, at the end of Sedgwick's 'A Vigil', which commemorates the dying Fisher, and which concludes by citing his, rather than her, words, she focuses on how "the dance" of Fisher's hands

> ...   begins again
> so elegant, and he specifies,
> "Inimitable.
> The dance is inimitable

---

96 Sedgwick, 'The 1001 Seances', 461.
97 James Merrill, *Collected Poems* (New York: Knopf, 2002), 219; cited in Sedgwick, 'The 1001 Seances', 480.

because it is so refined
and it is going on at every level, all the time".[98]

Thus, just as Sedgwick thinks *The Book of Ephraim* "sounds autobiographical in Merrill's characteristic way", so does 'The 1001 Seances' vibrate with Sedgwick's self-revelation, and thrills with her prospective, poetic ambition.[99] For example, anticipating the emphatic white spaces of *A Dialogue on Love,* Sedgwick characterized *The Book of Ephraim* as "a spacing machine"; a poem that "provides spacing" by "writing the letters in the pointed-at order" and "by introducing spaces between groups of letters, making words".[100] Similarly, just as Sedgwick expressed, towards the end of *Dialogue,* her wish to generate "A TEXTURE BOOK" that "WOULDN'T NEED A FIRST PERSON AT ALL, ANY MORE THAN WEAVING ITSELF DOES";[101] so '1001 Seances' praises *Ephraim*'s "pure pointing in the absence of either a pointing subject (the cup stands in) or a pointed to object (the alphabet stands in)".[102] Mostly, however, the essay anticipates the forms of Sedgwick's two "poetic *roman fleuve*" novellas, 'Trace at 46' and 'The Warm Decembers'.[103]

Like *The Book of Ephraim,* both feature "two intercalated type cases".[104] Both play with forms of dialogue and inter-subjectivity in the absence of quotation marks, a characteristic Sedgwick concern as we have seen, making such language "formally distinct but not entirely self-contained", "less conventional in import and more permeable to the contagion of surrounding tones

---

98 Sedgwick, *Fat Art, Thin Art,* 13–14.

99 Sedgwick, '1001 Seances', 457.

100 Sedgwick, '1001 Seances', 459–460. Later in the essay, Sedgwick defined the difference between the novelistic and poetic as a "highly charged interface between currents that differ not in their elements but in their spacing" (478).

101 Sedgwick, *A Dialogue on Love,* 207.

102 Sedgwick, '1001 Seances', 459. For a discussion of the deconstructive, as well as proto-Buddhist, sources of this desire, see Kent, 'Surprising Recognition', 503.

103 Sedgwick, '1001 Seances', 479.

104 Sedgwick, '1001 Seances', 459.

and grammars".[105] In addition, and like Sedgwick's essay, which concerns *Ephraim* and two earlier novels by Merrill, both interleave "novelistic" and "poetic incident",[106] narrative and lyric; more sociably "novelistic" and self-referentially "masturbatory" voices that "attempt to 'do' the same 'subject matter'", but also "interrupt one another". And we know the former to be masturbatory and orgasmic because of the way such scenes are often followed by a more-or-less dreamy and "instant surrender to sleep",[107] as at the free-associative end of Chapter 5 of *The Warm Decembers*.[108]

However, if Sedgwick admired the way in which Merrill's poetry articulated his "waxing and waning concentration", as well as his polarities of "gassy expansion and succinct collapse",[109] she also acknowledged that the "flow of his writing" could be both "awesome" and "awful", and that its "real drama" occurred in moments of "arrest".[110] Indeed, she specifically praised Merrill's "explicit effort to stop the flow of the poem for an instant in order to give an account of it", thinking that this was when his verse sounded best: "the instants when some resistance sends him back over the ground he has just covered, arresting the fluency of which he is rightly a little suspicious".[111] In saying so, '1001 Seances' provided a useful pointer to a number of Sedgwick's uncollected poems, in which, like Merrill, Sedgwick was unafraid of employing language that is "remarkable for its weight and repetitiousness", and whose "more than ordinarily" repetitive texture is designed to stop reader and writer from getting "carried away", beyond the scene of poetic representation and of genre.[112] In addition, just as *Ephraim*'s 'lost' novel

105 Sedgwick, '1001 Seances', 460.
106 Sedgwick, '1001 Seances', 461.
107 Sedgwick, '1001 Seances', 461–462.
108 Sedgwick, *Fat Art, Thin Art*, 131.
109 Sedgwick, '1001 Seances', 479.
110 Sedgwick, '1001 Seances', 480.
111 Sedgwick, '1001 Seances', 475.
112 Sedgwick, '1001 Seances', 476–477.

includes a character called Ellen,[113] so is there is an Ellen in *Uncle Miles,* the fictional novel within *The Warm Decembers*; and, like Beatrix's mother, in that same poem, Merrill's Ellen "can neither reach nor exorcise" her husband.[114]

Indeed, if '1001 Seances' acknowledges a vanilla "queasiness in writing about intelligent pornography",[115] the essay nevertheless anticipates 'A Poem is Being Written' in a number of ways: in its concern with masturbation, castration, and urination; with the sexual "thrust" of poetic lines and the queer resonances of the "structural issues" of verse; and with tableau of punishment, centred on the protagonist, reader and writer's temporal "expectancy" and spatial "attention" being "caught & held by 1000 details of the scene".[116]

Given this career-long identification with Merrill, it is no wonder that Sedgwick was delighted to discover, twenty years later, that she shared, with Van Wey, her love of a poet whose *Ephraim* she often quoted in the sessions.[117] The pair explicitly discussed Merrill's death on February 7, 1995, when Van Wey, in Ephraim's small-capitals script, documented Sedgwick's sadness at the fact that "MERRILL DIED YESTERDAY". Sedgwick then read

---

113 Sedgwick, '1001 Seances', 469.

114 Sedgwick, '1001 Seances', 469.

115 Sedgwick, '1001 Seances', 465.

116 Sedgwick, '1001 Seances', 462–465, 473. For example, as *Ephraim* makes clear, Sedgwick shared with Merrill her interest in the potential sadomasochistic implications of poetic rhythm, with Merrill describing how "Rod upon mild silver rod, like meter" was "broken in fleet cahoots with subject matter". Like Sedgwick, Merrill is prone to urinary aesthetics, as "when the urge / Comes to make water, a thin brass-hot stream / Sails out into the updraft, spattering / One impotent old tree that shakes its claws. / The droplets atomise, evaporate" (*The Changing Light at Sandover*, 20). Looking back on a sadomasochistic scene, meanwhile, one of Merrill's characters reflects: "That orgy must never be repeated! — as with a moistened cloth I dab primly at my mind, where there are telltale signs" (cited in Sedgwick, '1001 Seances', 464). This brings to mind Sedgwick's discussion, in *Epistemology of the Closet*, of how the "chalky rag of gender" was "pulled across the blackboard of sexuality" and the "chalky rag of sexuality across the blackboard of gender", leaving a "cloudy space" from which to speak (239).

117 Sedgwick, *A Dialogue on Love*, 137. The passage she quotes can be found in *The Changing Light*, 59–60.

part of Merrill's poem 'The Kimono', from the same 1976 collection, *The Divine Comedies,* that contained *Ephraim,* particularly the three haiku-like lines which encourage them both to

> Keep talking while I change into
> The pattern of a stream
> Bordered with rushes white on blue.[118]

In the midst of what Lynch called "these waves of dying friends",[119] or what Sedgwick, in a related more Spenserian idiom, described as the "great, upwelling flux of mutability" attendant upon the illnesses and deaths of so many of her poetic peers, Sedgwick's poetry "had returned", and she was emerging "a different person", which is the title of Merrill's own 1993 psychoanalytic memoir, to which we shall return.[120] Indeed, one might read *A Dialogue on Love* as a book-length equivalent, for Merrill, of the famous 'White Glasses' obituary Sedgwick wrote for Lynch, or as a kind of parallel necromancy, of Merrill, akin to the poet and his lover David Jackson's raising from the dead Ephraim, W.H. Auden, and others. Or, with *Ephraim* in mind, we might choose to read *Dialogue* as offering its readers what Merrill describes there as his "executive privilege vis-à-vis / Transcripts of certain private hours with E", where E, for Merrill, is the medium Ephraim, but where E, in *A Dialogue,* is Van Wey's shorthand for Eve.[121]

Indeed, Sedgwick tacitly gives not just Van Wey but, through him, Merrill, the last word in *Dialogue.* On the final page, Van Wey recalls Sedgwick telling him earlier how she waited, throughout

---

118 Sedgwick, *A Dialogue on Love,* 188–189.

119 Michael Lynch, *These Waves of Dying Friends* (New York: Contact, 1989).

120 Sedgwick, *A Dialogue on Love,* 136. Merrill himself uses the phrase repeatedly in his memoir. For examples, see *A Different Person,* 460 and 537,

121 Merrill, *The Changing Light at Sandover,* 41. Just as Van Wey gives Sedgwick access to his session notes, so, in *Ephraim,* "D lets me have the notes he made", while Merrill "went to [his] ex-shrink / With the whole story" (*The Changing Light at Sandover,* 27, 29). Similarly just as Van Wey warms to Sedgwick's "talents" (*The Changing Light at Sandover,* 72), so Ephraim warms to those of Merrill and Jackson (cited in Sedgwick, '1001 Nights', 460).

her life, for someone to tell her she can "STOP NOW — E.G. DIE".
She increasingly imagines him "DOING THIS SOMETIME IN THE
FUTURE" and she "TALKS ABOUT HAVING COME TO BE ABLE TO
HEAR A VOICE LIKE [HIS] VOICE INSIDE HERSELF WHEN IT IS
QUIET THAT SHE CAN TRUST AND HAVE CONFIDENCE IN". In the
final sentence of the book, Shannon "CAN IMAGINE THE VOICE
TELLING HER SHE CAN STOP".[122] In both of their minds, however,
that voice cannot just be Sedgwick's, or Van Wey's. It must also
be Merrill's. After all, in *Ephraim*, hadn't Merrill asked his medium "Can we stop now please?" before his queer-little-god re-
plied, with a reassuringly tacit yes: "U DID WELL JM".[123]

But *Ephraim* does not just echo across *Dialogue*. It reverberates across Sedgwick's narrative poetry. In 'The Warm Decembers', there is a further parallel between the moment, in *Ephraim*,
where Merrill, alluding to Dante Gabriel Rossetti's 1850 poem,
hopes that he and his lover, David Jackson, will "*both* be reborn"
which "at least spares one / Dressing up as the Blessed Damozel / At Heaven's Bar to intervene";[124] and the moment in *Uncle
Miles* where Ellen, thinking of her now dead uncle and his then
mistress, wonders "*Was this woman, that woman? / Companion
to the bulky, handsome man / got up as the Blessed Damozel…?*"[125]
Indeed, one might see *Ephraim* as the urtext of both 'The Warm
Decembers' and 'Trace at 46's interest in forms which, in Sedgwick's words, focus on "ontological thresholds" between "a person alive and dead; a person and a photograph; a sister and a
sister; a present and a past; a person child and adult; people with
the same name; a happening and the dream of it; a writer (or a

---

122 Sedgwick, *A Dialogue on Love*, 220.
123 Merrill, *The Changing Light at Sandover*, 43. The passage in which "Whatever E imagined", Merrill's novel "didn't / Press back enough, or pressed back
against him" (66) also speaks to the moment when Sedgwick more success-
fully "push[es] Van Wey] backward" (*A Dialogue on Love*, 93–94). Sedgwick
also wonders of one of her own characters, "What did I once think these two
would feel", noting that Merrill has an identical question at an "analogous
juncture" (*Fat Art, Thin Art*, 154; *The Changing Light at Sandover*, 84; and as
quoted by Sedgwick, '1001 Seances', 474).
124 Merrill, *The Changing Light at Sandover*, 25.
125 Sedgwick, *Fat Art, Thin Art*, 127.

model) and a character; an I and a she or he", and the "perverse, desiring energies that alone can move across them";[126] especially since *Ephraim* asks its interlocutors to "Trace me back to some loud, shallow, chill, / Underlying motive's overspill".[127]

Before completing our exploration of Merrill's repeated haunting of Sedgwick's corpus, however, we need to explore one last, to-date unattributed Merrill intertext for *Dialogue*: his 1993 memoir, *A Different Person,* a phrase Sedgwick explicitly employed, as we have seen, in her autobiography.

A Succulent Mouse to Lay at My Master's Door? A Dialogue on Love as Merrillian Memoir

Like the earlier *Book of Ephraim,* Merrill remained interested, in *A Different Person,* his later autobiography, in employing various fonts to signal different narrative voices, with each chapter composed of regular type for the main story, and italics to signal his present-tense reflections and addresses to the reader.[128] In addition, Merrill intermittently employed capitalised fonts, when conveying headlines — "RECITANO BAUDELAIRE VESTITI DA COWBOYS" — and when describing the sign of a shop he'd never "found open, its dark window dingily lettered in gold: LUST'S BAKERY".[129]

---

126 Sedgwick, *Fat Art, Thin Art,* 157.

127 Merrill, *The Changing Light at Sandover,* 33. In addition, the poem wonders "what / Traces, if any" a character "will then transmit / To her own offspring" when she reaches puberty (*The Changing Light at Sandover,* 18). Another spirit's "gibbous moans", meanwhile, anticipate the "gibbous belly" of the punakawan that ends 'Trace at 46' (*Fat Art, Thin Art,* 67).

128 Sedgwick, 'The 1001 Seances', 480. As Merrill explains early in the memoir, he would employ a "different typeface for the person I became"; a person who "will break in at chapter's end with glimpses beyond my time frame". Later, he notes that being "italicised" was a response to feeling "more elegantly slanted now, more emphatically set upon the world's page, than the blunt type of a year or two earlier" ('A Different Person: A Memoir' [1993], in J.D. McClatchy and Stephen Yenser, eds., *Collected Prose* [New York: Knopf, 2004], 467, 665–666).

129 Merrill, 'A Different Person', 460, 482.

Like *A Dialogue on Love, A Different Person* is also the account of a productive psychoanalysis with a therapist who initially seems under-skilled. Just as Sedgwick criticized Van Wey for wondering where the metaphor "Fasten your seatbelt" came from and judged him for "mispronounc[ing] / *folie a deux*";[130] so Merrill "silently congratulate[s] Dr Detre on having returning from his seaside holiday with a metaphor" and describes his relation to Ephraim as a "folie a deux".[131] Again like *Dialogue,* Merrill's memoir is the product of an encounter with mortality — in Merrill's case, his diagnosis with HIV, in Sedgwick's with breast and spine cancer — and both ponder what Merrill calls the *"slow erosion" of a "once military spine to a fragile question mark".*[132] In addition, just as *Dialogue* details Sedgwick's painful writer's block and results in the return of her muse, *A Different Person* leads to Merrill's renewed ability to write.[133]

Indeed, there are so many moments of dialogue between Merrill and Sedgwick that *A Different Person* sometimes seems to be addressed to her. Merrill more than once employs the phrase *Between Men,* suggesting he might have read her book.[134] Like Sedgwick, in 'A Poem is Being Written', Merrill discusses his own poetic schooling in *"Louis Untermeyer's anthology".*[135] The pair share a fondness for the "finger's-breadth" as a unit of measurement;[136] a tendency to find themselves in Faure;[137]

---

130 Sedgwick, *Fat Art, Thin Art,* 21.

131 Merrill, 'A Different Person', 659; *The Changing Light at Sandover,* 30.

132 Merrill, 'A Different Person', 597.

133 Merrill, 'A Different Person', 555, 669.

134 For example, see *A Different Person,* 567, where physical intimacy is "of course […] unthinkable between men"; and Dr. Detre's account of how "sex between men is by its character frustrating", since "[t]he anus is full of shit; the mouth is a well of flattery and untruth" and "the honest penis is left with no reliable place to go" (640).

135 Sedgwick, *Tendencies,* 181–182, 208; Merrill, *A Different Person,* 468.

136 See Merrill's description of a "finger's-breadth of wine" (*A Different Person,* 548) and Sedgwick's of "the finger's-breadth by finger's-breadth / dearly bought knowledge / of the body's lived humiliations, / dependencies, vicarities / that are stitched into the book / of The Sexualities, wasteful / and value-making specificity" (*Fat Art, Thin Art,* 149).

137 Merrill, 'A Different Person', 515; Sedgwick, *Fat Art, Thin Art,* 43, 59.

an interest in popular T-shirt culture;[138] a passion for Randell Jarrell;[139] and an aversion to injections;[140] as well as a predilection towards the aesthetics of the fat, the thin, and the flat.[141] Sedgwick and Merrill also both describe their experience of spanking as children,[142] and their strict, premature toilet training regime, with Merrill describing how he had been "so strictly trained in childhood to perform 'number two' each day or face the consequences (enemas, laxatives)" that he dragged himself "each morning to the toilet across the hall, where Herculean labours produced a few blood-smeared votive pellets". Later, when bowel troubles emerge, Merrill is confronted by a doctor who "asked his one question (*'Avez-vous fait quelque chose ce matin?'*)". The poet is "able to answer with a feeble but proud 'Oui'", a resonant word for Sedgwick, as we have seen.[143] In addition, like Sedgwick, Merrill is interested in medicalised, co-erced-consent scenes where he is forced to "drop [… his] pants", as, for example, when he suffers from haemorrhoids.[144]

Both Sedgwick and Merrill are also preoccupied with family photographs in the context of their therapies. Merrill notices that "Snapshots from years before" his parents' "divorce tell how something had already turned one brave, unlettered little boy astride a gigantic stallion into a sissy of six, posed, hands folded and ankles crossed, at the slide's foot".[145] In addition, in phrases that precisely anticipate Sedgwick's account of her photographer

---

138 Sedgwick, *Tendencies*, xi; Merrill, *A Different Person*, 585, which describes how a family member "must have sported a BORN TO SHOP T-shirt".

139 Merrill, 'A Different Person', 509; Sedgwick, *Fat Art, Thin Art*, 21, 113; *Touching Feeling*, 27.

140 Merrill, 'A Different Person', 478; Sedgwick, *Fat Art, Thin Art*, 29.

141 For example, Merrill compares "a fat, richly stamped letter" with a "flat parcel from Holland" (A Different Person, 681).

142 Merrill, 'A Different Person', 492.

143 Merrill, 'A Different Person', 478.

144 Merrill, 'A Different Person', 483. Cf. *A Dialogue on Love*, 176, where Sedgwick confesses her erotic fondness for the phrase "pull down your pants" (176).

145 Merrill, 'A Different Person', 574. "Snapshot" is also a resonant word in Sedgwick's vocabulary, with one of her collected poems entitled 'Snapsh'.

father, Merrill describes how "to anyone with identity problems", the camera was a "godsend, each shot proving (if nothing
else)" that the photographer had "composed *himself* for the split
second needed to press the shutter", and was also a "way to make
quick raids on life while keeping it at arm's length" since you
"look at things no longer quietly, for their own sake, but greedily, for the images they yield".[146] Similarly, like the Sedgwick who
chose a rose-tinted image of herself for the cover of *Fat Art, Thin
Art,* Merrill, too, purchased a "tinted monocle" for his camera.[147]
And like the Sedgwick taking pictures at the bedside of her
friends dying of AIDS, as in the lyric 'Grave, never offering back
the face of my dear',[148] Merrill describes the photographs he took
of the "beautiful head" of a sick friend "gazing mysteriously up
from the hospital pillows".[149]

Perhaps the most direct relationship between *A Dialogue on
Love* and *A Different Person,* however, comes in a metaphor of
human–feline relationality. Whilst Sedgwick described, to Van
Wey, the dream of having sex with her father as a particularly
"succulent mouse to lay / at my master's door",[150] Merrill noted that "before entering analysis", he fancied dreams to be the
"very meat on which patient and doctor breakfasted insatiably
together". "Each night", he therefore "set off in catlike pursuit of
a new one, and next day proudly laid the dead mouse at Dr. Detre's feet".[151] Finally, at the end of each poet's memoir, and partly
through a shared encounter with Buddhism,[152] there is a realisa-

---

146 Merrill, 'A Different Person', 491. For more on Sedgwick's father as a photog-
    rapher, see *A Dialogue on Love,* 19–22.
147 Merrill, 'A Different Person', 523. For other examples, see *A Different Per-
    son,* 578, which describes Merrill's mother as "too often blurred by excessive
    closeness if not by the trembling of the handheld camera" and the "tinted
    oval photograph" described on p. 597.
148 Sedgwick, *Fat Art, Thin Art,* 10.
149 Merrill, 'A Different Person', 611.
150 Sedgwick, *A Dialogue on Love,* 42.
151 Merrill, 'A Different Person', 609.
152 Merrill, 'A Different Person', 648. In *The Changing Light at Sandover,* the
    later séances are accompanied by a "bodhisattva / Green with age" (40), and
    there is a straining after "the elate / Burst of satori" (91).

tion that, in Merrill's words, whilst *"Freedom to be oneself is all very well; the greater freedom is not to be oneself"*, and that the "different person" both meant to become would be "more receptive to others" than they had been thus far, and "more conscious of their needs than greedy for [their] own fulfillment".[153] Indeed, I could never not hear, as a direct address to Sedgwick, as well as a description of a particular evening, Merrill's phrase "On Easter Eve we attended *Parsifal* at the Graz Opera".[154]

As with Derrida and Ferenczi, however, it is clear that Merrill and Sedgwick also differed in some ways. If Merrill repeatedly employed the phrase *Between Men*, he would have had little time for the *Epistemology of the Closet*, since he made light of his parents' *"expressions of mid-twentieth-century prejudice"* as *"harmless enough"*, and no different from *"hundreds of thousands of parents"* who *"spent the forties and fifties urging secrecy and repression upon their queer sons"*. Merrill also sets himself at a significant distance, in 1993, from the politics of shame that powerfully motivated Sedgwick's queer theory and activism,[155] when he reported that he was *"surprised to hear from Jerl"*, a *"young, politically correct friend who digs me like an archaeological trench of outmoded notions"*, that *"he and his 'support group' view[ed]"* Merrill's parents' prejudices as a *"form of verbal sexual abuse"*. *"He has to be joking!"* Merrill assumed, *"But no"*, Jerl assured him: *"a single shame-producing word"* could be as *"traumatic as an incestuous caress"*.[156]

But Sedgwick's deep admiration for Merrill should not distract us, as Katie Kent's essay in this volume further reminds us, from doing justice to some of Sedgwick's female muses. And, in the next two sections, I want to consider two: Emily Dickinson and Gertrude Stein.

---

153 Merrill, 'A Different Person', 565, 568. Compare Sedgwick's suggestion that "it means a lot, to be happy. / It may even mean: to be good. Ungreedy, unattached, unrageful, unignorant" (*A Dialogue on Love*, 215–216).
154 Merrill, 'A Different Person', 620.
155 Sedgwick, *Shame and its Sisters*, 35–66; *Touching Feeling*, 93–122.
156 Merrill, 'A Different Person', 532.

Dash It! Or "The Effect of the Horizontal Stroke": Channelling Emily Dickinson

Although there is no Sedgwick essay devoted to Dickinson, the poet frequently embossed Sedgwick's prose. In *Between Men,* Dickinson's 'Our journey had advanced — / Our feet were almost come / To that odd Fork in Being's Road' provided the epigraph for the coda.[157] In *Epistemology of the Closet,* Sedgwick employed Dickinson's 'The Fox fits the Hound' as a way of characterizing the relationship of Henry James' characters May Bartram and John Marcher.[158] In *Touching Feeling,* Sedgwick drew on Dickinson's '"Hope" is the thing with feathers — / That perches on the soul' as part of her theorization of the close relationship of hope and anxiety,[159] whilst Part 3 of the 1975 poem, 'Sexual Hum' employed, as a mantra, Dickinson's poem 822 as an "excellent chant" to distract the anxious poet in the "dentist's chair".

It is, however, in *Tendencies* where Dickinson loomed largest. The volume commenced with a photomontage of Sedgwick and Lynch leaning on Dickinson's grave, to which we shall return. In 'Queer and Now', marvelling at the miraculous queer survival of her "adult friends and colleagues doing lesbian and gay work", Sedgwick cited Dickinson's

> — an outgrown anguish
> Remembered, as the Mile

> Our panting Ankle barely passed —
> When Night devoured the Road —
> But we — stood whispering in the House —
> And all we said — was 'Saved'![160]

---

157 Sedgwick, *Between Men,* 201.
158 Sedgwick, *Epistemology of the Closet,* 209.
159 Sedgwick, *Touching Feeling,* 151.
160 Sedgwick, *Tendencies,* 1.

And the characteristic Bauhaus slant of Sedgwick's prose, on the first pages of each chapter, might owe something to Dickinson's 'There's a Certain Slant of Light', with its themes of the differences left by Death, even in the absence of a visible scar, especially since Dickinson reappears in 'White Glasses', Sedgwick's 'memorial' essay for Lynch. There, Sedgwick revealed that Dickinson was of the pair's "most durable" points of shared reference, leading to "tokens, readings", "impersonations", and "pilgrimages", including one to Dickinson's house in Amherst, the place Sedgwick lived and taught between 1984 and 1988, and fought to get Dickinson onto the curriculum.[161]

Dickinson's specifically clitoral poetics, meanwhile, figured in two further essays. 'Is the Rectum Straight' discussed the potential pleasure and danger of "clitorial eroticism", in James' *The Wings of the Dove* (1902), through reference to Dickinson's 'My Life Stood — a Loaded Gun'.[162] Sedgwick fleshed out this allusion in the following essay, 'Jane Austen and the Masturbating Girl'. This acknowledged the centrality, to Sedgwick's thinking about queer female writers, of Paula Bennett's *My Life A Loaded Gun: Female Creativity and Feminist Poetics* (1986) and *Emily Dickinson: Woman Poet* (1990).[163]

Sedgwick was also inspired, in *A Dialogue on Love,* by Dickinson's idiomatic use of punctuation. For example, readers might notice the way in which, like Dickinson, both Sedgwick and Van Wey repeatedly employed dashes. Each sub-section of the book is marked by a horizontal line of dashes; and Van Wey employed one, two or three horizontal lines, in his notes, to mark changes of topic in his otherwise under-punctuated prose. The evocatively Dickinsonian appearance of *A Dialogue on Love* can, perhaps, best be seen in the extract below:

---

161 Sedgwick, *Tendencies,* 257, 259. For more on Sedgwick's time at Amherst, see the 'Amherst' section of the Sedgwick biography at http://www.evekosofskysedgwick.net.

162 Sedgwick, *Tendencies,* 94.

163 Sedgwick, *Tendencies,* 115. For more, see Paula Bennett, *My Life a Loaded Gun: Female Creativity and Feminist Poetics* (Boston: Beacon, 1986); *Emily Dickinson: Woman Poet* (London: Harvester Wheatsheaf, 1990), 150–180.

> How they're intertwined —
> his permanence in me — my
> permanence in him –
>
> How, when I suppose
> him to be forgetting or
> dropping me — somehow —
>
> from his mind — I lose
> the Daedalian thread of
> ˌShannon in *my* mind — [164]

Here, as in Dickinson's poetry, Sedgwick used dashes to generate a number of effects. Whilst she was not much drawn in her textile practice to embroidery, the dashes of various lengths, both framing and within the trio of haikus, conjure the idea of threads "intertwined" in the first line and lost in the last stanza. The specifically *fraying* character of hope and anxiety that I alluded to earlier is also present here, in all those loose threads to be tied up together. The dashes additionally function as a kind of Sedgwickian *enjambment* marker, both separating out and connecting the various phrases, just as the passage explores the pain of being held close and pushed away, dropped, and let go. In so doing, the dashes affirm the silent and nonverbal, the spaces between words. They also resist stasis, the psychoanalytic idea of fixation that Sedgwick was so averse to in *Dialogue,* instead emphasizing the unfolding of time. While necessarily slowing down the given sentences, the dashes give little indication of the *length* of any pause between dis/connected thoughts that a more regular form of punctuation might have indicated. Readers have only the regular 5–7–5 haiku metre to stabilize their sense of rhythm, as if that stands in for the regularity of therapeutic sessions, if not their relational ebb and flow. The final dash also

---

164 Sedgwick, *A Dialogue on Love,* 122.

signals the difficulty of ending each session, a difficulty that pre-occupied Sedgwick at this time, as her poem 'The 58 ½ Minute Hour' testified.[165]

Many of the meanings of the phrase 'to dash' are also relevant here, particularly given Sedgwick's emphasis, in 'A Poem is Being Written', of the sexualized violence located at the heart of poetic genres. For example, as Kamilla Denman reminds us, to dash is "to strike with violence so as to break into fragments", a punctuation mark, therefore, signaling the pains and pleasures of the therapeutic deconstruction of the self, in *Dialogue,* particularly if we think of a dash as a "horizontal stroke", a language of whipping central to Sedgwick's broader poetics and one that Sedgwick brought into relation to "the effect of the horizontal stroke" through 'deleted' words in Merrill, as Katie Kent has pointed out,[166] and employed in her own verse, such as 'An Essay on The Picture Plane', where "The canvas dissolves at a horizontal stroke" and "at a stroke it is a canvas about distance".[167]

In addition, to dash is to "drive impetuously forth or out", to "cause to rush together" and to "destroy, ruin, confound, frustrate, spoil", signaling the strong positive and negative affects tying together this particular therapeutic couple and prying them apart. Dashes, along with dots, also form a key part of Morse code with three dashes making up the middle letter of the cry for help, S.O.S., here signaling perhaps both that international Mayday, and the exclamatory Romantic "O", in the form of both an ejaculation of pleasure and a cry of woe, especially since Sedgwick employs just such an 'O' in her uncollected poem, 'Epilogue: Teachers and Lovers'. Critics have also interpreted Dickinson's use of dashes as "the result of great stress and intense emotion, as the indication of a mental breakdown", another context appropriate to this therapeutic scene.[168]

---

165 Sedgwick, *Fat Art, Thin Art,* 26.
166 Sedgwick, '1001 Seances', 464; Kent, 'Surprising Recognition', 504.
167 Sedgwick, *Fat Art, Thin Art,* 72.
168 My thoughts on Dickinson's punctuation are indebted to Kamilla Denman, 'Emily Dickinson's Volcanic Punctuation', *The Emily Dickinson Journal* 2.1 (Spring 1993), 22–46.

But if Sedgwick was excited by the idea of Dickinson's dashes and her loaded clitorial gun, we should also recall the potential centrality to Sedgwick's poetry of another lesbian syntactic and clitoral muse, Gertrude Stein, and, in particular, her *Tender Buttons* of 1914.

The Masturbating Girls With Buttons or Tending Gertrude Stein

In Chapter 4 of 'The Warm Decembers', 'The Girls with Buttons', we hear about "a real snapshot" showing

> two girls, one fair, one dark,
> [As Jarrell begins his beautiful poem][169]
> in identical outfits of — 1952,
> say. The dark girl, who might be six, wears hers
> invigoratedly. The fair girl, half her age,
> is being chafed under the armpits by
> the waistband of her jumper, by wads of sweater sleeve.
> The dark child is heads-up. Her slender jaunty legs
> are crossed, knees cocked, to make a lap in plaid
> for the display of a big-headed round kitten.
> [Indeed, handwriting on the back that's slightly like mine
> names this composition: "The girls with Buttons".]
> The three-year-old — no neck, the crossed legs only stubs —
> sans pussy, what has she held in her plaid lap?
> Her hands. Which hold each other and her gaze
> as if they were anything *but* hers.
> The fictitious absorption of that gaze!
> The little squinch of brow, shielding her eyes
> from sunlight coarse as straw that animals

---

169 The poem is 'The Lost Children', *The Lost World* (1948; New York: Macmillan, 1966), 28–30. Sedgwick again refers to the volume at the end of her poem 'Sh', where when "it's Jarrell I need", Van Wey "reaches to the bookcase" and "has it, *The Lost World*" (*Fat Art, Thin Art,* 21). That volume also contains 'Hope' (32–40), the poem Sedgwick employs to introduce in 'Interlude, Pedagogic', as we have seen.

have been curled up on and disarranged, the rounding
of shoulders saying no to a coltish red wagon
near the gravel driveway, the patience with harsh grass
where her skirt is not pulled smoothly up
under her — how slavishly it all is,
yet, at the same time, it is independent.[170]

Later, we learn that the two girls here described, Sedgwick and
her sister Nina, originally had two cats: Nina had her Buttons,
while Eve, who "had the same colouring as her cat", had her Butterscotch. That was until Butterscotch was sent away, not because Eve was "too young", but because her parents, who, inap-
propriately enough, call one another "Lovekitten", thought "two
cats were two too many".[171] Their phraseology recalls Old Father
Time, in Thomas Hardy's *Jude the Obscure* (1895), at the equally
misguided Malthusian moment in which he murders his siblings, because they are also "too menny".[172]

Why, though, bring Stein into the discussion here? The answer is because the scene Sedgwick invites us to contemplate is
one in which she both is, and is not, able to tend to her Buttons.
On the one hand, she is "sans pussy", holding only "her hands"
in her "lap". Her diminutive knees are not "cocked", unlike her
big sister's, and she is forced to endure the "harsh grass / where
her skirt is not pulled smoothly up / under her". In addition,
the Kosofsky sisters have only "one Buttons between them". On
the other hand, as in Stein's *Tender Buttons,* whose relevance is
signalled, perhaps, in Sedgwick's italicized *"but",* the imagery is
suggestively masochistic, masturbatory, anal and clitoral. Sedgwick's sister's "legs are crossed" together, closed to the outside
world, but, as Luce Irigaray reminds us, her lips are adjacent
to each other.[173] In Nina's lap, is a "big-headed round kitten"
keen to be stroked. Sedgwick herself, meanwhile, suggestively,

170 Sedgwick, *Fat Art, Thin Art,* 113.

171 Sedgwick, *Fat Art, Thin Art,* 123.

172 Thomas Hardy, *Jude the Obscure* (London: Harper and Brothers, 1895), 399.

173 For more, see Luce Irigaray, 'When Our Lips Speak Together', *Signs* 6.1 (Autumn 1980), 69–79.

has "only stubs" for legs, and has her hands between her legs. That the Sedgwick sisters can, therefore, be seen to tend their Buttons invites Stein to the scene, especially since, as Kent has documented, she and Sedgwick revelled over the "injunction to 'tend her butt'" that Stein "embedded within the title of her long prose poem", and Sedgwick encouraged Kent to write an essay on Stein's clitoral poetics, and her sexual and textual practice of tending her button.[174]

Particularly relevant, in the context of 'The Girls with Buttons', was Stein's playful meditation, in *Tender Buttons*, on the erotic relations between a "sister and sister" and "a single set of sisters" with "no blisters", rather than on a "sister" and a "mister"; as well as Stein's interest in an owner and a "timely working cat", for whom it is an "occasion to be so purred". In addition, and again anticipating Sedgwick's vocabulary, Stein pondered the "sight of no pussy cat" and she suggested that "a plain lap, any plain lap shows that sign, it shows that there is not so much extension as there would be if there were more choice in everything".[175]

The scene of Sedgwick tending her Buttons also inspired the cover of this book. Like *Fat Art, Thin Art,* I selected a photograph from Sedgwick's childhood. The front cover of *Fat Art, Thin Art* depicted a "SLENDER, DISCRETE, RESOLUTE, SELF-CONTAINED GIRL", with "LONG HAIR", "JUST BEFORE ALL OF THE TURMOIL OF BECOMING GENDERED HAS COME DOWN ON HER". It also represented a Sedgwick already "WITH ONE BREAST",[176] and thus an image signalling the breast cancer that formed such an underlying motive for *Fat Art, Thin Art,* and the explicit subject

---

174 Kent, 'Surprising Recognitions', 498. For more, see Kent, "'Excreate a No Sense": The Erotic Currency of Gertrude Stein's Tender Buttons', in *Making Girls into Women: American Women Writers and the Rise of Lesbian Identity* (Durham: Duke University Press, 2003), 139–166.

175 For more, see Gertrude Stein, *Tender Buttons: Objects, Food, Rooms* (1914; New York: Dover, 1997), 17, 28, 37, 44, 49, 51–52, and passim. Sedgwick and Frank documented how the rhythms of Tomkins' paragraphs reminded them of Stein, "another writer who certainly knows the pleasures of lists" (*Touching, Feeling,* 96; *Shame and its Sisters,* 3).

176 Sedgwick, *A Dialogue on Love,* 193.

of at least three poems in the book's first section.[177] The repara-tive cover of *Bathroom Songs,* by contrast, self-consciously de-picts a younger, beaming Sedgwick, her pussy safely and happily in her hands and lap.

A Dialogue on Love or A Reader's Guide to Eve Kosofsky Sedgwick, Poet

If 'A Poem is Being Written' represented a reader's guide to Sedgwick's then-unpublished verse, *A Dialogue on Love* provid-ed an only more inclusive primer. For example, the comparative difficulties of losing her hair during chemotherapy and a breast after her mastectomy are the subject of a conversation with Van Wey and 'Mobility, speech, sight', a poem in the first section of *Fat Art, Thin Art.*[178] *A Dialogue on Love* reveals the person to whom 'When I got so sick it never occurred to me' is addressed is Sedgwick's former friend Benj.[179] The retrospectively "warm", "golden", and "intoxicating" institutional s/m fantasy scene of 'A scar, just a scar', looked back upon, through rose-tinted or "WHITE GLASSES", the subject of repeated discussions between Sedgwick and Van Wey.[180]

'Performative (Toronto)' and 'Performative (San Francisco)', the topic of an extraordinarily moving essay by Meg Boulton in this volume, are also brought to mind by a passage in *Dialogue.* This described Sedgwick being sat on a runway at the Canadian airport, "anti-icing fluid [...] suddenly running pink down the window" beside her, "looking like Pepto-Bismol" and coming on her "sight like horror". The moment recalled something she

---

177 See 'Mobility, speech, sight', 'A scar, just a scar', and 'When I got sick it never occurred to me', Fat Art, Thin Art, 28–30.

178 Sedgwick, *Fat Art, Thin Art,* 28; *A Dialogue on Love,* 64.

179 Sedgwick, *Fat Art, Thin Art,* 30; *A Dialogue on Love,* 65.

180 Sedgwick, *Fat Art, Thin Art,* 29; *A Dialogue on Love,* 45, 47–49, 172, 175–176, 192. With its account of "someone's soft tears / and a far murmur that only barely / wasn't my imagination, 'spread your legs'" (*Fat Art, Thin Art,* 29), the poem also resonates with Merrill's 'Sanctum', of five years earlier, in which "someone — myself perhaps — tries vainly // to hold back a queer / sob" (555).

"hadn't thought of from that day to this": the "bloody discharge from tubes in the week or so after surgery". As a "matter of fact", it was the anniversary of her diagnosis, but the larger tacit context of the passage included her farewell to Lynch, who had died of AIDS in the same city, and the end of 'Performative (San Francisco)', with its "horror in the taxi" and suddenly "unstanchable", "clotted gouts of blood" when a tragic pedestrian, in antiquity, picks a flower at a roadside.[181]

Perhaps unsurprisingly, Sedgwick's particular relation to Van Wey echoes across the memoir and a number of poems in *Fat Art, Thin Art,* as well as in one previously uncollected poem, 'Valentine', about the therapist included here. Like the thirteen-line, interrupted-sonnet form of 'The 58 ½ minute hour', that we have already briefly mentioned, many of the memoir passages negotiated formal strategies for dealing with the random, "awful stopping places", and the "histrionics of the dropped / patient" when the pair "have to stop now" at the hour's end.[182] A second *Fat Art* lyric, 'Crushed. Dilapidated', with its description of the morning "after a near tornado", also anticipate passages in *Dialogue,* where Sedgwick, after some difficult sessions, characterised herself as resembling a "big, loose footprint / like a messy hurricane" that "churns up the space" but maybe also "keeps / things aerated and fertile", although, there, Sedgwick, by contrast, welcomed "SOMETHING OF THE CALM AFTER THE STORM".[183]

A third category of poems from *Fat Art, Thin Art* that find their resonance in *A Dialogue on Love* are those final lyrics from the first section addressed, jointly, to Sedgwick's husband and sister. For example, where *Fat Art, Thin Art* documents that 'In dreams they're interchangeable — my husband, / my big sister', the title of one poem; on her sister's return to Sedgwick's life,

181 Sedgwick, *Fat Art, Thin Art,* 17–18; *A Dialogue on Love,* 88.

182 Sedgwick, *Fat Art, Thin Art,* 26; *A Dialogue on Love,* 50, 120.

183 Sedgwick, *Fat Art, Thin Art,* 25; *A Dialogue on Love,* 140, 166. Other collected poems about Van Wey include 'Not like the clownish, friendly way you talk', 'Sh', 'I can tune my mind today', 'All I know is I woke up thinking', and 'Snapsh'.

she reports to Van Wey the curious "SENSE OF BEING UNABLE
TO TELL HER SIS AND HAL APART" and her feeling that "HAL WAS
MY SISTER". In addition, we learn that the title of the volume as a
whole, *Fat Art, Thin Art,* resonates in this context, one in which,
when facing her sister for her first time, after years of being estranged, Nina looking "so very thin", Sedgwick "so very fat", they
both grasp at

> once that through eighteen
> years' separation, each girl
> must have looked in the
>
> mirror every
> morning to see, fearfully,
> the other's body.[184]

Sedgwick's memoir also reveals as deeply autobiographical the
kinds of body parts, actions, and contexts that make up the
mise-en-scène of a number of her thrillingly pornographic early poems, from part II of *Fat Art, Thin Art,* with their related
scenes of "butts, assholes" and "women's genitals", "institutional
or quasi-institutional setting", "relation of witness or overhearing", "waiting with dread", "speech or action of coerced consent from the person being punished", and their beating metric
rhythms.[185] In particular, a number of Sedgwick's poems return
to the scene of a traumatic visit to the dentist. For example, in
Part 3 of 'Sexual Hum', as we have seen, the speaker employs a
Dickinson poem as a mantra to distract herself from the pain-

---

184 Sedgwick, *Fat Art, Thin Art,* 32; *A Dialogue on Love,* 132–134. There is also
    a relationship between the poem 'It seems there are two kinds of marriage',
    where Sedgwick recalls reading *Daniel Deronda* on her honeymoon, and
    the moment, in *A Dialogue on Love,* where, re-reading *Middlemarch,* Sedg-
    wick wonders: "this time: George Eliot and the masturbating girl?" (*Fat Art,
    Thin Art,* 34; *A Dialogue on Love,* 175).
185 Sedgwick, *A Dialogue on Love,* 172. For examples, see *Fat Art, Thin Art,*
    72–85.

ful, frightening work going on inside her jaws,[186] whilst the astronaut, in the previously uncollected 'Ring of Fire', sensing his own impending death, is imagined to be

> like a dentist who has crushed a tooth
>
> that lies along the gum in rosy shards,
> but must to the gagged child whisper from the height
> of a taught fatherly vision, firmly, 'You're all right'.

Dialogue brings two explanatory contexts to these painful dental scenes. The first is Sedgwick having failed her orals in graduate school.[187] The second is a "PARTICULARLY TRAUMATIC", "EXHAUSTING AND VERY PAINFUL" visit to the dentist Sedgwick had when she was seven or eight, when she had "SEVERAL FILLINGS DONE IN ONE AFTERNOON". "UNABLE TO GET AWAY, AND PERHAPS UNABLE TO PROTEST", Sedgwick experienced the visit as "SIMILAR TO A CONCEPT OF RAPE", to her "MASOCHISTIC FANTASIES", and to her father's repeated scenes of taking a topic Sedgwick was interested in, and absorbing it, along with its accompanying energy, into himself, leaving her depleted. This paternal context reveals, perhaps, a phantasmatic, parricidal violence as a subtext to 'Ring of Fire', given that Sedgwick's father, a NASA lunar photographer, like the astronaut in the poem, couldn't have guessed "what harm his desire to see the moon had done".[188]

Perhaps because of Van Wey's own sci-fi interests, meanwhile, the single most returned to lyric, in *Fat Art, Thin Art,* is 'Not', with its thematics of a child protesting to its parents that it "didn't put in for a transfer to this planet". The poem is echoed

---

186 Sedgwick, *Fat Art, Thin Art,* 77–78.

187 Sedgwick, *A Dialogue on Love,* 64.

188 For Sedgwick senior's photographs, see *The Moon as Viewed by Lunar Orbiter* (Washington, DC: NASA, 1970). Sedgwick's father may also haunt 'Artery', with its discussion of how "planets may bear life" but "not she, her delicate continent / held rock and supported nothing / that moved from within itself"; and 'Lullaby', where the speaker seeks her beloved's gaze as the earth turns toward the "waning moon".

some five times in the memoir's insistence that Sedgwick was an *"exceptional"* kid whose parents were the "emperor and empress of Mars"; Sedgwick's sister describing her as if she were "FROM ANOTHER PLANET"; Van Wey describing Sedgwick's "OUTER-SPACE-LOOKING NECK BRACE"; and when Sedgwick's parents might have thought that she was "really the exiled // daughter of the king / and queen of Mars", but Sedgwick herself did not know it and just longed "to be // their own, peasant child".[189]

In addition, *A Dialogue on Love* provides crucial context for a number of Sedgwick's uncollected poems. We learn that Sedgwick's "embarrassing" early poem 'Stillborn Child', cited, in 'A Poem is Being Written', as an example of "angry self-pity" and "genuine morbidity", as well as of a "certain resistance and heroism",[190] documents a key scene otherwise edited out of the Kosofsky family album, since Sedgwick's mother had earlier had "a miscarriage or a still birth" between the birth of Sedgwick and her little brother, David. This was a baby who was, otherwise, not much mourned.[191] When thinking of the predominance of death as a theme in much of her juvenilia, Sedgwick again later acknowledged, in 'A Poem is Being Written', that she was a "morbid, / sentimental kid", for whom the "thought // of dying young was / a good friend", and to whom "to think of death / brought . . . a sense of safety", "rest" and "being held".[192] But, by contrast, *A Dialogue on Love* points to a number of genuinely tragic substrates beneath two further undergraduate poems.

'Two P.O.W. Suicides' invokes the "voice of a friend / young a couple of years back when he died / from a landmine in a programme of foreign aid", while *A Dialogue on Love* documents that, in 1970, the best friend of Sedgwick's husband had been "blown up in a landmine in Vietnam", aged twenty, a "very […]

189 Sedgwick, *Fat Art, Thin Art*, 36; *A Dialogue on Love*, 102, 136, 152–153, 155, 212.

190 Sedgwick, *Tendencies*, 184–185.

191 For more, see *A Dialogue on Love*, 61, 192.

192 Sedgwick, *A Dialogue on Love*, 16. Compare also her later account of the "sadness and morbidity inside me as a child" (62).

shocking" event because it was so "out of the blue".[193] 'A Death by Water' probably recalls the death, in 1971, of the couple's friend and father figure, Frank Rosenblatt, who had "died in a boating accident" that year.[194] Elsewhere in her memoir, Sedgwick documented that she had cut her thumb whilst whittling soap at girl scout camp aged 12,[195] a scene resonant with the start of the uncollected poem 'Artery' (which, "Like Plath", begins "with a finger sliced") and the scout camp Sedgwick described in 'Who Fed This Muse', where, like "generations of baby lesbians", Sedgwick was happy.[196]

In *A Dialogue on Love,* we also learn more about the cosmopolitan Monsieur O, subject of 'A Poem is Being Written' and of the uncollected poem 'Epilogue: Teachers and Lovers', the seventh-grade French tutor who so caught Sedgwick's imagination, and the revelation of whose homosexuality led, in some meaningful sense, to her identity as a poet and a paranoid reader.[197] In addition, in that context Sedgwick's admission that, "except for English", she was "awful at languages",[198] makes more resonant the bid for the cosmopolitanism of the young Eve Kosofsky in a number of her uncollected poems, given her pointed citation

---

193 Sedgwick, *A Dialogue on Love,* 63.
194 Sedgwick, *A Dialogue on Love,* 63.
195 Sedgwick, *A Dialogue on Love,* 73.
196 Sedgwick, *Fat Art, Thin Art,* 5–6. For more on the queer possibilities of girl scout culture and summer camps, see Kent, *Making Girls into Women,* 105–139; and "'No Trespassing": Girl Scout Camp and the Limits of the Counterpublic Sphere', in Steven Bruhm and Natahsa Hurley, eds., *Curiouser: On the Queerness of Children* (Minneapolis: University of Minnesota Press, 2004), 173–191.
197 For example, Sedgwick described how, following the revelation of Monsieur O's entrapment, she "BEGAN READING INSATIABLY" about male homosexuality, the "INTENSITY" of her investment "PROPELLED" by "HER CHAGRIN AT HAVING MISREAD THE FRENCH TEACHER SO COMPLETELY — HER PERCEPTUAL ACUMEN HAVING FAILED HER", but her "FASCINATION WITH IMPLICIT THEMES" subsequently "ENGAGED AND SHARPENED" (*A Dialogue on Love,* 74–75). For more on paranoid and reparative readings, see *Touching Feeling,* 123–152.
198 Sedgwick, *A Dialogue on Love,* 74.

from a range of German, as well as French and Latin, language poets.[199]

Our Favourite Poet and Dear Daughter, Eve: A Portrait of the Artist as a Newly Middle-Aged Poet

In addition to helpfully contextualising many of Sedgwick's poems, *A Dialogue on Love* documents the specific moment when her first poem comes after years of writer's block. This was a "mild and rainy" spring day, when Sedgwick was nervously looking forward to her next session with Van Wey, a little anxious she'd be able to "get centred and at home with him properly" and about whether she'd generate some interesting content for them to process together, but mostly thinking about the "strange form of address" between them: "the unmistakable one that's somewhere between talking to myself and talking to another person". Then, "invoking Shannon's wide sheltered room" in a "wet, calm outdoor space" that had so often been a scene of her past poetry[200] and finding herself centred, she heard a "quiet inside voice" noting, in a four-line, non-haiku stanza,

I can tune my mind today
to the story I think I want to tell you;
I can tune my eyes
already to your face, listening.

---

199 'When in Minute Script' addresses Aristotle; 'Falling in Love over The Seven Pillars' invokes Sophocles; 'Calling Overseas' sings of Virgil and of Abelard and Heloise; 'Epilogue: Teachers and Lovers' quotes Baudelaire, in the original French, while 'Die Sommernacht hat mir's angethan' alludes to a poem by von Scheffel, as we have seen. 'The Warm Decembers' quotes, again in the original German, Andrew Gryphius, whilst the later poem, 'Nicht Mehr Leben', again presumes readers fluent in German (*Fat Art, Thin Art*, 37, 109). Sedgwick's father spoke German.

200 For example, see "the sloppy landscape" of Norfolk and the "extensive and steamily beautiful / wetland view" of New Hartford in 'The Warm Decembers', the latter where Sedgwick sits, "a notebook open, its loose-leaves spread" (*Fat Art, Thin Art*, 111–112).

As she walks along, Sedgwick finds that her "little smile is enfolding a new thought". When she gets inside, maybe she will "put these words on a scrap of paper and see whether they look (as they sort of sound to me) like the possible start of a poem"; acknowledging that it had been years since she had "tasted this particular mild, speculative smile".[201] And, with a few small revisions and nine more lines, that thought became one of the collected poems: 'I can tune my mind today'.[202] A Dialogue on Love, then, documents the very moment in which Sedgwick's poetry returned and "with it, and with Shannon's escort", "some of the long-ago life of the girl whose first passion it was".[203] But the poetry was not just a therapeutic blast from the past or life raft in the midst of so many of her friends and family dying. It was a harbinger of a different future, in which Sedgwick would emerge "a different person"; a person with a crucial new identity as a fibre artist.[204]

Making Poetic Things, Practicing Emptiness, or How to Do Things With Poems

In the same period in which she was writing A Dialogue on Love, poetry proved increasingly important to Sedgwick's emerging practice as a fibre artist, and, in a late essay 'Making Things, Practicing Emptiness' (2007), she described the emergence of a "distinct artistic practice involving textiles". As in A Dialogue on Love, although to a lesser extent, Sedgwick partly emphasised the non-verbal aspects of that practice. She described how her textile practice had "little aptitude for being put into words". She emphasized the textural specificity of her "very material

---

201 Sedgwick, A Dialogue on Love, 123–124.
202 Sedgwick, Fat Art, Thin Art, 22. In the published version, Sedgwick tunes her "eye" singular, rather than "eyes"; and there is a lesser, comma- rather than semi-colon-length, pause at the end of the second line. The "mild and rainy" spring day, of the memoir, becomes, in the second stanza of the poem, "the rain of today, / which will rain all afternoon".
203 Sedgwick, A Dialogue on Love, 136.
204 Sedgwick, A Dialogue on Love, 136.

and pressing" textile practice, and she documented how the ico-nography of "hands and handiwork" were central to her textile projects, as well as the "deep inherent relationality of touch and texture". In addition, Sedgwick followed F. David Peat's account of the fascinating "dimensionality of string", with its simultane-ous, multiple existences at different scales, as a "single thread", a "twisted line", "long cylinder", or "three-dimensional figure", and as composed of "individual fibers, tiny twisting lines", empha-sizing the importance, in her own works, of "hypervisible [...] dangling bits of thread".[205]

And yet, Sedgwick's account of fibres as "tiny twisting lines", often "dangling", recalls her poetic predilection for multi-claus-al, parenthetical sentences and *enjambment*. And, later in the es-say, Sedgwick emphasized that her "sluttish", "easy", and "funky" textile practice did not represent a complete "change of iden-tity" from her former persona as a "literary critic" and "poet". Taking Sedgwick's cue, we can hear a connection, in the highly sexualized language of "sluttishness" and her description of how her textiles were the result of a "Buddhist penetration", the clear overlap with her former queer theoretical interests. Her fondness for the "enfoldment" offered by fabrics, meanwhile, brought to mind her *c.* 1993 poem, 'The Use of Being Fat', which described how, in the context of the AIDS epidemic — and with an allusion to Thom Gunn's then-recently-published *The Man With Night Sweats* (1992) — she had a

> superstition that
> there was this use of being fat:
> no one I loved could come to harm
> enfolded in my touch —
> that lot of me would blot it up,
> the rattling chill, night sweat or terror.[206]

---

205 Sedgwick, *The Weather in Proust*, 69–122.
206 Sedgwick, *Fat Art, Thin Art*, 15; *The Weather in Proust*, 69–122. Thom Gunn, *The Man with the Night Sweats* (London: Faber, 1992).

In addition, Sedgwick's description of how her "mushrooming array of 'arts and craft' projects and supplies" were "pinning [her] to the table" evokes precisely the sadomasochistic lyric *tableau* of 'A Poem is Being Written'. Her account of the ways in which her hands were "very hungry" for fabrics recalls the digestive aesthetics of *Fat Art, Thin Art*. Her description of her interest in the "fractional", "dimensional betweenness" of shibori, often "left in a kind of springy, elastic state", in the context of the similar two-and-a-half dimensions of the perspectival "picture plane", recall her career-long interest in the "between" and specifically 'An Essay on the Picture Plane'.[207]

Towards the end of the essay, Sedgwick emphasized that an interest in the "texture and materiality" of language "obviously animated a lot of [her] work as well", with the result that "the complete exclusion of language from [her] art was never in the cards". After all, "that exclusion would have consolidated the dualism" between word and image that she could have never countenanced. Sedgwick also documented how important to her had been a number of Japanese death poems from the seventeenth to the early twentieth whilst she was at work on her exhibition, *Bodhisattva Fractal World,* shown at John Hopkins University in 2002, before moving on to Dartmouth College in 2003. She found this particular form of haiku evocative because while such poems often had a first person, it wasn't her first person, and it was a "first person at the very edge of its decomposition". She also had an ongoing "sense of urgency" to try to discover "what it feels like to die" or "a way it can feel to die, if you've got your mind properly wrapped around the reality of the process",[208] a preoccupation also in evidence in Sedgwick's fascination with Merrill's *Ephraim,* as we have seen, and in her earlier poems 'A Ring of Fire' and 'The Last Poem of 'Yv*r Wintrs', contained in this volume.

---

207 For more on shibori, see Yoshiko Iwamoto Wada, *Memory on Cloth: Shibori Now* (Tokyo: Kodansha, 2002); and Wada, Mary Kellogg Rice, and Jane Barton, *Shibori: the Inventive Art of Japanese Shaped Resist Dyeing* (1983; Tokyo: Kodansha, 1999).

208 Sedgwick, *The Weather in Proust,* 111.

In the essay, Sedgwick reproduced four such works inspired by Japanese death poems. These were Choko's c.1731 haiku 'This Final scene I'll not see / to the end — my dream / is fraying'; Sai-kuku's c. 1730 'I borrow moonlight / for this journey of a million miles'; Shagai's c. 1795 'Reality is flowerlike: / cold clouds sinking through / the dusk'; and Bashō's c. 1692–1694 'While sweeping the yard / it forgets about the snow / a broom'.[209] In addition, Sedgwick generated other works drawing on related material, including Ryoho's c. 1669 'Now I understand how / the third verse of moon and flowers is interwoven'; Fusen's c. 1777 'Today, then, is the day / the melting snowman is a real man'; Saiba's c. 1858 'I shift my pillow / closer to the / full moon'; Ro-shu's c. 1899 'Time to go ... / they say the journey is a long one: / change of robes'; and Kyotaro's c. 1928 'Tender winds above the snow / melt many kinds / of suffering'.[210] Sedgwick also explored Ariawara no Narihara's c. 825–880 'I have always known that I would take this path, but yesterday I did not know it would be today'.[211]

209 For more, see Yoel Hoffmann, ed., *Japanese Death Poems Written by Zen Monks and Haiku Poets on the Verge of Death* (Boston: Tuttle, 1986), 154, 275, 286–287; and Ueda, ed. *Bashō and His Interpreters*, 346.

210 For more, see Hoffmann, *Japanese Death Poems*, 164–165, 237–238, 267, 272, 278.

211 Whilst this is not the precise translation Sedgwick employs, for more see Ariwara no Narihara, *Tales of Ise* (trans. Henry Harris; Boston: Tuttle, 1972), 158. Whilst commentators, including Sedgwick, have often pointed to the importance of Merrill's 'Prose of Departure', and, behind it, Bashō's haibun, to *A Dialogue on Love,* that Sedgwick employed the final poem from the ninth-century Japanese text indicates the potential importance of this text to *Dialogue.* Like both Merrill and Bashō's source texts, *The Tales of Ise* is composed of episodic narrative prose interspersed with lyric verse. In Nari-hara's case, this is in the form of uta, a 31-syllable (5-7-5-7-7) form closely related to haiku. In addition, unlike both Bashō and Merrill's source texts, The *Tales of Ise* is composed primarily of the dialogues between two cross-gender lovers, in which, as Harris notes, the poetic and relational effects "rise unmistakably as much from the spaces between the short sentences as from the sentences themselves" (*The Tales of Ise,* 12). Sedgwick's lines occur in the final section of the poem, which tells how "Long ago a man fell gravely ill", who "always knew" in "his heart that he was to die", but "yester-day or today ... / no! never had I thought it" (158).

In 2007, Sedgwick described *Japanese Death Poems* as having been "recently published". In fact, Yoel Hoffmann's edition of *Japanese Death Poems Written by Zen Monks and Haiku Poets on the Verge of Death* had been published more than twenty years earlier in 1986. This is the first instance of a curiously queer temporality present in the essay, and one that points further to the significant overlap, in Sedgwick's idiom, of her practice as a poet and textile artist. For example, Sedgwick located the emergence of her interest in textiles "almost a dozen years ago" from 2007, so around late 1995. Later in the essay, however, Sedgwick suggested that both "textiles" and "Buddhism" came "bounding into [her] life" sometime "about eleven years ago", so 1996, along with a "stamp of mortality" derived from the "diagnosis in 1996" that her breast cancer had metastasized to her spine. It was also around "age forty-six", thus in 1996, that Sedgwick gave up the "pretext of self-ornamentation" in favour of a more abstract, pictorial textile practice. The poem that Sedgwick tacitly evokes here is clear. 'Trace at 46' similarly begins with a "middle-age" transformation and one already enamoured of textiles, as Sedgwick depicts Trace delighting fondling "handsome / individuable wovens" in "desaturated beige, / a lovely champagne" that call to mind Sedgwick's later weaving practice: "folded money-purses in dry pouchy kid" that speak to Sedgwick's later delight in textiles of "enfoldment"; "silk cords, thick and thin ones, in blues and greens" that anticipate Sedgwick's later use of "rolled up bundles of silk and paper" to be "dyed in indigo"; and a "scarf / stained with feathery mauve-and-azure waves ('Marbled by Hand'), like endpapers" that anticipates Sedgwick's later shibori marbling techniques.[212]

Poetry was also central to Sedgwick's practice as the maker of artist's books and, in particular, to a *c.* 2007 altered book that collaged together an illustrated edition of Edward Bulwer-

---

212 Sedgwick, *Fat Art, Thin Art*, 43, 47–49. 46 represented an unusually over-determined age for Sedgwick, since it was also at aged "forty-six or forty-seven" that Sedgwick's brother in law, Stan, developed metastatic cancer (*A Dialogue on Love*, 126).

Lytton's *Last Days of Pompeii* (1834) and excerpts from 22 poems by Cavafy.[213] This explored, in a parallel visual idiom, what Sedgwick described, in her Cavafy essay, as the Greek poet's interest in the "relations of selection and quotation", "the intimate spatiality of the shrine", and the aesthetics of "a little house within a house", "one oriented towards its missing fourth wall, like a doll-house, a diorama, a hearth, or puppet theatre". [214]

Finally, poets and poetry were central to Sedgwick's practice as a photo-collage artist, a fact we might have anticipated from her *c.* 1993 poem, 'Grave, never offering back the face of my dear'. This described Sedgwick taking photographs from a "dramatic low angle by the footstool" at the hospital bedside of one of her male friends dying of AIDS, as we have seen, before taking the film to the "1-Hr. prints", so that she can assemble a "big pseudo-David Hockney photo collage". [215]

Four of Sedgwick's photo-collages depict poets. *Jacket Night at the ID450 Collective* (July 1988) captures various members of the feminist writing collective Sedgwick was a part of, that also included acclaimed poet Mary Baine Campbell, who contributes a key essay to this volume.[216] *Listening to Dionne* (April 1992) depicts Gary Fisher, at Sedgwick's then house in Durham.[217] 'Terrible Scrabble' (February 1988) documents Michael Lynch playing scrabble with his son Stephen and Sedgwick's husband, and 'Eternity's White Flag', employed on the dedication page to *Tendencies,* depicts, as we have seen, Sedgwick and Lynch tenderly interlocked over Dickinson's grave in Amherst,

---

213 Edward Bulwer Lytton, *The Last Days of Pompeii* (London: Marshall Cavendish, 1976, with illustrations by Felix Gluck Press).

214 Sedgwick, *The Weather in Proust,* 44, 66.

215 Sedgwick, *Fat Art, Thin Art,* 10.

216 For more, see ID450 Collective, 'Writing the Plural: Sexual Fantasies', 293–307 which may contain an otherwise unattributed poem by Sedgwick, there read by Campbell, 'Marcel looked as virile as he was able' (301–302). For Campbell's poetic work, see *The World, The Flesh and Angels* (Boston: Beacon, 1989) and *Trouble* (Carnegie Mellon University Press, 2003).

217 For more, see Sedgwick, *Gary in Your Pocket.* In spite of the title, Fisher was also a poet, and the volume includes a number of his poems. For examples, see 6, 17–18, 23, 32–36, 45–48, 62, 68, 90.

each wearing a pair of Lynch's signature white glasses. The collage, of course, takes its title from the last lines of Dickinson's 'Our Journey Had Advanced':[218]

Our journey had advanced
Our feet were almost come
To that odd fork in Being's road
Eternity by term.

Our pace took sudden awe
Our feet reluctant led.
Before were cities, but between
The forest of the dead.

Retreat was out of hope
Behind, a sealed route,
Eternity's white flag before
And God at every gate.

Eternity's White Flags or The Melancholy Poetics of The Long Goodbye

In her remarkable, poignant essay in this volume on Sedgwick's two 'Performative' poems from *Fat Art, Thin Art,* Meg Boulton considers the idea of saying goodbye to the people that we love as an impossible, unhappy performative, one that we hope will never be truly necessary. Questions of "saying goodbye" also come to the fore in the final sentences of Sedgwick's last essay on poetry: 'Proust, Cavafy and the Queer Little Gods'. *Bathroom Songs* exists very much in that vulnerable, stubbornly resistant space of Boulton's refused goodbye to Sedgwick, in its unwillingness to accept that there will be no more new poems by Sedgwick found, and no more new books by or about Sedgwick, even though she, through the voice of Cavafy, asked her readers not to "mourn […] uselessly" and had "long prepared" us,

---

218 Sedgwick, *Tendencies,* 252–266.

as best she could, so that, "graced with courage", we could "say goodbye to her". I can't quite do that yet. Instead, let's "listen with deep emotion", in what I am confident will not be "our final delectation, to the voices" and "exquisite music" of Sedgwick's uncollected poetry and, first, to the voices of our six commentators upon her collected verse.[219]

219 Sedgwick, *The Weather in Proust*, 67–68.

CHAPTER I

Look With Your Hands

Angus Connell Brown

I began writing this essay in what used to be a child's bedroom. Perched at the small desk by the doll's house, I looked away to my right and saw how the enormous sash window smoothly held my reflection among the lights and the trees outside. This uncanny framing, this return to the fascination of reflection among the tactile technologies of childhood imagination feels like a fitting place to begin thinking about one of the first poems Eve Kosofsky Sedgwick ever published: 'An Essay on the Picture Plane'.

According to *Fat Art, Thin Art,* Sedgwick composed the poem in 1973 but the tiny discrepancies — a missing line here, an extra comma there — between the publication of the poem in *The Poetry Miscellany* in 1975 and the collection of the poem in 1994 hint that the latter text is the product of a slight return to a younger muse, a muse still theorizing the world around her. My own return to 'An Essay on the Picture Plane' oscillates between a question and an instruction that Sedgwick's poem scratched up from my own childhood. The question: "What are you looking at?" The instruction: "Look with your eyes, not with your hands". I learnt both at school. And both, like 'An Essay on the Picture Plane', left me tongue-tied.

In her memoir — her 'texture-book' — *A Dialogue on Love* (1999), Sedgwick described a way in which she would gently break this kind of fraught silence, the kind of silence that often followed poems and stories in her creative writing class.[1] As the tension reached breaking point she would murmur:

> "What's this piece doing?"
> or even, "What does it know?"[2]

'An Essay on the Picture Plane' asks "What are you looking at?" It's there in the title, "What are you looking at? A poem? An essay? A picture?"

We learnt the power of this question on the playground. "What are *you* looking at?" It took your silence from you. You were no longer just quiet; you weren't allowed to talk. The paranoid aggression of this question turned the boy or girl asking it from a "who" into a "what". An inanimate menace: subject to, impervious from, and terrified of, the possibility of desire. The obscene magic of that question "What are *you* looking at?" shamed *you* with the queer connotations *it* generated, *it* publicized, and still, entirely without conscience, blamed you for.[3]

Now, when 'An Essay on the Picture Plane' asks that question, any belligerence softens into the same throaty murmur of, "What's this piece doing?" It is curious and only a little stung by the nervousness of becoming an object so subject to desire or scorn. Reading this poem, my confused tongue only began to loosen when I realized that when 'An Essay on the Picture Plane' asked, "What are you looking at?" it was talking directly to me. *I* was the *you* the poem addressed. 'An Essay on the Picture Plane' is a letter to the reader.

Take the poem's second stanza:

> The vertical plane makes the absence present
> to you, who are absent both from the horizon

---

1 Eve Kosofsky Sedgwick, *A Dialogue on Love* (Boston: Beacon Press, 1999), 207.

2 Sedgwick, *A Dialogue on Love,* 42.

3 Sedgwick treats playground performativity in her writing on wussiness in *Touching Feeling: Affect, Pedagogy, Performativity* (Durham: Duke University Press, 2003), 69–70.

and from the fabric itself before you
which is too articulate.[4]

In reading this poem, *you* — by which I mean *I*, so let's call it
we — render the vertical plane, the page itself, absent. The fibers of the fabric in front of us are "too articulate" for us to see.
Reading instead of looking, we blur the page into the poem. But
even if we do look, even if we shift our focus past the words on
the page and onto the grain of the recto and verso we are still,
surely, separate from the poem itself. Safe in the extraordinary
privileges of looking and reading, wrapped in their strange and
yielding silences, we once again excuse ourselves from the poem's tableau. Or we would if the poem would let us. 'An Essay on
the Picture Plane' continues:

My project, really, is a street at 8 or 9
in cold weather — after all, there is a point
in late dark evening when the formalism leaves you.
Are you wrapped warmly?

I want big houses of two kinds:
in the first kind no one's visible and that's OK
where nothing belongs to it but its windows that are dark
which just reflect the night, and its windows
that are lit, which make a small transparent space, the room
that while distant is both visible and perspicuous.
For you on the street, hot and chilly:
there are bright places free entirely of you
and there at the same time, of course, for you.[5]

Here, in my reading, Sedgwick presses us firmly into the poem
as both reader and character. As character we are tickled warm
and cold, looking into a house that now accepts, now reflects,

---

4   Eve Kosofsky Sedgwick, *Fat Art, Thin Art* (Durham: Duke University Press,
    1994), 72.

5   Sedgwick, *Fat Art, Thin Art*, 72.

our gaze from window to window. As reader, we are presented with a bright, white space — the page — free of us and yet for us. We are invited to look through it, to test its resistances. In the final paragraphs of her essay, or the final two stanzas of her poem, Sedgwick describes the second house and, in doing so, juxtaposes the window and the page, mapping the poem's second person onto *you*:

> you with your confusing purchase on the space
> of fears, inflections, and ambitions (for who
> might not now walk in, putting on all the glamor
> of the lit stage, perfectly irresistible,
> and you out here dark, with no means
> at all of yielding), I'm saying,
>
> for you, there is no free or distant space.
> Across the dark around you, the bright window is
> only as transparent and no more
> than this designed and speckled page.[6]

As you struggle to maintain your confusing purchase on its pages, the poem plucks at your fingers. Gently rethreading the needle of its playground logic, 'An Essay on the Picture Plane' calls you out for staring. It lights you up and looks back, inscrutable among the glinting windows of the poem's surface. In this final stanza, the reader finally becomes the poem's second person, rendered inanimate within the text, subject to desire and scorn.

Sedgwick's other essay on a picture plane, 'A Poem is Being Written' (1987), notoriously ties the optics of form to spanking. In doing so, it quietly gives the source of her window trick. In a parenthetical aside, Sedgwick admits, "I planned for each poem in a booklet I made at eight to be closely framed by a golden proscenium hung with curtains, carefully labelled 'The Magic

---

6   Sedgwick, *Fat Art, Thin Art*, 73.

Window"".[7] In 'An Essay on the Picture Plane', this precocious fantasy of the poem, the window, and the handmade comes together, and again it is framed by fabric. While the poem is astringent in its optical interrogation of what "are often blandly called" reader-relations, its insistence on materiality invites us to look, not with our eyes but with our hands.[8]

Sedgwick makes her most tangible invitations to look with our hands in her textile art. In the part-published paper 'Come As You Are', she writes about this art, describing "the rub of reality" and "tactile interrogation".[9] Still, Sedgwick's most sensational work might be *Touching Feeling*. Since the book's publication in 2003, theorists like Sianne Ngai and Heather Love have generated an illuminating critical friction from the feeling of Sedgwick's title. Both critics extend Sedgwick's treatment of affect to a certain degree. In *Ugly Feelings* (2005), Ngai briefly draws on Sedgwick's work with Adam Frank in her discussion of Silvan Tomkins.[10] In *Feeling Backward* (2007), Love engages much more explicitly with Sedgwick's work on shame.[11] Love and Ngai's titles both borrow some of the poetry of Sedgwick's. As *Ugly Feelings* and *Feeling Backward* echo the twin trochees of *Touching Feeling*, they show the extent to which subsequent theories of affect have numbed the physical connotations of Sedgwick's *Feeling*. The ambiguous gerunds of Sedgwick's title do not let us forget that affect and embodiment make for inseparable bedfellows in her work. The insistence of 'An Essay

---

7   Eve Kosofsky Sedgwick, *Tendencies* (Durham: Duke University Press, 1993), 183. In *Touching Feeling*, Sedgwick returns at length to the figure of the proscenium in order to explore the spatiality of performativity and, in particular, "marriage itself as theater" (72), an idea she also explores in her poem 'Our'.

8   Eve Kosofsky Sedgwick, *Epistemology of the Closet* (Los Angeles: University of California Press, 1990), 3.

9   Sedgwick, 'Come As You Are' unpublished MS, 4. Parts of this paper were published in various chapters of *The Weather in Proust*. My thanks to Jonathan Goldberg for sharing the manuscript with me.

10 Sianne Ngai, *Ugly Feelings* (Cambridge: Harvard University Press, 2007).

11 Heather Love, *Feeling Backward: Loss and the Politics of Queer History* (Cambridge: Harvard University Press, 2007).

on the Picture Plane' on materiality massages some blood back into Sedgwick's *Feeling* and allows us to consider her neglected *Touching*. *Touching*: her work so often is. It trembles with affect's weight but still clasps to cutaneous and digital connotations. Perhaps this is what the manicules, the small pointing fingers that begin each chapter of *Touching Feeling* are pointing towards so elegantly: touch is a heuristic.

Fat Art, Thin Art is full of the touching that might shape this heuristic. As Sedgwick's work changes, the meaning of skin on skin began to change. In the later poems, the muse of masturbation becomes the touch of teaching. Lines like:

> The
> actual, slightly numb, and wakeful touch
> of bodies in the dream ('Sexual Hum') [12]

> Last night, fingers beating ('Sestina Lente') [13]

and,

> the touch of dead cat ('Sestina Lente') [14]

turn to lines like:

> The touching made us feel absurdly vital ('Performative (Toronto)') [15]

and, my utter favourite — from 'The Use of Being Fat' —

> no one I loved could come to harm
> enfolded in my touch. [16]

---

12 Sedgwick, *Fat Art, Thin Art*, 76.
13 Sedgwick, *Fat Art, Thin Art*, 84.
14 Sedgwick, *Fat Art, Thin Art*, 84.
15 Sedgwick, *Fat Art, Thin Art*, 17.
16 Sedgwick, *Fat Art, Thin Art*, 15.

This kind of enfolding touch is a different version of "a steady touch in an inky room" ('Everything Always Distracts'),[17] though one we're all equally, adolescently, and adultly familiar with. It is the touch of reading.

We know this touch already, and we have come to know it intimately, by imagining its impossibility. The language of close reading provides the impossibility of touch with its most insistent and enduring aesthetic: the image of edging closer and closer towards an object that we'd dearly love to put our hands on but daren't. In this way, 'An Essay on the Picture Plane' holds up a mirror to the close reader. When I look at my reflection, I see myself where, I think, I've always been as a reader: quietly blurred between the impossibility of touch and the imaginative worlds that belong to that impossibility, wavering on the edge of fantasy. But, when I look again, I can see something else. I am already touching 'An Essay on the Picture Plane'. I am holding the poem by the pages' curves. I can feel their grain, light on my thumbs. I am learning to look with my hands.

---

17 Sedgwick, *Fat Art, Thin Art*, 74.

CHAPTER 2

The Abject Animal Poetics of 'The Warm Decembers'

Ben Westwood

Sedgwick's long, unfinished verse novel, 'The Warm Decembers' (*c.* 1978–1986), invites us to think carefully about the relations between humans and animals, the value of animals in poetry, and how these ideas might link to the abject. In what follows, these points of connection emerge as functions of the "perverse, desiring energies" which, Sedgwick suggests, animate and colour the poem's representation of boundaries between states of being, between, that is, beings dead and alive, past and present, real and fictional, and human and animal.[1] In 'The Warm Decembers', animals are figures of the abject, which intensify and diversify the poem's expressive capabilities. They are represented as something other than the simple outside of humanity, as parts of structures which are never stable but constantly folding in on themselves or dissolving into indistinctness. And, in this linguistic and conceptual reconfiguration, Sedgwick offers a vision of how the category of the abject can help us re-describe our relations with different forms of animal life and a vision of how animals can offer writers uniquely flexible models for articulation and expression.

Juxtaposed with the discussion of the poem's conceptual work are short accounts of the conditions governing the lives

---

1   Eve Kosofsky Sedgwick, *Fat Art, Thin Art* (Durham: Duke University Press, 1994), 157.

of billions of real-world animals in the hope of widening the scope of what might be meant by Julia Kristeva's idea of the abject territories of the animal.[2] Part of the aim of this chapter is to suggest some connections between the linguistic representation of animals and the harsh realities of existence for many actual animals by putting side-by-side fictional, poetic accounts and non-fictional ones. My other hope for this split structure is that it retains some of the character of the work it discusses, which itself twines together a fictional literary-historical past and an emphatic autobiographical present, and conveys the sense of non-linear thinking which the poem seems to encourage or even require. For though there is a clear narrative strand running through the figure of Beatrix, its progression is constantly interrupted or turned back on itself and many aspects of Sedgwick's poem resist clear understanding or simple explanation: its split parallel timelines ("The present tense of the poem is 1880, except where it is circa 1980");[3] its striking and sometimes oblique use of figurative language; its strange mix of personal lyric and third-person narrative, and the hybridity of its generic make-up (epistolary, realist novel, civil rights protest poem, journal); and the fact that it remains unfinished. This chapter is, therefore, an attempt to follow a certain thread through what is a thoroughly knotted text. But, ultimately, these crossed wires are what allow for unexpected connections, and are what make this poem such a generous one to think with.

Drawing on a spectrum of more or less figurative embodiments, Sedgwick continually places animal life in key points or relations, and they play an important role in expanding the poem's imaginative range — both of action and imagery. Therefore, one of the questions I want to ask here is: what kind of work might these animal figures be doing in the poem? They appear as metaphorical qualities of objects — "tapeworm swags

2   Julia Kristeva, *The Powers of Horror: An Essay on Abjection,* trans. Leon Roudiez (New York: Columbia University Press, 1982), 12.

3   Sedgwick, *Fat Art, Thin Art,* 88.

of linen",[4] "shrimp light breasting the tub".[5] As ways of acting
(or not acting): Beatrix stands "silent — her father / would have
said, she imagined, like a horse".[6] They appear as images of visual
confusion, and tactile proximity — as Beatrix makes her escape,
"swans, cows; in the sloppy landscape anything / condensed in
front of her"; thinking she had fallen "asleep under a windmill",
she realises that "the creaking noise she still heard / was a cygnet — climbing up and down / on top of her. She could have
hugged it".[7] They are richly and symbolically suggestive — Butterscotch, the kitten, is removed from the young narrator's lap,
because "two cats were two too many" for young girls to have as
pets, according to their father.[8] Animals help describe the qualities of art — in Beatrix's landscapes, the grass looks like "the fur
of an animal / too sick to tend itself";[9] and both human and
nonhuman animals are themselves drawn from, and form part
of, these landscapes — "extents of vital texture… / only at the
last extremity nipped in / to make an animal form".[10] Animals
are food, good and spoiled — "broken meat" and "miles" of
ham[11] — but they are also companion animals, as in the "almost
exactly the same dog" joke.[12] They are even models for sexual
play when Richard Burton is quoted on "whole" boy prostitutes,
and the use of their scrotums as a "bridle for directing / the
movements of the animal".[13] Indeed, in Sedgwick's 'Notes' on the
poem, she says that her initial idea for the poem was to have "a
man named Miles and a hound named Miles", who, at "the formal climax of the poem […] would somehow get their narrative

---

4   Sedgwick, *Fat Art, Thin Art*, 116.
5   Sedgwick, *Fat Art, Thin Art*, 100.
6   Sedgwick, *Fat Art, Thin Art*, 109.
7   Sedgwick, *Fat Art, Thin Art*, 111.
8   Sedgwick, *Fat Art, Thin Art*, 123.
9   Sedgwick, *Fat Art, Thin Art*, 114.
10 Sedgwick, *Fat Art, Thin Art*, 114–115.
11 Sedgwick, *Fat Art, Thin Art*, 130, 98.
12 Sedgwick, *Fat Art, Thin Art*, 135.
13 Sedgwick, *Fat Art, Thin Art*, 148.

points-of-view inextricably fused".[14] That this fusing of narrative viewpoints both was planned and fails to materialize is revealing of the poem's boundary-skirting impulses. Sedgwick herself notes that, while borders between states of being are "sought out with longing" in the poem,[15] inevitably such seeking is as likely to run up against these borders as to flow along and across them. Recounting the unrealized germ of the poem — particularly its metamorphic quality — is then, perhaps, a limited way in which Sedgwick can have her cake and eat it, a way of seeking out or recalling a boundary to be crossed, and running up against the impossibility of doing so, or the acknowledgement of not having done so. The difficulty of knowing what such perspectival confusion would look like appears to be tacitly admitted, when, in retrospect, Sedgwick leaves out the ontological boundary between human and animal in her list of the distinctions the poem seeks out and plays with:

> between a person alive and dead; a person and a photograph; a sister and a sister; a present and a past; a person child and adult; people with the same name; a happening and the dream of it; a writer (or a model) and a character; an I and a she or a he.[16]

This implicit acknowledgement of a barrier between human and animal experience can help us understand why the poem's animal figures frequently correlate with images of abjection. Though, as I note above, animals are all over 'The Warm Decembers', I want to think closely about animals of the poem that

---

14 Sedgwick, *Fat Art, Thin Art,* 157. Narratologist David Herman is currently working on critical strategies for exploring the ways an array of writers and texts have refracted nonhuman experience or perspectives through fiction. For example, see 'Modernist Life Writing and Nonhuman Lives: Ecologies of Experience in Virginia Woolf's *Flush*', *Modernist Fiction Studies* 59.3 (2013), 547–568, and, 'Storyworld / Umwelt: Nonhuman Experiences in Graphic Novels', *SubStance* 40.1 (2011), 156–181.

15 Sedgwick, *Fat Art, Thin Art,* 160.

16 Sedgwick, *Fat Art, Thin Art,* 157.

might be considered, in different ways, abject. Paying attention to bacteria, cow's milk, and hunted 'vermin' or 'pests', what
emerges from the text is not only a poetics of animals and the
abject, but a poetics of abject animals.[17]

Sedgwick's incorporation of animals into the poem enriches
its scope, resulting in a more nuanced layering of questions of
subjectivity and subjection, agency, will, and life itself. But the
relation between animality and poetics is two-way. Poetry itself may be a way of saying more with less (or indeed, less with
more), as well as of articulating the inarticulable, and the animal
poetics of 'The Warm Decembers' extends the range of the work
it can do and the ideas it can encompass. Animals therefore allow Sedgwick's poem to speak about more and more widely,
but the range of reference opened up would be, in its particular complexity and messiness, nearly impossible to reproduce
in expository, non-fictional prose; not only do animals enable
Sedgwick's poetry to say more, but Sedgwick's poetry is itself
able to say more about, and do more with, animals. Messiness
is, in fact, a necessary structuring principle of this chapter, and
my aim has been throughout to resist, wherever possible, the
assignation of too-ready or too-easy burdens of signification
on the animals and animal-figures of this strange text. In this
way, I am responding here not only to Kristeva and deconstruction, but to Donna Haraway's explorations of the "knot[s] of
species coshaping one another [...] sticky with all their mud-
dled histories".[18] One significant lack those explorations suffer

---

17 In a different context, Mark Payne has explored the links between animals,
    poetry, and the abject, considering emotionally continuous feelings of ag-
    gression between humans other animals in the poetry of ancient Greece
    and William Carlos Williams, as articulated through a poetics structured by
    abjection (*The Animal Part: Human and Other Animals in the Poetic Imagi-
    nation* [Chicago: Chicago University Press, 2010], 27–58).

18 Donna Haraway, *When Species Meet* (Minneapolis: University of Minnesota
    Press, 2008), 42. A poetics of abject animals with its attendant implications
    of recuperation, worldly entanglement, and increased attention to diver-
    sity and scale, necessarily owes an important debt to Haraway: "I think we
    learn to be worldly from grappling with, rather than generalizing from, the
    ordinary. I am a creature of the mud, not the sky. I am a biologist who has

from, however, is the lack of scope or space for a sensitivity to the equally — if not more — knotted relations between species *in language,* especially literary language, a question which this chapter takes up.

The poem's animals' intersections with the abject often involve the binary processes of consumption and abjection, and, within this framework, the text performatively enacts a similar analysis to *Epistemology of the Closet,* that is, the "deconstructive procedure of isolating particular nodes in a web of interconnected binarisms".[19] While the oversimplified dichotomies I discuss here (such as consumption/abjection, edible/inedible, companion/vermin, captivity/freedom) are drawn from the text itself, they also help structure Western conceptualisations of human-animal relations, and this overlap in the linguistic patterning of poetry and broader philosophical patterns of thinking about other animals speaks to an ongoing reconfiguration

---

always found edification in the amazing abilities of slime to hold things in touch and to lubricate passages for living beings and their parts. I love the fact that human genomes can be found in only about 10 percent of all the cells that occupy the mundane space I call my body; the other 90 percent of the cells are filled with the genomes of bacteria, fungi, protists, and such, some of which play in a symphony necessary to my being alive at all, and some of which are hitching a ride and doing the rest of me, of us, no harm. I am vastly outnumbered by my tiny companions; better put, I become an adult human being in company with these tiny messmates" (3–4). *When Species Meet and The Companion Species Manifesto* (Chicago: Prickly Paradigm Press, 2003) both stand as important and idiomatic contributions to the field of animal studies, although I should note that I harbour certain reservations surrounding Haraway's approach, particularly over the totalizing and homogenizing power of the overarching metaphor of all species as "messmates at table, eating together" (301). The risk being that, for all the insistence on attention to the messy specifics of interspecies response and interaction, the metaphor itself implies a lack of differentiation between these "messmates", thereby creating a more or less sophisticated continuance of justifying the killing of animals for human use or, to put it in Haraway's own words, "simply a different way of making killable" (80).

19 Eve Kosofsky Sedgwick, *Epistemology of the Closet* (Los Angeles: University of California Press, 1990), 132.

within deconstruction of the relation of language to animals.[20]
(It is also, I contend, what makes possible and productive the
juxtaposition of poetic and factual representations of animals).
Jacques Derrida has long claimed that, for him, the distinction
between human and animal has been the foundational structure
of Western metaphysics,[21] and more recent work has sought to
ask how we can account for the fact that the logic of the trace
and the iterative structure of human language seem to have
"something strangely animal at work" in them.[22]

As I have so far suggested, 'The Warm Decembers' is a productive text with which to think about the relations between animals, desire, and human language, and part of the connection
between the latter two terms is hinted at by a remark of Sedgwick's on the poem. The concept of the trace — distinguished
from, perhaps, but also related to the trace of deconstruction
referred to in the previous paragraph — becomes important to,
and metamorphozed by, Sedgwick throughout her career; this
mix of confluence and departure marks a potentially fruitful
site of interplay between Sedgwick's readings of desire, and her
deconstruction-influenced reading practices.[23] In 'The Beast in

20 For the most influential contributions to this discussion, see Jacques Derrida, *The Beast and the Sovereign,* vols. 1–2, trans. Geoffrey Bennington,
eds. Marie-Louise Mallet et al. (Chicago: University of Chicago Press,
2009–2010), and *The Animal That Therefore I Am,* trans. David Wills (New
York: Fordham University Press, 2008); Cary Wolfe, *Animal Rites: American Culture, the Discourse of Species, and Posthumanist Theory* (Chicago:
Chicago University Press, 2003); Lynn Turner, ed., *The Animal Question in
Deconstruction* (Edinburgh: Edinburgh University Press, 2013).

21 Jacques Derrida, "'Eating Well', or the Calculation of the Subject', in Elizabeth Weber, ed., *Points... Interviews, 1974–1994,* trans. Peggy Kamuf et al.,
(Stanford: Stanford University Press, 1995), 255–287; 268–269.

22 Sarah Wood, 'Swans of Life (External Provocations and Autobiographical
Flights That Teach Us How to Read)', in *The Animal Question in Deconstruction,* 13–33; 26.

23 Indeed the point may be that the notion of Queer itself exists as trace. In
Tendencies (Durham: Duke University Press, 1993), Sedgwick hopes that
"the essays collected in this book [...] make, cumulatively, stubbornly,
a counterclaim against [...] obsolescence: a claim that something about
queer is indistinguishable. Queer is a continuing moment, movement, motive — recurrent, eddying, troublant" (xii). Also worth seeing is the long,

the Closet: James and the Writing of Homosexual Panic', she suggests that, in "refusing or evaporating" elements of his lived homosexual desires in his writing, James "reliably left a residue both of material that he did not attempt to transmute and of material that could be transmuted only rather violently and messily".[24] The trace here becomes not only a part of the function of language but a part of both the function of secrets and homophobia. This question of the trace or residue of desire that has been thwarted, disavowed, rerouted, Sedgwick suggests, is also inscribed into 'The Warm Decembers'. In 'A Poem is Being Written', she asks "How far can or will an already gendered and physically very localized desire swerve, how radically will it misrecognize itself in its need to join a preexisting current of discourse through which to become manifest [...] to become, in short, meaningful?"[25] The answer is, she believes the poem suggests, "quite far indeed", but "not without cost, nor perhaps without leaving a trace of its own particular itinerary".[26] The boundary-seeking, boundary-skirting, and indeed boundary-loving impulses mentioned earlier are then liable to leave a trace, both in terms of language and desire (though how far these terms are separable is, perhaps, always in question), in the poem. What is remarkable, given the absence of the boundary between human and animal in Sedgwick's list to which I have referred, is just how much of a trace animals seem to leave.[27]

---

quasi-narrative poem, 'Trace at 46', in *Fat Art, Thin Art,* where Trace is the name of the middle-aged male protagonist, experiencing a case of writer's block and mid-life crisis ("Why can't he work on getting the current chapter written, / on Fauré?" [43]), what you might call an experience of anxiety surrounding his trace. A reference to this poem appears as the first sentence of chapter nine of *Between Men: English Literature and Male Homosocial Desire* (New York: Columbia University Press, 1985), 161.

24 Sedgwick, *Epistemology of the Closet,* 197.

25 Sedgwick, *Tendencies,* 206.

26 Sedgwick, *Tendencies,* 206.

27 This assertion would run contrary, as Derrida has pointed out, to a long-running and decisive strand of Western philosophical thinking on the animal: "even those who, from Descartes to Lacan, have conceded to the animal some aptitude for signs and for communication but have always denied

An exploration of animal poetics needs both to account for the overlap between human language and the other animals it can refer to and remain attuned to the differences between the two. But Derrida's insistence on the similarities between conceptual structures of thought or language and the real-world conditions that it both sustains and generates is nonetheless particularly useful here. These patterns of thought and representation, he argues, are frequently couched in "commonly accredited oppositional limits between what is called nature and culture, nature/law, *physis/nomos*, God, man, and animal",[28] and these limits are framed by the real-world conditions described in *The Animal That Therefore I Am*:

> However one interprets it, whatever practical, technical, scientific, juridical, ethical, or political consequence one draws from it, no one can today deny this event — that is, the *unprecedented* proportions of this subjection of the animal. [...] No one can deny seriously any more, or for very long, that men do all they can in order to dissimulate this cruelty or to hide it from themselves; in order to organize on a global scale the forgetting or misunderstanding of this violence, which some would compare to the worst cases of genocide. [...] It is occurring through the organization and exploitation of an artificial, infernal, virtually interminable survival, in conditions that previous generations would have judged monstrous, outside of every presumed norm of a life proper to animals that are thus exterminated by means of their continued existence or even their overpopulation.[29]

In contrast, Kristeva's seminal 1980 work, *Powers of Horror*, offers a less clear, but nonetheless provocative link between language, animals, and the abject: stating that "the abject confronts

---

it the power to respond — to pretend, to lie, to cover its tracks or erase its own traces" (*The Animal That Therefore I Am*, 33).

28 Derrida, *The Beast and the Sovereign*, 1: 15.

29 Derrida, *The Animal That Therefore I Am*, 26–27.

us, on the one hand, with those fragile states where man strays on the territories of *animal*".[30] 'Animal' is italicized in the text, and the sense that Kristeva requires the word to signify perhaps both too expansively and too securely is hard to avoid (as is the sense of a missing definite article).[31] Simply grammatically, for instance, it is not clear whether in this sentence *animal* is a noun (as in "the territories of *animals*") or an adjective (as in "territories which are *animalized* or *animalistic*"). This ambiguity, though, is nonetheless important to a more expansive sense of the links between animals and the abject. The "fragile states" between "man and animal" is another way of characterizing and understanding the variety and fecundity with which animals signify poetically in 'The Warm Decembers', as well as another way of describing the often occluded links between conceptual or linguistic categories and their possible counterparts in more praxis-based contexts. For it is in the flexibility and ambiguity of written language that these "fragile states" can be recovered and explored. What are the links between the abject and animals, or "the animal"? And what links the grammatical or semantic function of an animal in a text with an individual animal's wider relational interactions? Are the territories of animals always necessarily abject? Sedgwick's poem, of course, provides no answers to these questions, but its animal poetics create room in which they can be explored. In considering these questions of structure and meaning making, what follows is a series of meeting points between abjection and consumption and human and animal, which attempt to render some sense of the messiness with which these two complicated categories of human identity-construction and meaning-making can interact.

***

---

30 Julia Kristeva, *The Powers of Horror: An Essay on Abjection,* trans. Leon Roudiez (New York: Columbia University Press, 1982), 12.

31 On the impossibly expansive corralling that the term 'the Animal' is allowed to achieve, and on the idea of the animot, see Derrida, *The Animal That Therefore I Am,* 32–39.

Parts of characters, memories, images, and objects are all consumed and/or ejected throughout the text, and the idea of what
is kept inside and what is thrown up or ejected keeps resurfac-
ing — indeed it will not stay down. In particular, the juxtaposition of infant and parasite registers a certain uncanny analogous-
ness between the two as invasive and (initially) unrecognisable
foreign species, who must ultimately be expelled to preserve
the health and integrity of the carrier. Baby Henry is thrown
up in "tapeworm swags of indigestible linens", beached "like
the stove-in carcass of some ship", oscillating between outside
and inside — ejected, swaddled, and stoved-in. Prior to Beatrix's
hiccupping into the world, though, the fine but important line
between foetus and parasite is more insistently foregrounded.

Lucinda's pregnancy shares a timeline and a body with the
tuberculosis that kills her (which is also, of course, known as
consumption), a simultaneity which manifests not only the potentially radical strangeness of pregnancy and birth, but the potency of Kristeva's figuration of the abject in this context. One of
the most distinctive characteristics of what is abject is its "[dis]
respect [of] borders, positions, rules";[32] while the "stranger" in
Lucinda's lungs only brushes its "heavy tail matted with dung /
and leaves" up against her chest,[33] the intimate tactility of brush-
ing in this case is the most complete violation. This strain of
mycobacteria inhabiting and destroying Lucinda's lungs is a
creature with a "fine snout" and "dry feet": a distinctly animal if
not precisely porcine, figure, and, above all, a "stranger". While
the "oxygenless hue of radishes" — Beatrix — is ready to "hurl
herself" in any direction,[34] it is another involuntary muscular
spasm, a "yawn", which signals the departure of both the tuber-
culous stranger and Lucinda. The occupation of her body leaves
practically no room for Lucinda herself, dispossessing her of the
capacity for action and agency, so that neither the exit of the
stranger or Beatrix are voluntary actions. A yawn and a hiccup

32 Kristeva, *Powers of Horror,* 4.
33 Sedgwick, *Fat Art, Thin Art,* 91.
34 Sedgwick, *Fat Art, Thin Art,* 92.

are all that Lucinda has left, and, as Steven Connor has suggested, the hiccup, like the sob, enacts a strange kind of incapability within desire, as the manifestation of an obstacle. A hiccup is parasitic: "countermanding speech, [it] nonetheless seems to cling to it; it strains for articulation, and is empty and abstract until it has bound itself to it, like the virus with no DNA of its own which it must acquire of its host".[35] During the pregnancy, a similarly involuntary breaking in of voice on speech permeates borders between Lucinda and Lucy Lucas: "Death [...] / uttered its sentence in [...] / the very tattoo, of Lucy Lucas".[36] The hiccup, the yawn, the unconscious rhythmic tattoo: Lucinda's pregnancy is characterized by moments of involuntary oral abjection, and by the confusion and permeability of borders between lovers, children and parasites, and life and death. What is abject, we seem to learn, has profoundly different ontological possibilities and ambiguities; pregnancy and birth itself are not so much contrasted with the stranger in the lungs, as uncannily juxtaposed.

Procreation and gestation are the processes by which life is continued, but in placing a vividly realized animal life inside Lucinda, alongside the foetus, Sedgwick queers the culmination of the reproductive process, perhaps anticipating a kind of deconstruction within the paradigmatic act of reproductive futurism, where pregnancy and birth itself is already queered.[37] All of us carry nonhuman life within our bodies — and both baby and the animalized mycobacteria of TB are "strangers". If, as is certainly the case, the category of the human is produced at least in part through the abjection of what is "animal" or (what this is often synonymous with) other, the strange knotting of the fates of Lucinda, the baby, and the creature complicates this claim,

---

35 Steven Connor, *Beyond Words: Sobs, Hums, Stutters, and Other Vocalizations* (London: Reaktion, 2014), 55.

36 Sedgwick, *Fat Art, Thin Art*, 92.

37 For the seminal polemic attacking 'reproductive futurism', see Lee Edelman, *No Future: Queer Theory and the Death Drive* (Durham: Duke University Press, 2004).

and reminds us of the different ways in which a human subject is intimately inhabited by something other.[38]

In locating the territories of the animal within the pregnant female body, Sedgwick also draws together the abject with a certain model of both fertile and fragile femininity and animals. While the link between animals and the former two terms appears to be an insight unique to the poem, Sedgwick notes intriguingly during the period of the poem's writing that "the relation between the traffic-in-women paradigm [...] and Kristeva's [hypothesis] in *Powers of Horror*, of a primary fear in men and women of the maternal power of women, is yet to be analyzed".[39] Less of such an analysis, but more of a thinking, would seem to be happening in this complex reconfiguration of Kristeva's formulation of the abject, which employs a remarkable, arresting, almost vehemently anti-conventionalist poetics in which abjection-gestation is an evacuation and obliteration of the female body, but at the same time produces a protagonist to which perhaps our own, but certainly Sedgwick's, identificatory desires are focused towards: Beatrix.[40]

***

The dairy cow surely has pride of place among farmed animals. Historically, she has been revered, and she is frequently portrayed as a symbol of maternal nurturing. The life of the majority of cows used for dairy, however, is very harsh.

---

38 Diana Fuss articulates just this kind of resistance to simplification in the face of definitions of the human: "Our purpose in this volume is not to broaden the category of the human to include previously abjected and excluded others, but to engage in a more radical interpretation of the process by which the human comes to mean in the production of cultural difference" 'Introduction', in ed., *Human, All Too Human* (London: Routledge, 1996), 1–2.

39 Sedgwick, *Between Men*, 18.

40 In a much later essay on Proust, Sedgwick identifies Kristeva's readings of the same author as sharing a certain anti-Oedipal kinship (*The Weather in Proust* [Durham: Duke University Press, 2011], 5, 37).

The young female, or heifer, can produce her first calf at around two years of age. In a natural environment, she would let her calf suckle several times a day — in between, she would leave him in a sheltered, safe area, probably with some other calves, and wander off to graze, thus fuelling her own milk supply. After a couple of weeks, the calf would start eating grass as well, and over the next eight months or so, he would gradually wean himself off his mother. The maternal bond is very strong. There are records of cows traveling several miles on their own to find calves who have been taken from them and sold to other farms. In all cases they somehow manage to scent out their own calf in completely unknown territories.

In the high-tec dairy industry, the calf is taken away from his mother at just a day or two old. This causes apparent anguish to both. The cow is then milked to capacity, often producing ten times as much milk as her calf would have suckled from her, had he been allowed to do so.[41]

***

Using her revulsion to milk as an example of the way abjection works to create and maintain a human subject, Kristeva recalls the

sight-clouding dizziness, nausea [that] makes me balk at that milk cream, separates me from the mother and father who proffer it. "I" want none of that element, sign of their desire [...]. "I" expel it. But since the food is not an "other" for "me," who am only in their desire, I expel myself, I spit myself out, I abject myself within the same motion through which "I" claim to establish myself. That detail, perhaps an insignificant one, but one that they ferret out, emphasize, evaluate, that trifle turns me inside out, guts sprawling; it is thus that

---

41   Joyce D'Silva, 'The Welfare of Cows', in Andrew Linzey, ed., *The Global Guide to Animal Protection* (Urbana, Chicago: University of Illinois Press, 2013), 173–175; 173–174.

they see that "I" am in the process of becoming an other at the expense of my own death. During that course in which "I" become, I give birth to myself amid the violence of sobs, of vomit.[42]

There is a certain resemblance between the process Kristeva describes and the account of Lucinda's pregnancy, a kind of lit- eralization performed in Sedgwick's poem. The human body which Lucinda expels was forced onto her by Cosmo, and as this growing body inside Lucinda takes up more and more of her TB-depleted resources — takes up, more and more, the body of Lucinda — the final hiccup of expulsion occurs at precisely the same time as "out the other end" life leaves Lucinda.[43] The subject that is produced through this abjection in Sedgwick's version, however, is the abject being itself, Beatrix.

Later in the poem, Beatrix herself is forced to negotiate a threat to her own sense of subjecthood, and, curiously, this is, in part, precipitated by, and resolved through, a revulsion to milk and other animal products. That milk is, in both Sedgwick's and Kristeva's imaginary, a prominent feature of a scene of difficult negotiations between parent and child is perhaps paradoxically appropriate, given that the production of milk involves do- ing such violence to the maternal bond, a violence that is both physical (forcibly removing the calf, for male ones often to veal crates), and psychological. But if the production processes of dairy in some ways set the scene for their appearance in *Powers of Horror* and 'The Warm Decembers', so too do the rhetorical and conceptual lives of milk chime with Sedgwick's poem.

Beatrix's account of her dream in Chapter Five describes a conversation with her mother, who tells her that her dead father "had / always disliked" Beatrix, as well as featuring an encounter with the same father. His intense dislike of Beatrix, she learns, was meant "to conceal something the opposite, / a strong, un- derlying desire", and it is this "whiplash of hatred and love"

---

42 Kristeva, *Powers of Horror,* 3.
43 Sedgwick, *Fat Art, Thin Art,* 92.

which, for the space of the dream, "keep[s] him a little / longer from dispersing in that death- / that-comes-just-after-death".[44] He enters, carrying a "pudding" or "trollope", "an architectural mayonnaise, / rounded, and swaggy with arabesques, and huge" (ibid), which more and more seems to represent a fascinating horror of dissolution and incorporation. The trollope is "forgetful" of the plate it is on, a "sucking rift / of pudding pulling pudding", "slewing across the tipsy platter when / already it was broken meat, burst dimpled milk, / the protein girdle ruptured, / or almost" (ibid), and ultimately the forgetful pudding is a figure of her father's disregard of ontological boundaries — "like his forgetting he was dead".[45] What saves Beatrix, it would seem, from the "spreading turbid place of that / ruinous thing" (ibid) is precisely the repulsion to the "burst dimpled milk" and "the dead breath of milk" on her father's breath (ibid); the instinctive recoil they generate are signs of a separate being. In this dream, Beatrix reaches out beyond the boundaries of death (in a passage which seems to anticipate Sedgwick's interest in Tibetan Buddhism later in her life),[46] and her mother struggling to articulate a feeling that death might not mean abjection from the realms of the living and that the reactive process of abjection might delay spiritual death. There is something so pungent and nauseating about the smell of decaying cow's milk in both *Powers of Horror* and 'The Warm Decembers' that the instinctual retch of abjection it produces is itself a sign of life, and that retch bears some similarity to the powerful and contradictory energies of desire that protracts her father's death. And indeed it also bears some similarity to the unconscious "rhythmic tattoo", the hiccup, and the yawn that accompany Beatrix's birth. But the point must also be that dairy and eggs are what Carol J. Adams describes as "absent referents".[47] Talking about "dairy", "milk",

---

44 Sedgwick, *Fat Art, Thin Art,* 129–130.

45 Sedgwick, *Fat Art, Thin Art,* 131.

46 For more on this, see Sedgwick, *Touching Feeling: Affect, Pedagogy, Performativity* (Durham: Duke University Press, 2003), 153–182.

47 Carol J. Adams, *The Sexual Politics of Meat: A Feminist-Vegetarian Critical Theory* (London: Continuum, 1990). Here, if there were time, would also

"eggs", and "meat" instead of "cow's milk", "chicken's eggs", or "dead cow" are ways of hiding the facts of their production and of the lives that are ended in bringing them to the plate, and so the actual animals that these consumable objects (should) signify become absent referents.[48] Absence, then, is inscribed at the heart of the milk and eggs — the "architectural mayonnaise" and "sour milk" — which signifies, for Beatrix, the strange presence of the absence of her father.

But if the involuntary reaction to milk is a way of affirming some kind of selfhood, it also crosses what Derrida has identified as a foundational, structuring binary of the human/animal dichotomy: the distinction between response and reaction. In several places, Derrida argues that the enduring legacy of Descartes has continued to depict animals as mere automata, incapable — crucially — of the capacity to *respond*. In a footnote (always a productive place for Derrida), he states:

> Here we would need, as I have tried elsewhere, in a rereading of Descartes, to unfold what I shall here call the question of the response. And to define the hegemonic performance of this "Cartesianism" that dominates the discourse of human and humanist modernity — as to the animal. What the programmed machine, like the animal, supposedly cannot do, is not to emit signs but, says the *Discourse on Method* (part 5), to "respond."[49]

"The question of the response" is pursued in *The Beast and the Sovereign* through a reading of Lacan (whose influence on Kristeva is, of course, fundamental), who, for Derrida, exemplifies the way even the most theoretically sophisticated thinkers can present "*simultaneously* a theoretical mutation and a stagnant

---

be an opportunity to open up the question of the relation of the abject to absence.

48   I owe this insight to Emelia Quinn. For more on this see her MA dissertation, "'Is He a Martyr Or Is He a Fucking Jalfrezi?": Reading Islamophobia Through a Vegan Lens', University of York, 2014.

49   Derrida, *Beast and the Sovereign*, 1: 111–112.

confirmation of the legacy [of Cartesianism], its presupposi-
tions and its dogmas".[50] But, he argues, when these presupposi-
tions and dogmas are interrogated, it becomes clear that exactly
what it means *to respond* is unstable and ill-defined itself—a
problem, therefore, for anyone who insists that humans alone
possess the ability to respond, and to distinguish response and
the lack thereof in other beings. The retch of abjection, then,
constitutes a human subject in a moment of instinctive reaction, thereby straying on the "territories of the animal", in
Lacan-through-Kristeva's formulation. These fragile states are
then, in one way, points at which our oppositional definitions
of the human — of ourselves — are troubled and, at least in this
case, troubled by the para-linguistic affects caused by an animal
product which has been culturally transformed for human consumption.

***

And eating animals is one of those topics, like abortion,
where it is impossible to definitively know some of the most
important details (When is a foetus a person, as opposed to a
potential person? What is animal experience really like?) and
that cuts right to one's deepest discomforts, often provoking
defensiveness or aggression. It's a slippery, frustrating, and
resonant subject.[51]

I wouldn't eat George, because she's mine. But why wouldn't I
eat a dog I'd never met? Or more to the point, what justifica-
tion might I have for sparing dogs but eating other animals?
[…]
    Dogs are wonderful, and in many ways unique. But they
are remarkably unremarkable in their intellectual and expe-
riential capacities. Pigs are every bit as intelligent and feeling,
by any sensible definition of the words. They can't hop into

---

50 Derrida, *The Beast and the Sovereign*, 1: 113.
51 Jonathan Safran Foer, *Eating Animals* (London: Penguin, 2009), 13.

the back of a Volvo, but they can fetch, run and play, be mischievous, and reciprocate affection. So why don't they get to curl up by the fire? Why can't they at least be spared being tossed on the fire?

Our taboo against dog eating says something about dogs and a great deal about us.[52]

***

The inedibility of burst milk that causes the retch of Beatrix and Kristeva links to another thematic thread in the poem. While cow's milk has long been designated edible by agrarian northern/western cultures, 'The Warm Decembers' also draws attention to the role inedible, abject animals — often classified as vermin — play in the scenes around Bluefields.

Jonathan Safran Foer argues that the labels of edible and inedible come not from "a law of nature" but "from the stories we tell about nature",[53] but in 'The Warm Decembers' these labels are rather explored through stories told about hunting and photography, stories, one might say, about the processes by which humans make nature mean something. Bluefields is, like Trollope's novels, the site of regular fox hunting. Hunting, that is, as a sport and not as a means of sustenance is an activity that aims at the capture, not consumption, of an inedible quarry. "Hounds do not eat the fox that they kill, and fox does not constitute part of their diet. Hounds are neither capturing food for themselves, nor are they doing so, as in many other hunting events, for humans".[54] In a canny juxtaposition of the masculine, homosocial hunt and Beatrix's personal photographic hobby, Sedgwick in contrast highlights the terminology of consumption that photography is couched in. If the men hunt to kill rather than to eat, Beatrix's hobby is considerably less wasteful: when asked by

52 Foer, *Eating Animals*, 24–25.
53 Foer, *Eating Animals*, 25.
54 Garry Marvin, 'Unspeakability, Inedibility, and the Structures of Pursuit in the English Foxhunt', in Nigel Rothfels, ed., *Representing Animals* (Indiana: Indiana University Press, 2002), 139–158; 149.

Trollope, "you with your light and camera have consumed / how many plates?", Beatrix replies, "It's slow, but I'm omnivorous".[55] And as she captures the landscapes around Bluefields, the scene of hunting is indeed omnivorously gobbled up by her camera: "the wheatfield hoofed to silver after fox, / hounds, horn, huntsmen, horses: the / photographic light that eats the plate".[56] This photographic metaphor is engaged alongside more familiar ideas of capturing and shooting (Trollope finds Beatrix "hiding" "from the hunters", trying "to shoot / the Priory ruins"),[57] and, in doing so, the text points towards the proximity, as well as the shifting demarcations, of the edible and inedible, of, perhaps, fox hunting and hunter-gathering. However, that Beatrix is the photographer and that we never properly witness a hunt also suggests that Sedgwick is sensitive to what Giovanni Aloi has identified as "traditionally masculine perceptions and attitudes towards the wider world [and] animals" and "the synergic conflation of gun, camera, gaze and the desire to possess" that such attitudes found artistic footholds in.[58] Beatrix's photography equipment is a hand-me-down from her violent husband, and both this second-hand equipment and her gender combine perhaps to decentre the photographing subject.

The hunt also raises questions of agency, will, and waste, which intersect with Beatrix's failed escape attempt from the boarding house to which Cosmo confines her, her mother, and her sister; an escape attempt, that is, in which she is the pursued. The inedibility of the quarry in the foxhunt is the counterpart of Beatrix's camera's omnivorous ability to capture and consume anything and everything. But if inedibility is an important part of the hunt, it is no less critically structured, anthropologist Garry Marvin suggests, by the possibility of the

55 Sedgwick, *Fat Art, Thin Art,* 99.

56 Sedgwick, *Fat Art, Thin Art,* 100.

57 Sedgwick, *Fat Art, Thin Art,* 127.

58 'Art and Animals: An Interview with Giovanni Aloi', *The Discerning Brute,* http://www.thediscerningbrute.com/2013/03/04/art-animals-an-interview-with-giovanni-aloi/.

quarry escaping.[59] What the fox hunt relies upon, we might say, is the hunted animal being capable of resisting the aims of the human participants, of what Vinciane Despret has called *agentivity*.[60] This describes a capacity to affect other beings that only emerges in the interaction between individuals, rather than an idea of agency as an attribute of those individuals. Rather than thinking of agency as "intentional, rational, and premeditated",[61] Despret urges us to see it as a function of reciprocal actions. The rules of the foxhunt necessarily allow the possibility for the fox to escape, to thwart the hunters. And so we can see how similar law-bound structures might create limited conditions for the exercise of individual will. The possibility of resistance to, or escape from, a given structure might offer a more flexible model of agency than is generally still relied upon.

At the risk of over-extending the homologies between structures of hunting and Beatrix's photography, it is important to remember that Beatrix is, in many ways, a failed escape artist. She only barely manages to escape the womb, at the loss of her mother; she is unable to step out of her husband's shadow in the eyes of the other guests at Bluefields; the "demented pup" and Trollope "nose" her out when she tries to shoot the priory ruins in solitude; and her attempt to escape from the work of a "slavey in a rooming-house" leaves her bedridden in the very house she fled.[62] Thus the focus above on "subject/agent boundaries" is useful for highlighting the fact that Beatrix's own failed escape attempt from Great Yarmouth, and the subsequent urinary tract infection she develops, in part redraws her own subjectivity and free will.[63] Her escape is foiled by her regard for the rules of propriety and gender-appropriate behaviour and her sense of shame, and ultimately she thwarts her own attempt by not being willing to get rid of her own bodily waste when necessary.

---

59 Marvin, 'Structures of Pursuit', 151–155.
60 Vinciane Despret, 'From Secret Agents to Interagency', *History and Theory* 52 (2013), 29–44.
61 Despret, 'Secret Agents', 30.
62 Sedgwick, *Fat Art, Thin Art*, 108.
63 Despret, 'Secret Agents', 37.

This failure to escape given social and personal structures makes legible a confusion regarding agency and will, a confusion not so much caused by the "middle ranges of agency" (a question in which Sedgwick is deeply engaged critically)[64] as by the kind of paradoxically impossible escape from discipline which D.A. Miller outlines in *The Novel and the Police* (1988).[65] To what extent does Beatrix stop herself, and to what extent is it an inevitability derived from restrictive social conventions? To what extent can the fox exert its own will in the fox hunt, and is escape properly possible? If, to mix Despret's and Marvin's terms, agentivity is possible in the structures of pursuit, but not a rational, intentionalist style of agency, we might remain suspicious, as I think Sedgwick does, of the efficacy of such redefinitions or new terminologies alone in fundamentally altering the repressive structures of either patriarchy or human exceptionalism.

During Beatrix's escape, Sedgwick's turn to an animal poetics, once again a linked poetics of dissolution and elision, coincides with a foregrounding of this question of will or agency. When the "will so local in the distended bladder of this woman too shy (of course) to / urinate in the light and air was let to lapse",[66] the stream of piss morphs into a snaking, coiling waterhose in 1960's Alabama, dropping civil rights protestors as "glistening offal" and pulling out the feet of those trying to direct it. From out of this knotted, self-defeating and uncontrollable image of supposedly agentive will — "the running noose; Bea's control, let out / of her control" — distinctions between subject and object, animate and inanimate, become blurred:

---

64 For example, see *The Weather in Proust,* 69–122; *Tendencies,* 130–142; the question of the active/passive binary in auto- and alloeroticism raised in both 'Jane Austen and the Masturbating Girl', 109–129, and 'Is the Rectum Straight? Identification and Identity in The Wings of the Dove', 73–103; and the poetics of rhythm and spanking in 'A Poem is Being Written', 177–214, all in the same volume.

65 D.A. Miller, *The Novel and the Police* (Berkeley: University of California Press, 1988).

66 Sedgwick, *Fat Art, Thin Art,* 110.

Swans, cows; in the sloppy landscape anything
condensed in front of her.
Not only the land
and the water, or the sea water and the fresh water,
but the water and the air, over and over the same places,
sometimes invisible and sometimes visible.

And the "creaking noise" she thought was a windmill turns out
to be a cygnet, "climbing up and down / on top of her".[67] These
dim, nebulous moments threaten a coherent sense of individual
selfhood — as do both Trollope[68] and the trollope — but they
also prove artistically productive for Beatrix, who, while bedridden, scratches landscapes in chalk, "extents of vital texture, slabs
of it / only at the last extremity nipped in / to make an animal
form".[69]

***

Pigs also have an inborn tendency to use separate areas for
sleeping and defecating that is totally thwarted in confine-
ment. The pregnant pigs, like most all pigs in industrial sys-
tems, must lie or step in their excrement to force it through
the slatted floor.[70]

In Smithfield's case, the number is about 281 pounds of shit
for each American citizen. That means that Smithfield — a
single legal entity — produces at least as much fecal waste as
the entire human population of California and Texas combined.
    Imagine it. Imagine if, instead of the massive water-treat-
ment infrastructure that we take for granted in modern cities, every man, woman, and child in every city and town in

---

67 Sedgwick, *Fat Art, Thin Art,* 111.
68 Sedgwick, *Fat Art, Thin Art,* 153.
69 Sedgwick, *Fat Art, Thin Art,* 115.
70 Foer, *Eating Animals,* 184.

all of California and all of Texas crapped and pissed in a huge open-air pit for a day. Now imagine that they don't do this for just a day, but all year round, in perpetuity.[71]

***

These "extents of vital texture" "nipped in" to make animal forms is perhaps the best way to understand the animal poetics of 'The Warm Decembers'. "Nipping in" is a kind of gathering that is always fluid, contingent, and improvisatory: as liable to come apart as it is to get stuck. And so the poem, gathering as it does fluid and various "ontological thresholds", is about what it means to self-fashion and be fashioned into a human subject. But in the poem, not only are the attachments and pressures that shape a subjectivity probed and enlarged in scope, but subjectivity, volition, and the continuance of our identities become impossible to think without an animal presence. Sedgwick's poetic language is one which embraces the fantasies and horrors of dissolution, of spiritual and material elision, at the same time as it boldly seeks out the fragile boundaries erected to stave them off. And its animal poetics are, Sedgwick seems to suggest, ways of raising related questions that complicate and thicken our sense of this. That these poetics are underlaid by her familiarity with object relations psychoanalysis[72] (as I hope to have shown) suggests that, for her, the animal poetics of 'The Warm Decembers' are, in some ways, another attempt to find a language, or vocabulary, for how we fashion semi-coherent selves. But, perhaps most importantly, the *animal* in these animal poetics is another way of exploring the "transitivity" at the heart of queer.[73] That queer "tend[s] toward 'across' formulations" is central to Sedgwick's definition, and what is evident in 'The Warm Decembers' is that it at no point takes either the boundaries separating, or the vectors of relation between, human and other

---

71 Foer, *Eating Animals,* 175.
72 For example, see *The Weather in Proust,* 123–143.
73 Sedgwick, *Tendencies,* xii.

animals for granted. These borders and paths, when they occur in the poem, tend to differentially move across other forms of relationality and subjectivity that are also kept in play, to the extent that to speak only of an animal poetics is perhaps artificially to pick a single thread in a beautifully tangled skein. What 'The Warm Decembers' messily, strangely points out is that the lines separating, and the lines joining, human and other animals can — maybe should — be part of a queer constellation of thought. I leave the final word to Sedgwick, who sums up this messiness succinctly: "The immemorial current that *queer* represents is antiseparationist as it is antiassimilationist. Keenly, it is relational, and strange".[74]

---

74 Sedgwick, *Tendencies*, xii.

CHAPTER 3

Eve's Muse

Kathryn R. Kent[1]

> *"Poetry [was] both my first love, I guess, and first self —*
> *always with the most excruciating blockages".[2]*

> *"I don't know if it was depression that drove this muse away or it*
> *if was the long rocky strand of her loss that made depression".[3]*

In 'A Poem is Being Written', Eve Kosofsky Sedgwick declares:

I have spent — wasted — a long time gazing in renewed stu-
pefaction at the stupidity and psychic expense of my failure,
during [my teen years], to make the obvious swerve that
would have connected my homosexual desire and identification with my need and love, as a woman, of women. The

---

1   This essay benefited greatly from the insights of many people. Special
    thanks go to the Fellows at the Oakley Center for the Humanities, Fall 2014,
    for their comments on an early draft. Jason Edwards kindly asked me to
    write the paper that became this piece, and the ensuing essay is infused with
    his brilliant insights and was greatly improved by his editorial aplomb. Hal
    Sedgwick shared important information with me — his generosity never
    ceases to astound me. Sarah McCarry helped me locate crucial documents.
    John Limon gave this essay his piercing, careful critical attention. And Ben
    Weaver read numerous drafts and sustained me in ways too plentiful to
    count.
2   Eve Kosofsky Sedgwick, *A Dialogue on Love* (Boston: Beacon, 1999), 65.
3   Sedgwick, *A Dialogue on Love,* 65.

gesture would have been more a tautology even than a connection. Yet it went and has still gone unmade.[4]

Sedgwick's coming out as, to put it crudely, *not* a lesbian is sand-
wiched in between her description of her deep depression as
a teenager and a self-identification that has earned her some
praise, lots of scorn, and even more virulent forms of criticism:
"In among the many ways I do identify as a woman, the identification as a gay person is a firmly male one, identification 'as'
a gay man; and in among its tortuous, and alienating paths are
knit the relations, for me, of telling and of knowing".[5] Related to
this, she explains, is the fact that, instead of a "will-to-live", she
possesses an "aggressive will-to-narrate and will-to-uncover".
"Un-covering" can mean revealing in an epistemological sense
but also to ferret out a secret, lay bare, or, literally, to reveal one's
body, all practices also related to various kinds of (often paranoid, to use Sedgwick's term, and extremely productive) knowing, and in 'A Poem is Being Written', Sedgwick exposes her ass
as a site of shame and pleasure, just as she confesses her attach-
ment to other forms of ideological exposure.[6]

Yet in this narrative of her teenage years, in a passage immediately preceding the sentences I just quoted, Sedgwick also
reveals that "the depression [I endured...] I survived through
passionate and loving relationships with — have I mentioned
this? — women".[7] How are we to understand, though not nec-

---

4   Eve Kosofsky Sedgwick, 'A Poem Is Being Written', in *Tendencies* (Durham:
    Duke University Press, 1993), 209.
5   Sedgwick, *Tendencies,* 109. Sedgwick critiques the dynamics of interpre-
    tive exposure in her later essay, 'Paranoid Reading and Reparative Reading,
    Or, You're So Paranoid, You Probably Think This Essay is About You', in
    Touching Feeling: Affect, Pedagogy, Performativity (Durham: Duke Univer-
    sity Press, 2003), 123–151. From now on I will refer to this work as 'Paranoid
    Reading, Reparative Reading'.
6   "Un-covering" also related to the complex dialectic of knowing/unknow-
    ing, the "open secret" that connects sexuality to larger epistemological tra-
    ditions, that Sedgwick went on to delineate in *Epistemology of the Closet*
    (Berkeley: University of California Press, 1990), 1–5, 67–75.
7   Sedgwick, 'A Poem', 209.

essarily reconcile, these moments of (dis)identification — the complex processes by which she simultaneously identifies *with* female–female desires and *as* a woman and yet subordinates these affiliations to a story, one might even say a confession, of her identification with gay male subjectivity and with a male–male, adamantly anal, erotics?[8]

'Who Fed This Muse?', the poem that inaugurates and frames *Fat Art, Thin Art,* provides one set of possible answers to this question. It constitutes an exception to most of Sedgwick's other writings in that it places the speaker's, who I will assume for the purposes of this essay is Sedgwick's, relationship with her female muse in a set of queer, female–female homoerotic frames.[9] In examining the work's form and metaphors, its remaking of the idea of the muse and the genre of her invocation, I will elucidate how the text reveals, even as it withholds Sedgwick's understanding of the relation between her depression and her poetry: to reiterate the epigraph that frames this essay: "Poetry [was] both my first love, I guess, and first self — always with the most excruciating blockages [...] I don't know if it was depression that drove this muse away or it if was the long rocky strand of her loss that made depression".[10] Poetry is personified as Sedgwick's first love and also as (part of) her self: here Sedgwick alludes to an autoerotics of (self)-creation that is inseparable from female–female erotics. In so doing, 'Who Fed This Muse?' provides a counterpoint to Sedgwick's male homoerotic identifications and desires, one that explores the complexities

---

8   Sedgwick, 'A Poem', esp. 209–211.

9   Without rehashing all the debates about the relation between an author and their writings, let me just say that I am choosing to read this poem biographically, while I realize there may be many other ways of approaching it that challenge this assumption. This is because this essay represents part of a larger project: an experimental, book-length biography of Sedgwick. I see my role in interpreting the poem as one of creating a dialogue between the central concerns, images, metaphors, and formal aspects of the poem and Sedgwick's own account of her growing up, her relation to writing and to life. At times, however, I also go beyond this frame, interpreting in ways that ignore the limits of the biographical.

10   Sedgwick, *A Dialogue on Love,* 65.

of female–female intimate relationships as it charts the connections between the muse, the poet, and the worlds through which they travel, both separately and together.

However, this essay does not seek to redeem Sedgwick in the eyes of those critics, who early on found (and to some degree still find) her supposed inattention to lesbians to be a political problem.[11] I am not going to argue that she was always already or secretly or essentially "really" a lesbian. To do so would be to employ the "hermeneutics of suspicion" that, following Paul Ricœur, Sedgwick wants to challenge.[12] Instead, I engage Sedgwick's own proposal that, first and foremost, criticism "think […] other than dualistically"[13] and that it replace a "paranoid reading" (based on the impulse to anticipate and expose secret — or poignantly obvious — structures of power and/or knowledge that always already control us) with a "reparative" one.[14] Sedgwick importantly notes that not all paranoid readings are bad, that, in fact, they are often crucial, but that in their tendency to subsume nuance in order to make "strong" claims (for example, to "insist […] that everything means one thing"), and to focus solely on negative affect, they rule out other kinds of affective relations to the world and objects and selves within it.[15] Sedgwick defines reparative reading as "additive and accretive"; "it wants to assemble and confer plenitude on an object that will then have resources to offer an inchoate self".[16] She also connects reparative reading to Melanie Klein's notion of the "depressive position"; in describing the Kleinian distinction between this

---

11   For key examples, see Blakey Vermeule, 'Is There a Sedgwick School for Girls?', *Qui Parle* 5.1 (1991): 53–72, and Terry Castle, *The Apparitional Lesbian: Female Homosexuality and Modern Culture* (New York: Columbia University Press, 1993), especially 12–15 and 250–252, n. 3.

12   Sedgwick, 'Paranoid Reading and Reparative Reading', 124–125.

13   Sedgwick, *Touching Feeling*, 1.

14   Sedgwick, 'Paranoid Reading and Reparative Reading', 123–151. My essay is part of a larger work that examines Sedgwick's relation to female–female erotics/lesbianism over the course of her career, as well as other critics' and activists' interpretation of this relation.

15   Sedgwick, 'Paranoid Reading and Reparative Reading', 136.

16   Sedgwick, 'Paranoid Reading and Reparative Reading', 149–150.

position and the "paranoid" one, Sedgwick highlights the use of the term "position" as providing a kind of flexibility that can distinguish various kinds of critical *practices,* not theoretical ideologies, of "changing and heterogeneous relational stances".[17]

'Who Fed This Muse?' performs, as it presents a set of "changing and heterogeneous relational stances" between the muse and the poet and, in so doing, produces its own reparative reading of Sedgwick's relation to women and to the writing of poetry.

'Who Fed This Muse?' is not easy to summarize, especially since to describe it in prose risks making it much more linear and narratively cohesive than it actually is. But given the poem's relative obscurity, the risk is worth taking. The poem details the complex relation between an "I", putatively Sedgwick, and her muse from the muse's infancy through the two's shared childhood and adolescence. At various points the muse deserts the "I", sometimes for other friends and/or families, sometimes for long periods. The "I" wonders throughout the poem "who fed this muse", meaning who provided the muse with literal and metaphorical nourishment, especially since, as the "I" remarks, "for years, while she was homeless, I was housed. / Was nourished and gave nurture". At the end of the poem, the muse and the poet are reunited, and, in a sort of coda, the work ends with an expression of "both our gratitude to those / beloved, who fed this muse".

This summary fails in many ways, not least of which in its inability to convey the queerness of the relation between the poet and the muse. By queer, I mean not just outside normative heterosexuality (although this is key), but outside normative homosexuality, and outside the norms of familial relationships.[18]

---

17 Sedgwick, 'Paranoid Reading and Reparative Reading', 128.
18 Here I draw upon Sedgwick's influential set of definitions of the term, especially queer as "the open mesh of possibilities, gaps, overlaps, dissonances and resonances, lapses, and excesses of meaning when the constituent elements of anyone's gender, of anyone's sexuality, aren't made (or can't be made) to signify monolithically" and queer as "hang[ing] much more radically and explicitly" than "gay" or "lesbian" on a "person's undertaking

For example, in remaking even as it draws upon the classical notion of the muse, the poem, from the very beginning, challenges the traditionally heterosexual "relational stance" between the being that inspires and the one receiving the inspiration. In Greek verse, to put it *very* simply, poems often begin with the invocation of a muse, personified as female. Ostensibly, this is to glorify the god who, in the form of this muse, provides inspiration to the male poet. An obvious hetero-erotics thus grounds the relationship between the poet and the muse.[19] Moreover, this generic requirement also serves another purpose: it brings glory to the poet by association, as the chosen one whom gods have blessed with the ability to channel the muse. In other words, it is a moment of simultaneous self-abnegation and self-promotion.[20]

From the beginning of 'Who Fed This Muse?', Sedgwick plays with this trope, in that the relationship between the muse and the "I" she charts is never stable enough to achieve this vision of poetic power. The muse is never fully subsumed, devoured, or incorporated by the narrator: rarely is she gathered into a "we" with the "I" but, for most of the poem, usually remains separate, and often absent. The identity and identifications of the "I" and her relation to the muse shift dramatically along a continuum (and here my echoing of Adrienne Rich's famous lesbian continuum is deliberate).[21] Sedgwick moves loosely for much of the

---

particular, performative acts of experimental self-perception and *filiation*" (*Tendencies,* 8–9, emphasis mine).

19 Sidenote: interestingly enough, although traditionally there were nine muses, Sappho sometimes was referred to as the "tenth".

20 For more on Sedgwick's relation to "gods", see *The Weather in Proust* (Durham: Duke University Press, 2011), 42–68.

21 In her famous essay, 'Compulsory Heterosexuality and Lesbian Existence', Rich posits the idea of the "lesbian continuum", a term which "include[s] a range — through each woman's life and throughout history — of woman-identified experience, not simply the fact that a woman has had or consciously desired genital sexual experience with another woman". She fleshes this out to argue, "As the term lesbian has been held to limiting, clinical association in its patriarchal definition, female friendship and comradeship have been set apart from the erotic, thus limiting the erotic itself. But as we deepen and broaden the range of what we define as lesbian existence, as we

poem within the skin of a jealous sister, but also occupies the place of mother and homoerotic female "*friend*".

The locution "friend" recurs frequently in Sedgwick's autobiographical writings as a sort of placeholder for a set of relations that exist on a spectrum from the usual understanding of the word, to a way to describe someone on whom she has a passionate crush, to someone with whom she has a sexual relationship. In this poem, for example, she refers to "our friend Hal", an unusual locution for describing one's husband. Such unmoorings indicate Sedgwick's refusal to allow the usual trope of the muse to run fully its course, making this *not* a drama of the poet's glory but instead one of writer and muse in constant, complex, unstable relation.

Thus, the question that begins the poem focuses not on who nourished the poet (although the unstable relation between the "I" and the muse means we might as well, at least at moments, ask "*Who fed Sedgwick?*") but ostensibly on the literal and metaphorical care, epitomized through the literal and metaphorical feeding of another, semi-differentiated entity:

> Who fed this muse?
> Colicky, premature,
> not easy to supply, nor fun to love:
> who powdered her behind and gave her food
> the years when ("still a child herself almost")
> her mother was too blue?
>   "Almost" — I was a child.
> Blue, I was blue; even more I was green.

---

delineate a lesbian continuum, we begin to discover the erotic in female terms [...]." (Rich, in Henry Abelove, Michele Aina Barale, and David M. Halperin, eds., *The Lesbian and Gay Studies Reader* [New York: Routledge, 1993], 239–240. Elsewhere in the larger essay of which this piece is a part I discuss some of the drawbacks of this claim. Nonetheless, in its historical context and even to some degree today, it universalizes female–female erotics against the normative assumption of heterosexuality.

Most obviously, it is the poet herself who provides the sustenance. In the first stanza, the "I" identifies as a slightly older
child. But who is blue? Is the "I" the mother of both of them,
"almost a child herself", a quasi-narcissistic self-description
of the forties child-bride too young and beautiful to be giving
birth — young Rita Kosofsky?[22] Is the "I" the *mother substitute,*
forced to step in because the mother suffers post-partum depression? Is the "I" somehow both: a mother/sister who is so
close in age to the muse so as to be almost her twin, a mother
so "blue" and so "green", i.e., depressed and envious, she could
not care for her?

Rather than not "easy", this muse is "no […] fun" to love.
This substitution recalls the disapprobative declaration, "You're
no fun!", one child might make to another. Such echoes enforce
the sense that the "I" is but herself a "child" with some of the
self-centeredness, but also abject dependence, that goes along
with youth. Being self-centred then gets redefined in the next
few lines of the poem, as the "I" then queers female genitalia
and reproduction:

> They mystified me too,
> the red protuberant
> organs hypertrophied with self-abuse
> from which we thought back then
> a muse like this emerged.

Notice here that suddenly a "we" appears in the poem, just at the
moment the work articulates a theory of how "a muse like this
emerged". The phrase "[l]ike this" again distinguishes this muse

---

22 Sedgwick's mother. In *A Dialogue on Love* (Boston: Beacon, 1999), Sedgwick describes Rita as having an air of "kiddishness", and her therapist
notes that Sedgwick's "mother seemed to have presented a desired and oft-
spoken-about picture of prepubescent girlhood for her father" (78). Such
descriptions make the confusion of mother and daughter even more acute.

from the usual one; this is a different kind of muse, a hungry, fussy, unlovable, pleasurable, but sore one.[23]

The poem also disrupts traditional expectation when it employs the description "red protuberant organs" to represent female genitalia. Traditionally, these are represented, if at all, as hidden, even absent, and serve as a contrast to male genitalia's flagrant visibility. By contrast, these images invoke the colourful, undeniable presence of the clitoris — but also, as signalled by the plural "organs", the vagina, or at least its lips. Masturbation, until recently, has traditionally been pitted against reproduction as a wasteful, narcissistic sexual practice. The description of these "organs" as "hypertrophied with self-abuse" — a word whose half-rhyme links "abuse" with "muse" — employs both medicalized language ("hypertrophy" most commonly denotes pathological, "excessive growth") and the language of moral condemnation that distinguished late-nineteenth and early-twentieth-century discourses against getting off alone.[24] This choice reminds the reader that, to some degree, the "we" views these actions as transgressive, outside the bounds of normative sexuality.

A queer female vision of the muse (one who still needs her behind powdered) "emerg[es]". In 'A Poem Is Being Written', Sedgwick describes the more anal erotic — and for her gay-male identified — pleasure she took in enjambment and rhythmic meter, as invocations of, and metaphors for, anal sex and spanking respectively.[25] In 'Who Fed This Muse?', we see poetry's power coming from the solitary, self-centred (and here I use the term in a more positive light — more positive even than Sedg-

---

23 And again, this language echoes very closely the description of the poem as child in 'A Poem Is Being Written' (184).

24 That "hypertrophy" also is the antonym of "atrophy" hints that the poem also is invoking possible "positive" resonances of the term. For more on the history of masturbation, see Thomas Laqueur, *Solitary Sex: A Cultural History of Masturbation* (New York: Zone, 2003).

25 Another practice considered anti-reproductive and wasteful, at best. For more, see *Tendencies*, 177–214.

wick's in the poem), pleasures of masturbation.[26] Similarly, in *A Dialogue on Love*, written during the same time period as 'Who Fed This Muse', she reports that her own deepest sexual feelings and expression occurred through masturbation coupled with fantasy and, with her therapist's help, comes to the conclusion that this act of self-care rivals only writing in how it provides a kind of "heldness".[27] Sedgwick's poem offers a vision of auto/homoerotic, thoroughly queer (love of self, love of muse, birth of self through birth of muse) reproduction. The poet produces, queerly gives birth to, inspiration, but not the pure lyric of earlier poetry. Yet this birth is not idealized, nor is the genitalia, as it has been in much second-wave lesbian feminist art and writing.[28] Instead, in employing, even as she challenges, terms such as "self-abuse", Sedgwick displays ambivalence towards this process.

The next stanza continues this ambiguity even as it appears momentarily to stabilize the female lineage with the appearance of a grandmother:

> Her grandmother was willing, so I kept her,
> lucky I could so choose.
> My family fed this muse.

Who is this grandmother? Is it Rita, Sedgwick's mother, who is "willing" to care for the muse, Sedgwick's daughter?[29] In this reading, "kept" and "choose" signal the discourse of reproductive freedom: having the "choice" to "keep" the baby. The "I" is thus "lucky" to have the support of her family, and her invocation of the "family" constitutes the first answer to the question

---

26 Elsewhere, namely in 'Jane Austen and the Masturbating Girl', Sedgwick also explicitly connects masturbation itself to creativity. For more, see *Tendencies*, 109–129.

27 Sedgwick, *A Dialogue*, 44, 76.

28 For one famous example, see the work of Judy Chicago.

29 "Or is it Eve's grandmother, who figures so often, as in Proust, as a figure of tenderest love" (Jason Edwards, personal communication, 1 September 2015).

"Who fed?" that begins the poem. But, was the "I" willing, also? Again, we find ambivalence about the muse and the vocation she represents.

Sedgwick is perhaps, here, deliberately responding to the way other female poets have expressed ambivalence toward their muses. Most notably, Sylvia Plath's 'The Disquieting Muses' (1957)[30] provides an even more specific image of one's relation to a muse or muses, and of familial relations. 'The Disquieting Muses' first stanza reads:

> Mother, mother, what ill-bred aunt
> Or what disfigured and unsightly
> Cousin did you so unwisely keep
> Unasked to my christening, that she
> Sent these ladies in her stead
> With heads like darning-eggs to nod
> And nod and nod at foot and head
> And at the left side of my crib?

Plath's muses are terrifying, "[m]outhless, eyeless, with stitched bald head", but perhaps also resonant to someone like Sedgwick, who is steeped in textile culture. By extension, poetic inspiration, the need to create art, becomes a burden, a curse, and a christening gift brought by wicked "godmothers" from whom Plath's mother failed to protect her.

Plath belongs to the group of women poets immediately preceding Sedgwick's generation, and 'Who Fed This Muse?' recalls the milieu immediately preceding U.S. feminisms' second-wave that Plath's work also invokes, the world from which Sedgwick and her muse emerge. It can be found in the description of the "domestic politics/of postwar" (stanza 11), its complacencies ("nothing could be very different from this or much better")

---

30 Sylvia Plath, 'The Disquieting Muses', *The Collected Poems* (New York: Harper Perennial, 2008), 74–76. For readings of Plath that have influenced my own, see Lynda Bundtzen's extensive writing on the poet, including *Plath's Incarnations: Woman and the Creative Process* (Ann Arbor: University of Michigan Press, 1983).

(stanza 3), its gender norms and concomitant emergent consumer mass culture ("the Musketeers") (stanza 3), and its persecutions and violence as illuminated through allusions to the Hollywood 10 and the civil rights movement (stanza 11).[31] *A Dialogue on Love* provides more details about this context. At one point, Sedgwick shows her therapist a selection of family photos that reflect a similar worldview. Her choice of them, Sedgwick notes, echoes the original intentions behind the snapshots (taken mostly by her father, staged by her mother): the photos are intended to provide evidence of a "handsome, provincial / Jewish family", to create a set of "tableaux", for example, Sedgwick and her sister in matching outfits.[32] Pictures of the Kosofsky siblings and their parents reading in various combinations serve as "a chain of testimonials to literacy", and also art (there is one of "three kids doing blunt-scissored arts and crafts around a table").[33]

The image of the "blunt […] scissors" invokes maternal protectiveness and the strictures placed on mothers of this era: they must protect even as they cultivate their children.[34] In *A Dialogue on Love,* Sedgwick describes her mother as "suffer[ing] from 'photo face', the painful dissociated clamp-eyed rictus tugging at the cords / of her neck to make her look / like Nancy Reagan or a tiny Anne Sexton".[35] The reference to Sexton, with whom Plath is often grouped, invokes again the critique of heterosexual gender norms that characterized both of their works.[36] Moreover, the description of Rita Kosofsky, posing the children in part to present an idealized image of family for the grandparents, also recalls Plath's description of her own mother. In particular, Plath

---

31   For more on the Hollywood 10, see also Eve Kosofsky Sedgwick, *Epistemology of the Closet*, 243.

32   Sedgwick, *A Dialogue on Love,* 18–19.

33   Sedgwick, *A Dialogue on Love,* 19.

34   If not of every era since the emergence of the idea of white bourgeois motherhood in the nineteenth century.

35   Sedgwick, *A Dialogue,* 19–20.

36   For one notable example of this argument, see Jo Gill, *The Cambridge Introduction to Sylvia Plath* (Cambridge: Cambridge University Press, 2008).

details various ways her mother makes up heroines and embellishes fairy tales with happy endings —

> Mother, who made to order stories
> Of Mixie Blackshort, the heroic bear,
> Mother, whose witches always, always
> Got baked into gingerbread...

— perhaps as a way to cover over post-war terrors such as the fear of nuclear annihilation. But these stories bear no resemblance to, and have no effect upon, the muses who haunt Plath.[37] The mother, like Sedgwick's, also attempts to provide Plath with the accoutrements expected of successful upper-middle-class girls, such as dancing and piano lessons, at which Plath fails (as does her muse, and as did Sedgwick herself). Yet Plath's mother never teaches her how to exorcise these muses, "traveling companions" who "stand their vigil in gowns of stone". In the penultimate stanza, Plath describes her mother ascending

> in bluest air
> On a green balloon bright with a million
> Flowers and bluebirds that never were
> Never, never, found anywhere.

While her mother may be able to deny reality and be buoyed up, literally, by a Technicolor fantasy of superficial complacency that echoes a fifties vision of the perfect woman, Plath must live with the secret of her own grim burden: these muses that terrorize, rather than inspire her. As she puts it, "[N]o frown of mine/ Will betray the company I keep".

Plath details a queer relation to other women, one outside the normative (nominally Freudian) processes of gender formation in which the daughter learns femininity through her identification with/killing off of the mother. Contrary to this narrative, Plath's speaker indicts the mother for birthing her into "this

---

37 Plath, 'The Disquieting Muses', 75.

kingdom" but failing to provide her with any example or tools with which to resist the sinister presence and influence of these chilling muses. Poetic inspiration becomes a form of menace.[38]

In contrast, Sedgwick equates her mother with a more complex version of "imagination". In *A Dialogue on Love,* Rita shields her children from "acknowledging [...] [d]eath, or pain, or systemic injustice [...]. All the things we'd learned to be so proud of magicking away, as kids — waving the Rita-conferred wand of 'ambiguity,' imagination". But while this wand can hide harsh realities, it also privileges "[n]uance/Ambivalence". These are qualities Sedgwick's critical work privileges and brilliantly embodies, against "plodding dualisms" such as the ones she describes her mother rejecting.[39] In turn, "ambivalence" is the quality that distinguishes Sedgwick's feelings towards both her mother and her muse in both autobiographical writings and 'Who Fed This Muse?' This serves as a contrast to the unequivocal menace Plath's muses pose and to the equally unequivocal way Plath condemns her mother.[40]

Sedgwick's poem, as in Plath's, never solidifies the "I"'s identification with the muse and/or the mother and vice versa (again, the "I" acts sometimes as mother to the muse), and 'Who Fed This Muse?' often represents the estrangement between the two. But Sedgwick's invocation of nurture offered, withheld, and refused, and the poem's constantly shifting relation of the position of the "I" vis-à-vis the muse makes it difficult identifying any stable relation of mother, daughter, sister, muse and self, if not impossible. While the beginning of stanza three describes the muse and the "I" in a similar milieu, perhaps sisters or schoolmates, their positioning suddenly turns with the description of a parent–teacher conference, and the voice of the "I" seems to be more of a mother than a sister. That the parent-teacher confer-

---

38 Again, see Bundtzen's work on Plath.

39 Sedgwick, *A Dialogue on Love,* 28.

40 As Jason Edwards suggests, this may also signal a Kleinian achievement of the depressive position, and thus may display a less agonistic relation to her female predecessor's than Plath's (Edwards, personal communication, 1 September 2015).

ence was a potent site of fantasy for Sedgwick, but also a frame for conceiving how she, as parent, and her therapist, as teacher, could discuss a younger Sedgwick's "resistance to the pedagogies [they were] used to administering", just emphasizes the ambiguity of this positioning and of the muse's relation to the "I".[41]

The muse turns to teachers, goes with her friends to other "wonder-moms", rather than to Eve, and most significantly, the muse "refuse[s]" the nourishment provided by the "I" (and again hear the rhyme: this muse is constituted in and through refusal). Instead, the muse is literally and metaphorically fed elsewhere and suffers a hunger so great, and fluctuating so much in size, that the "I" claims the muse had an eating disorder. That Sedgwick herself struggled with "being fat" and came to advocate for a different body politic is something I detail elsewhere in the project of which this chapter is a part. This description of the dramatic variations in girth the muse can undergo in a single day also recalls the title of the collection the poem appears in, *Fat Art, Thin Art*. Moreover, the mention of "one crumb" and overwhelming hunger recall moments in Emily Dickinson's poetry, where the desire for food often stands in for other unmet, or deliberately denied, desires, including but not limited to erotic ones. Paula Bennett controversially connects images of small items in Dickinson's poems — beads, seeds, jewels, pearls, dews, pebbles, pellets and yes, crumbs — to the clitoris and to an understanding of "female sexual and creative power" as both "'little' and *great* at the same time".[42] In particular, Bennett cites the poem that begins, "God gave a Loaf to every Bird — / But just a Crumb — to — Me — / I dare not eat it — tho'/ I starve — / My poignant luxury".[43] Sedgwick is simultaneously invoking and riffing on this reading and on the connections between the dramas of need, refusal, and satisfaction through denial that Dickinson's poems and the "I" relationship with her muse enact.

---

41 Sedgwick, *A Dialogue*, 58.

42 Paula Bennett, *Emily Dickinson: Woman Poet* (Iowa City: University of Iowa Press, 1990), 173.

43 R.W. Franklin, ed., *The Poems of Emily Dickinson: Reader's Edition* (Cambridge: Harvard University Press, 199), 748.

The messiness of boundaries between the "I" and the muse comes again to the fore in stanza eight: "Of course, I was *in love* with her a lot", although whether the muse can "use" (again note the rhyme) the "I"'s love is a question that goes unanswered. Moreover, in this stanza, the confusion of the "I" and the muse is more fully articulated: "By the time she was 12 / I was cemented to my muse's moods. / Maybe you'd say she didn't have a self?" At first, this seems to be one version of the muse's relation to the poet: the muse inhabits the poet and inspires her with her moods, the poet feels taken over by her obsession with the muse, possessed literally by (desire for) her. But it is the muse, not the poet, who lacks "a self", and the line, "my eyes that dwelt then in her face", confuses any neat demarcation between the two. At this point in the poem, the muse and the poet are so intertwined that each lacks a separate identity. At the same time, the poem highlights the erotic differences between the two. It is the muse who "court[s]" the femme narrator, doing a "gruff, butch thing" that the "I" "ate up". Here the muse feeds the "I".

Yet what does the muse provide? The "I" questions what "taking care" means.

> Did I know
> how all the grim sublimity
> in the tight-budded, clumsy ingénue
> could have been called as easily
> depression as (what she would call it) speaking true?
> Enough to worry: *that,* yes, I did know.
> Worry, the only gift we always gave each other freely.

The poem describes "care" as "all this grim sublimity" that "could have been called as easily / depression", or what the muse would call "speaking true".[44] While the half-rhyme embedded in this phrase between "grim" and "sublime" links these two terms,

---

44 And here again the poem echoes Plath's description of her life with the muses: they "stand their vigil in gowns of stone", "[t]heir shadows long in the setting sun / That never brightens or goes down".

"grim" denotes both "fierce, cruel, savage or harsh in disposition and action" and, "in weaker senses, daring, determined, bold", while "sublimity" indicates "nobility or greatness of nature, character, or conduct; moral, spiritual, or intellectual excellence; perfection".[45] Such a coupling delineates so poignantly the position of the precocious, over-aware teenager. Is depression really just seeing the world for what it is, "speaking true", the "I" asks. Is depression also the proper relation to the world as it is? Knowing that Sedgwick suffered from depression for much of her life, but also sought the depressive, it is hard not to see this image of the "clumsy ingénue" as referring both to herself and the muse, intertwined and interdependent.[46] Yet the "I" "knows" "[e]nough to 'worry'" about the consequences of making this equation. And it turns out "worry", this noun/verb/embodied affect, is something that, in their sometimes rivalrous, sometimes flirtatious, economy of debt and gift, owing and paying, feeding and being fed, she and the muse "g[ive] each other freely".

In the next stanza, the speaker reflects back on what she implies was a "*pl*easantness" to their childhood suburb, as distinct from "*pl*easure". The alliteration continues with "a cautious *pl*enty" that alludes to a meeting of needs — again the food metaphor reemerges — that, in their naiveté, the "I" and the muse "thought we could assume / — lucky we: almost imagined the world could [...]" (emphasis mine). These lines confirm the sheltered existence of their white, middle-class lives, while the locution "lucky we" jars the reader in its slippage from "lucky me". Such a moment adds resonance to the sarcasm of "lucky" but also, in departing from the usual phrasing, emphasizes again the slippage between the "I" and the muse. Here, one of the few moments in the work they are joined in the first-person plural, they enjoy the privilege of at least a momentary fantasy of the

---

45 http://www.oed.com/search?searchType=dictionary&q=grim&_searchBtn=Search.

46 Sedgwick 'Teaching/Depression', *The Scholar and Feminist Online* 4.2 (Spring 2006), http://sfonline.barnard.edu/heilbrun/sedgwick_01.htm.

whole world fed, even as it is bookended by "heterosexuals out the wazoo". Whether compulsory heterosexuality and the concomitant gendered and other norms it represents are also what bookend the possibility of this fantasy is a question the poem raises here.

That the next line offers one significant respite — the homo-erotic space of Girl Scout camp — from both worry and these norms is no accident:

> what that place had been
> for generations of baby lesbians
> it was for her. And I, as well, was happy there [...]

Sedgwick here draws upon a set of traditions of women find-ing homoerotic spaces — e.g., the summer camp, the boarding school, self-imposed exile to another country — outside of the (hetero)normative "domestic politics of [U.S.] post-war", poli-tics she describes in detail in the next few stanzas as perhaps a reason her muse deserts her and retreats into silence and "untes-tifying", an allusion to the McCarthy hearings. At camp, both are fed, although they are not a "we". The muse is the "baby lesbian", the "I" simply "was happy there".[47] Why such a flat description? Does the speaker lack, perhaps because of the bland homoge-neity of her world, anything more complicated in terms of an affective register with which to describe her feelings? (Recall "pleasant" versus "pleasure"). Or is something else going on?

Much in the same way Sedgwick's construction of the muse recalls Plath's, her deliberate use of such a flat term connects the

---

47 Sedgwick attended Girl Scout camp and, in *A Dialogue of Love,* she de-scribes the female–female homoerotic community it provided her. She and I were also in on-going conversations about this space, as it is one I explore in my own writings (Kent, "'No Trespassing": Girl Scout Camp and the Limits of the Counterpublic Sphere', *Women and Performance: A Journal of Feminist Theory* 8.2 (1996), 183–203; reprinted in Steven Bruhm and Nata-sha Hurley, eds., *Curiouser: On the Queerness of Children* (Minnesota: Uni-versity of Minnesota Press, 2004), 173–189. In *A Dialogue on Love,* Sedgwick uses the term "happy" once in a way that seems more affectively alive, but when she does so, as if to create this effect, she italicizes it (207).

poem to another American woman writer, Elizabeth Bishop's, use of such techniques in 'Crusoe in England' (1976).[48] Crusoe, looking back to his time on the island, tries to represent the way Friday made him feel:

> Just when I thought I couldn't stand it
> another minute longer, Friday came.
> (Accounts of that have everything all wrong.)
> Friday was nice.
> Friday was nice, and we were friends.[49]

The use of the bland term "nice", as well as the seemingly innocuous yet loaded "friends" (and recall Sedgwick's use of the term) fails deliberately, flauntingly, to convey the complexity of Crusoe's relationship to Friday. Bishop uses these words to signify an inability to put into language homoerotic desires, both because of the prohibition against their revelation, and because of the way no language exists to do justice to such a relation. Read biographically, 'Crusoe' is often seen to allude to Bishop's relation to Lota de Macedo Soares, Bishop's Brazilian lover (and the description of their life together on the desert island likened to Bishop's choice to live as an expatriate), and the ways in which their own desires could not be openly represented in the fifties culture of Sedgwick's childhood.[50]

But while "Crusoe mourns the loss of Friday", the "I" confides that the she "fe[eds]/as much on the longing for [the muse], / on the body of her long refusal / to be with me" as on anything else. That is to say, the poet is nourished erotically and otherwise by

---

48 Elizabeth Bishop, 'Crusoe in England', *Poems: The Centenary Edition* (New York: Farrar, Straus, and Giroux, 1987). 162–166.

49 Bishop, 'Crusoe in England', 165.

50 For an extended reading of this poem and its erotics, one with which Sedgwick was intimately aware, see Kent, *Making Girls into Women,* 224–227. Helen Vendler addresses the flatness of a more generic, universalizing love in 'Elizabeth Bishop: Domestication, Domesticity, and the Otherworldly', in *Part of Nature, Part of Us* (Cambridge: Harvard University Press, 1980), 106. Sedgwick was very familiar with my work on Bishop, having co-chaired my dissertation, which formed the basis for my book.

the *lack* or absence of the muse and the productive unfulfilled desire this produces.[51] Indeed, the poem describes how the "I" learns to live her own life apart from the muse:

[I] [w]as nourished, and gave nurture.
Had my own queer enough aesthetic, it turned out.
Had even my own loves, which weren't all hers.
Fat amazon, found courage, such as it was,
including if I had to,
the courage to survive her.
Learned more about the shape
my own refusals took:
never to claim. Never to disavow.

These lines delineate the process by which the "I", in part because of the muse's desertion, develops her singularity and her own "queer enough aesthetic". "Queer enough" resonates with "good enough" — while it may not live up to some regulatory vision of homosexuality, it is enough for her. "Aesthetic" signals the ability to create art without the muse. There is a sense of self-sufficiency, along with shared "loves", and the "I" has some that are all "her own". The speaker names herself a "[f]at amazon", a reference to lesbian feminist iconography — the warrior woman able to exist without men, although this time without her female muse as well. The "I" also describes the courage she has "found" — a courage to "survive" the muse. "To survive" means to endure and to overcome the loss of, but also to *live through,* the muse's moods and those she creates in the speaker — including the ebb and flow of depression. "To survive" is also to live beyond, as in survive *after,* whether an absence, which is likened to a death, or an actual death. Finally, in the face of the muse's

---

51 In *A Dialogue on Love,* in the same paragraph in which the epigraph to this paper appears, Sedgwick describes how writing poetry was for her always a struggle and that losing the muse, the "loss of poetry" altogether, which happened in her thirties, was one of the great losses of her life, equal to the loss of a significant relationship and to the deaths of some crucial people in her life.

repeated refusals, the "I" has "learned more about the shape / my own refusals took: / never to claim. Never to disavow".

But to refuse to claim or disavow what? Most obviously, in the logic of the poem, this description might indicate a stance toward the muse, as toward a lover, a child, a friend, or an object: "I will not claim, i.e., possess you, but nor will I repudiate you". On another level, this description resonates with the processes of subject formation in relation to the other. "Claim" and "disavow" do not mark exactly the same processes as the Oedipal, where one must identify with the parent (and thus kill off and repudiate them) that characterize the normative Freudian account of the daughter's relation to the mother. Nor do they fully match Klein's "paranoid position": "For Klein's infant or adult, the paranoid position — understandably marked by hatred, envy, and anxiety — is a position of terrible alertness to the dangers posed by the hateful and envious part-objects that one defensively projects into, carves out of, and ingests from the world around one".[52] Nonetheless, the terms invoke a binary that the "I" rejects in favour of something else, an embrace of an in-between, "changing and heterogeneous relational stances", to bring back Sedgwick's description of the reparative position. This part of the poem advocates a different, reparative stance towards the muse and the world, not trying either to claim the muse for her own purposes or to disavow her with a kind of finality that defensively anticipates or even repeats the muse's prior disavowal.

In *A Dialogue on Love*, Sedgwick charts how, in the midst of surviving [my word] the approaching deaths of a relative and a dear friend,

> my poetry has returned. And returning with it, and with [her therapist's] escort, is some long-ago life of the girl whose first passion it was. What it's feeling like to me isn't death, but a great, upwelling flux of mutability

---

52 Sedgwick, *Touching Feeling*, 128.

> as if, falling in,
> you'd emerge young — old — dead — a
> different person —[53]

She does not "feel like" death, but transformation. On the other hand, when the muse finally, in the third-to-last stanza, returns in 'Who Fed This Muse?', while there is a similar experience of falling and of the "flux of mutability", of becoming "a different person", the affective valences of this reunion are more complex. The "I" describes how she is changed by the presence of the muse:

> This morning somehow she was at my side again —
> it seemed so natural,
> an "I" I guess I am when she is there.
> But maybe not the old one…

The muse "enfold[s the poet] with her" and the poet "[falls] into it all / the vat of [the muse's] unmakings, her returns, / bottomless eyes, her halting narrow tongue". But the moment cannot last. The erotic resonances of these images are immediately complicated by the fact that the muse also brings back "all the old saturnine / ways", i.e. gloom, depression, and "utopian" here can finally only mean "hearing her / silent No to the last / loamy reverberation".[54] Once again the two have found the homoerotic connection that constitutes a joining the "I" has longed for throughout the work (and for much of her adult life, the length of time the muse has been away). But while the slippage throughout the poem between the "I" and the "muse" deliberately alludes to theories of lesbian (inter)subjectivity, this couple is never idealized as it is in the writings of Rich, Luce Irigaray or Monique Wittig. Sedgwick's "I" and "muse" are neither perfectly

---

53 Sedgwick, *A Dialogue on Love*, 136.
54 Jason Edwards' reading of *A Dialogue on Love* picks up on this trend in Sedgwick's work. For more, see *Eve Kosofsky Sedgwick* (London: Routledge, 2009), esp. 130.

equal (Rich) nor disruptive of patriarchal linguistic conventions (Irigaray). Their joining never dissolves the subject/other binary (Wittig).[55]

In the quotation from *A Dialogue on Love* cited above, in which Sedgwick tells her therapist about the return of her ability to write poetry, she does not actually say "my muse", she says "my poetry". What is the connection between the two? And what distinguishes poetry from prose for Sedgwick? How far away is it from her critical writing, which is itself, at moments, very literary (even Jamesian)?[56] What is the generic divide, if any, between her poetry and her prose? *A Dialogue on Love* calls into question this divide as it experiments with the imposition of an extremely constraining poetic form on content by alternating, in a seemingly arbitrary way, between conventional prose and haiku. To some, 'Who Fed This Muse?' might itself not be considered "great" poetry. Sedgwick anticipates this criticism in her description of the muse's lack of traditional female talent: "[A]nother thing — [the muse] couldn't sing". The muse can't sing and can't dance "with her bad feet" (an obvious connection to poetic meter and form) though she adores — in a more than a slightly sadomasochistic fashion — her dancing lessons.[57] Making poetry becomes analogous to various forms of literal, aesthetic performance, and the muse fails, at least in terms of conventional standards of what "good" singing and dancing mean for a suburban girl.

In the poem it is Hal who insists that the muse has poetic power, that

it was in her nature as she was born

---

55 Rich, 'Compulsory Heterosexuality and the Lesbian Existence'; Luce Irigaray, *This Sex Which Is Not One* (New York: Cornell University Press, 1985); Monique Wittig, *The Lesbian Body* (Boston: Beacon Press, 1986).

56 And here I am revealing my opinion — elsewhere in the larger project I discuss at length critiques of Sedgwick's prose style, which was parodied and considered by some to be impenetrable, needlessly baroque, etc.

57 See Sedgwick's discussion of ballet in *Tendencies*, 186.

>to be elastic, even graceful; she somewhere had
>a voice to sing that was mobile
>and affecting[.]

The enjambment here, especially in the line that invokes elasticity, recalls Sedgwick's theorization of this technique in 'A Poem Is Being Written': the ability to take in, to take it, to be anally penetrated, and the rhythm of spanking, that for her are instantiated in certain forms of poetry. Sexual allusions proliferate at this moment in the poem, but one thing is clear: Sedgwick is well aware of the criticisms one might make of her art, and, by extension, her muse; in this work she anticipates them and performs them, not only at the level of content, but of form: at various points, the lines appear to stumble into iambics or assonances or alliterations, but the more one studies such moments, as I have demonstrated above, the more one sees how significant they are. In so doing, the poem, and Sedgwick through it, addresses the criticisms of her writing's "gracelessness", even accepts them "if graceless be" the muse's way.

'Who Fed This Muse?' also addresses the critics who fault her because, in her critical writing, she focuses almost wholly on male–male homoerotics in male-authored fiction. The poem returns to that moment in 'A Poem is Being Written' I cited at the beginning of this essay to reconsider the "passionate and loving relationships" Sedgwick had with women, including a female muse who, at times, embodies depression and, at other times, inspires love. But while this poem and its contexts illustrate how she did, at times, make a not-so-"obvious swerve that would have connect[ed] my homosexual desire and identification with my need and love, as a woman, of women", to claim Sedgwick for the lesbian nation would be to foreshorten and foreclose the many, complex ways she moved back and forth, backwards and forwards, temporally, physically, and psychically, between so many different, thoroughly queer, kinds of forms of love and desire.[58] In so doing, Sedgwick refuses to idealize or isolate the homoerotic couple at the heart of her poetry: she and her muse were fed by so many more diverse "beloved[s]", more than can be contained in any particular minoritarian, political, dare I say "paranoid" vision, or in any normative view of what constitutes "literature". Similarly, their relationship itself never settles on, claims or disavows any one model, whether it be rosy (lesbian-feminist) or maternal-filial-homicidal (Freud and others); if anything, it answers current calls, such as Sharon Marcus', to think more fully and complexly about relationships "between women" and her title itself an echo of Sedgwick's *Between Men*.[59]

Indeed, this poem constitutes one of the instances, if not the most important and thorough instance, in Sedgwick's entire oeuvre where she addresses and taxonomizes her desires, identifications and dis-identifications, debts and gifts, to and from other women. The last line of the stanza in which they are reunited reads: "[The muse's] presence seemed a promise to me, and I was happy". Yet even this line carries with it twinges of ambivalence and ambiguity; the alliteration of presence and promise bespeak commitment and continuity, but the "seemed" calls into question any certainty that the muse will stay. Similarly, the flatness of happy, while it recalls the blissful homosociality of scout camp, also reminds us that the muse incites as many or more strong feelings through her absence and at least as much depression (albeit often productive) as contentment. Furthermore, as much as queer self-pleasuring gives birth to the muse, as much as the muse is the "butch" to the "I"'s femme, the "I" never identifies as a "baby lesbian". Recall, however, that the "I" states she "was in love with [the muse], a lot" and implies by the line "But she would court me too!" that the "I" has also

---

58 For related readings of Sedgwick's relation to lesbianism, see Melissa Solomon, 'Flaming Iguanas, Dalai Pandas, and Other Lesbian Bardos (A few perimeter points)', in Stephen M. Barber and David L. Clark, eds., *Regarding Sedgwick: Essays on Queer Culture and Critical Theory* (New York: Routledge, 2002), 201–216 and Edwards, *Eve Kosofsky Sedgwick*, 43–5.

59 Sharon Marcus, *Between Women: Friendship, Desire, and Marriage in Victorian England* (Princeton: Princeton University Press, 2007).

worked hard to court her. Writing poetry appears to be not only the performative coming together — whether it be produced by the sister-lover like tangle of the "I" with the muse's moods, the eroticized loss and reunion of mother and daughter, or the subject-shattering fantasy of self-other that distinguishes some feminist valuations of lesbian sex — but also the performative splitting apart of the muse and the "I". Finally, then, whether or not the "I" identifies as a lesbian, writing poetry as Sedgwick theorizes it here constitutes a female–female (auto)erotic act. And the traditions this poem draws upon link her to other women writers and critics, some of whom also considered how to make female–female (auto) erotics part of the form and the content of their work.

In performing this reading, I, in the main, am following Sedgwick's lead, have chosen "reparative motives" over paranoid ones.[60] Perhaps this reading is "merely reformist", and it certainly carries with it the "pleasure" of the "merely aesthetic", in its choice to privilege close readings over any particular theoretical purity or "insistence that everything means one thing".[61] But as Sedgwick asks, "What makes pleasure and amelioration so 'mere'?"[62]

---

60 Sedgwick, *Touching Feeling*, 144.

61 Sedgwick, *Touching Feeling*, 136.

62 Sedgwick, *Touching Feeling*, 144. In her essay, 'Melanie Klein and the Difference Affect Makes', Sedgwick does a reading of another one of her own poems from *Fat Art, Thin Art*, 'What I Would Be When I Grew Up'. This reading resonates, yet differs, from my own of 'Who Fed This Muse?' The former poem personifies her "talent", rather than her muse, and, in it, Sedgwick positions herself unambiguously as the talent's "big sister". She explains, in the essay, that, having read Klein, she can now understand this little sibling as an example of a "good internal object", and she conceives of the relation between them as one that "is conceived of as virtually intersubjective, profoundly ambivalent, and a locus of anybody's special inventiveness" (*The Weather in Proust*, 127). Sedgwick views her "talent" as this object, as what "makes a relational space for me, however troubled, in which an orientation toward futurity and creation becomes possible" (128). While it is tempting, especially after reading this last description, which resembles, in many ways, my reading of the muse, to equate Sedgwick's talent with her muse, they are not the same and neither is her relation to them. Her talent is some-

thing she feels she never loses, something that stay with her even though she has "abused, betrayed it a thousand times", as she puts it in the poem (128). Sedgwick's muse, by contrast, deserts her — while by the end of the poem some kind of reunion occurs with the "I", their shifting, unstable relation makes it a much more complex relationship of self to (internal) other/ object. Moreover, Sedgwick's talent guides everything she does, not just the writing of poetry. But the resemblance still indicates the moves toward the reparative I would argue Sedgwick is trying to initiate in 'Who Fed This Muse?'.

CHAPTER 4

'Shyly / as a big sister I would yearn / to trace its avocations,' Or, Who's the Muse?

Mary Baine Campbell

'Sisterhood is Very Complicated': there's a reason that epithet was ditched in favour of a dactyl with half the syllables. Still, it's the truth, if not exclusive of its shorter, slighter sister slogan. Here's a story of how Eve Kosofsky Sedgwick taught me that complexity. And its power too, even sorcery, a word that comes (no, not from *soror* but) from Latin *serere,* to arrange things in a sequence — particularly, in the case of sorcery, the lots ("sorts") that make a fortune. It's a story about poetry and making poetry. Or about making fortune, *fortuna.*

I used to feel kind of left out, in the ID450 Collective of women faculty and grad students (and a boat-builder, a math tutor, a childcare worker), mostly studying and teaching literature and writing at, or near, Boston University in the early 1980s.[1] By nature, just because I usually do arrange that, but also, and more particularly, because I wasn't *fat,* or rather wasn't seen as fat or understood as fat (though I'd always been fat secretly). Those I loved most in that group were, or anyhow saw themselves that

---

1 For more, see ID450 Collective, 'Writing the Plural: Sexual Fantasies', *Criticism* 52.2 (Spring 2010), 293–307.

way, above all Eve. Not that I didn't love us all. But half of us were thin and half of us were fat, as far as we knew, and indeed I was at my very thinnest then, or so it scarily appeared, as I'd responded to the major heterosexual experiment of my youth (a traumatic one) by losing my appetite for two years. And the fat ones seemed to have a lot more quiddity: they were more radiantly, as the expression goes, themselves. There was *more to them.*

I was writing poetry like a house afire. It was not just a burning house, though it was certainly that, but the ski slope on which I, always acrophobic, skied down out of a prison into the humid world below. And then and there it seemed that Eve (an Eve who was writing *Between Men* but hadn't written it, who didn't have tenure and knew she wouldn't get it there, who knew she was a genius) was writing poetry too, had always written poetry, and was a poet.

Not that I liked her poetry. I didn't know what to say when she showed it to me, lots of it as I recall, though I recall from that first shock on encounter only 'Sestina Lente', the one poem I haven't dared to reread since then, until I wrote this piece, the poem that sends a lover the dead severed head of her cat to beat off with and he does. It was way too grown-up for me. I felt bad for the cat. Others were full of French expressions and Fauré, references to expensive shops and to France itself, million-dollar words, abstractions like 'this motion over time is a space' ('Penn Central: New Haven Line') or 'the confusion of the absence of the erotic' ('Sexual Hum'). I mean I knew she was a genius, but I liked my poems better. I was, as you might guess if you're old enough, in love then with short lyrics neither I nor anyone would want to explicate. I wrote in sentences like Eve, and like Eve I love sentences. But I was a model of 'How Not to Be There', in the immortal phrase of her own short lyric later on: that was what I wanted. Not to be there. No wonder I felt left out! Those mere slips of poems were to be there instead, precipitated (as I explained) from the ether.

I was really, really glad Eve was a poet. And I adored every phrase and sentence and even single word — "snout", "drag", "gesture", "funny", "whiff", "vastation", "granulated", "rebarba-tive", "pudeur" — of her prose, and of the "sexual fantasies" she wrote for ID450, often in verse, during our long drunken meet-ings: she of course drank Bloody Virgins, but tolerated infinitely the rest of us louts. Her poetry was, I knew, a resource, another infinity, along with the live, sap-swollen ramification of her sen-tences; it was good that something so "smart" (in her word) and nuanced and refined and fully-uttered existed, could exist in this brutal world. I pressed her to write more of it, to stay with it; I organized a reading for her and two other shy faculty poets at Boston University so she could come out as one. But I didn't like it. And she returned the favour — I remember a certain slant of light, one summer afternoon at her Amherst house around the corner from Emily Dickinson's place, when she said she "couldn't get interested in short poems", that there didn't seem to be anything there to get hold of.[2] By coincidence, my own just-published first book of short lyrics was lying within reach on an end table in the living room. 'Oh well', I thought sadly. I'd hoped she'd like them, as it turned out — but why did I think that was possible? Because they'd been precipitated from the ether? We had our only ever fight the next day, over the word 'gifted'. She said she loved the idea of having been given a gift by what she didn't yet call the 'queer little gods'; I gritted between my teeth a savage line about tearing mine from my own side.[3] The struggle went on, or does in my memory, for kind of a while, everyone watching in silence. I can call back the light and the feeling even now, and the chair I sat on across the room from Eve's, facing her, though I know whose side I'd have been on if I were watch-ing, and it isn't mine.

That disappointment must have been the beginning, my first incoherent single-celled knowledge that Eve was becoming my muse. A fuller, closer, happier moment of that unfolding, a cell division, came when we gave a reading at Harvard together a few

---

2   For a related discussion of chunky ideas, see Eve Kosofsky Sedgwick, *The Weather in Proust* (Durham: Duke University Press, 2011), 123–124.

3   For more, see Sedgwick, *The Weather in Proust*, 42–68.

years later: the poster (later the cover of *Novel Gazing*) showed two women in large, lush Victorian party dresses facing each other through a piece of glass — window? mirror? — touching each other's fingertips. We introduced each other, we picked poems with each other's ears in mind, we ended, at my urging, by reading 'Pandas in Trees', which is still my favorite poem of Eve's, with the help of our friend Carolyn Williams as a Louise for the ages. That was the first time I ever played Eve on stage, or at least one of her: the last time face to face with my maker. I felt better loved, certainly, than I had in Amherst's oppressive cathedral. But once again aware of myself as somehow skinny (which I hadn't been lately, in the visible dimensions), ravenous, embattled, manic, *perched* there at most, hardly breathing.

By the time of my second experiment with heterosexuality, more successful and longer, Eve was simply my Muse, or rather a major avatar of that Muse, one I shared with my partner, a paleoecologist studying the end of the last Ice Age. Whenever either of us had anything to write, we began by reading something of Eve's. For me, anything would do, it was the *fingerprint* of her writing that did the magic, not so much its touch as its graphic quiddity. I could open any of her books, anywhere, like fortune-tellers opening Virgil and reading the first verse their finger found. (For Jason, it was usually though not always her writing on the "depressive script", as Sylvan Tomkins termed it and Eve immortalized it). Reading her gave me permission, the permission to think, and to think better than I would without her, to think with all my heart, and also to *speak,* rather than to inscribe the terrible sentences of academic "rigor" ("You can *say* that?").[4] I remember her asking, one late night at an ID450 meeting, surrounded by boozed-up ladies with their heads in each other's laps: what's so great about *rigor mortis* that academics should aspire to it?

This was around the time of getting excited by fractals, and by (as we had both separately done, for seemingly unrelated

---

4   'In dreams on which decades of marriage haven't', Eve Kosofsky Sedgwick, *Fat Art, Thin Art* (Durham: Duke University Press, 1994), 39.

reasons) the twentieth-century Marxist-Buddhist-Neoplatonist genius of quantum physics, David Bohm, for whom:

> What I mean by 'thought' is the whole thing — thought, felt, the body, the whole society sharing thoughts — it's all one process. It is essential for me not to break that up, because it's all one process; somebody else's thoughts become my thoughts and vice versa. Therefore it would be wrong and misleading to break it up into my thoughts, your thoughts, my feelings, these feelings, those feelings [...]. I would say that thought makes what is often called in modern language a system.[5]

That's a passage that makes it hard to talk about muses but easy to open Eve's books, as I still do, to just anything, as if every moment, every character, were a portal into the implicate/explicate/generative manifold of the mind's hologram, which is exactly like the universe, or at least David Bohm's universe.

According to Bohm's partner Basil Hiley at Birkbeck, his last academic perch — where I too found myself for a while when the second heterosexual experiment failed, "things, such as particles, objects, and indeed subjects, exist as 'semi-autonomous quasi-local features' of an underlying activity".[6] But does it seem likely that on the night I delivered the paper that became this chapter, the audience and I would have been drawn from all the odd far corners in which we were born to meet on Valentine's Day in the ancient market town of York in northeast England, not far north of the tide-pool where the oldest human footprints outside Africa were found and lost again last year by the force of a "semi-autonomous quasi-local feature"?

---

5 David Bohm, *Thought as a System* (London and New York: Routledge, 1994), 18. For a related idea in C.P. Cavafy's poem 'Anna Dalassini' that Sedgwick discussed, see *The Weather in Proust*, 65.
6 Basil Hiley, 'Process and the Implicate Order: their relevance to Quantum Theory and Mind', unpublished conference paper (1 October 2005), 5, https://www.ctr4process.org/sites/default/files/pdfs/lsi/Hiley%20paper.pdf.

Maybe so. I think of the pre-Neanderthal footprints of Hap-pisburgh, in the silt of a prehistoric Thames, exposed by erosion to people to whom the estuary still matters, even as its matter dissolves. Local certainly, and like our own footsteps on the way, theirs were only semi-autonomous. But the difference between that phrase and Eve's semi-autonomous muse is the difference *poetry* makes. Eve wasn't or isn't the muse of my *life*. She was, she is, the one who proved, in great swoops, enfolded curlicues, and slender, fraying tendrils of art and song, that 'you can *say* that'. There were words to all her songs (even to her textile art). As soon as death knocked, she took voice lessons and wrote the lyrics of *Fat Art, Thin Art.*

I was very overexcited when the lyrics started to come! My muse writing short poems! My own poems, in turn, ground soon to a ghastly halt — or imitations of them arrived as a re-sponse to some imagined muse-sent permission to slack off, to not write my lyrics in defiance anymore but in the safe shadow of Eve's, relaxed (as if *hers* were!), autobiographical (as I've never wanted or known how to be), trusting in that "ragged right mar-gin" to make poetry where there was little more than the notion that if *my* shrink was a bad listener, and she was, surely there were better ones out there buying *APR* and *Poetry Now.* One of the minor regrets of my life is that I sent any of them to Eve. But she was of course kind and therefore silent. Her training in "How Not to Be There" hadn't been wasted — I needed her not to be there, in the worst way!

Still, it interests me that we couldn't both write short lyr-ics at the same time. Not that her own eruption into lyric had anything to do with me, but I suspect my own reduction then to junk poems and shamed silence had to do with her. How strange, when I was ecstatic over her poems, which soon be-came the interior wall-paper of my life! And I say "wall-paper" with love — I have always loved wall-paper, though only seldom does it live entirely up to my expectations for the genre. Still, those times have been enough to feed a love that, kindled in infancy, continues in the direction of my sixty-second birthday. The fibrous, powdery texture of the paper, the French pallor of

the colors, the weird two-dimensional world of the images drift-
ing like untethered astronauts off into empty space, evenly in all
directions: the writing on the wall.

So when I read *Fat Art, Thin Art*'s capacious dedicatory
poem, it seemed obvious to me that the muse — in one amid
a cornucopia of ways to read its 'I/her' — was Eve's 'thin' sister
Nina, who had indeed run away with her 'terrifying revulsions'
to maintain "her grueling aptitude for silence / and aversion"
somewhere unknown to anyone. And she had recently come
back: "This morning, she was at my side again. / It seemed so
natural".[7] "My eyes that dwelt then in her face": I remembered
Eve telling me how her sister had been her mirror when they
were kids, though they were soon articulated into 'fat' and 'thin'
by the family. I remember too, as others may who were in Man-
hattan that night, the shock of the photographs that looped
among us continuously at the CUNY-sponsored celebration of
Eve's life in 2009:

> she wasn't a fat
> child, she hadn't been fat — not
> even in the 80s

and early '90s when we were in ID450 together!

I wondered, wonder, if that sense of myself as paper-thin,
one of the thin ones who write short, slender lyrics — the sense
of myself as manic, brittle, breath-held, birdlike, perched to
fly — was a way of incarnating Nina, whom I've never met —

> she wasn't there at
> Eve's memorial and
> neither was Eve —

and who seems to have flown away again. If so, it's something I
do a lot, without willing it. I find myself at the movies wearing
the same heightened expressions on my face as the characters

---

7   Quotations are from 'Who fed this Muse?', in *Fat Art, Thin Art*, 3–8.

whose subjectivity the camera highlights. I wanted desperately to be an actress after I saw my first play and for years thereafter — to be able to *become* someone, someone called into being by a desire. How stranger still to imagine *Eve* doing that, in the pair of poems about her sister:

> Of course I identify with her [the kid tap-dancing at the
> > airport]. Also with
> the 3-year-old sister who (embarrassing)
> clumsy from servitude
> mimes every move she makes,
>
> […] simply because her big sister is making them.[8]

Strange because it asks us to see her opus, the love-child of her muse, as somehow Nina's: as brought into being by Nina.

> The only touch today, it seems,
> the breath of my desire can make on Nina's, is
> through her shy windows now licked from within,
> the joining of their gaze toward some other form of life.[9]

That second sonnet about Nina is about making poetry (surprise!). "As if / the furrows of my path to her / wore almost to the quick" — as if the ploughman's furrows, the sharp-dug lines of verse turning at the bottom of each furrow to the next (that's why it's a "verse", as in "re-verse" and "uni-verse"), were the whorls of a painfully deep-graven fingerprint; "as the eye's ear from syllable to line / staggers its numb repeated drag / of the foot, mauled and mauling, that still though numb feels pain", the feet of her iambic lines stumbling in the furrows of her craft "across the never again to be resistances / to meter — ". It's a very hurting account, both of ploughing and of writing poetry, not to mention of walking (did Eve already have that bone spur on her

---

8   Sedgwick, 'Little kid at the airport practicing', in *Fat Art, Thin Art*, 31.

9   Sedgwick, 'In dreams they're interchangeable', in *Fat Art, Thin Art*, 32.

heel?), also of reaching, lame and worn, that muse who appears in dreams as "someone [to be with] to make *us*" (the middle two letters of 'muse'), and not just anyone, but: "my husband, / my big sister".

'Interchangeable'? Hardly that in the world of persons! But in the world of structures, it either is someone to be with "to *make* us", as if it took two to tango, even just to be alive. That line about the eye's ear reading is as mauled and mauling as it can be (at least if by line 8 of this sonnet you were still holding on to some notion of iambic pentameter promised in the first triplet): "of the foot, mauled and mauling, that still though numb *feels pain*". Thirteen syllables, enjambed at both ends (and we know how that hurts!),[10] an anapest, two trochees, two iambs and the mighty spondee: 'feels pain'. I'm an intermittently, cane-dependent sufferer of plantar fasciitis, bunions and arthritis myself—as I write, my recently operated bunion 'still though numb feels pain'—and that line gets right down into my foot. But what does it mean?

The reaches of "middle agency" are hard to get your mind around (no doubt they were harder still to find language for).[11] 'Who fed that muse?' for instance—how many of us read that poem first, at least partway through, as a poem about Eve-the-poet, wondering if we'd fed her?

The first woman poet to publish a book of poems in 'America', Anne Bradstreet's book was entitled, probably by her husband, *The Tenth Muse*. It's a slip people often make. I've been making it right through this little story (including the sentence introducing Bradstreet's book!), calling Eve my muse when it's her *poetry* I'm trying to think about. Or is it her *making*? (That verb in English has meant both 'compose poetry' and 'take a shit'.) Anyway, the fusion of the syllabic feet and the bodily feet (hers, becoming mine) in that line—especially in their hurdling resistance to the meter that makes them feet at all—is like the

---

10 Cf., if you haven't, 'A Poem Is Being Written', in Sedgwick, *Tendencies* (Durham: Duke University Press, 1993), 184–186.

11 For more, see Sedgwick, *The Weather in Proust,* 79.

impossibility of telling apart Eve and her muse, Eve and her sister, and her sister and her husband. In this rereading anyway, where the "by heart / dull impulse of memory first speaks its part". A line I never quite seem to understand, but rereading and memory, they're like sisters, mirrors, lovers too. Spenser famously compared two lovers to two facing mirrors, but that's not — quite — right.

And what are we to make of that "other form of life" toward which Eve's gaze joins Nina's at her "shy windows" ('my eyes that dwelt then in her face')? Or when

> One of us falls asleep on the other's shoulder.
> An hour later when we peel apart:
> in the fat of the shoulder, artful, improbable
> brand, the double outside curve,
> an ear.[12]

It is perhaps strangest of all that Nina reappeared, after her long years of invisibility, a month or so after *Fat Art, Thin Art* appeared in August, 1994. It's as if the book — so wrapped/rapt in reflection, as it were, on or of Nina, so dedicated in its more recent layers to understanding the possibility, or maybe probability, of poetry as a touching of fingers to the mirror glass, a joining of gazes in the windows of the head, a food to serve a starving muse, who goes to the same school and the same summer camp — it's as if poetry had *called out*. Poetry is, after all, an art of the voice, and the sign of it is the ear, branded (there's that pain again) in the shoulder-fat of an "interchangeable" sister/ husband/ muse. And it's as if the muse had answered. Who says "poetry makes nothing happen"?

> But still
> the writer herself has been transfixed.
> Whether by that premature intuition of success

---

12 Sedgwick, 'One of us falls asleep on the other's shoulder', *Fat Art, Thin Art*, 35.

early in the chapter, or by the lordly yoking to it
there at the surface where I draw my breath
of the submerged and wreathy Medusan sister muse
melancholia by whose silence and rebellion
gagging on coral — comes, at best,
I guess any buoyant illusion of
the ordinary joie de vivre.

Two arts that feed as one.

Fat art, thin art.[13]

---

13 Everyone knows there is one last line of poetry after these in *Fat Art, Thin Art*, but no one knows what it means: "Not iron, but the tin thrust in the soul..." That's as it should be. In Bishop's final words: "freed — the broken / thermometer's mercury / running away", if I may mix my elements. Eve did.

CHAPTER 5

Queer Therapy: On the Couch with Eve Kosofsky Sedgwick

Monica Pearl

Successful therapy (or, for that matter, unsuccessful therapy) is a long conversation that goes nowhere. It does not have a structure, or an obvious end point, or genre. "From an outside perspective", writes Benjamin Y. Fong, "the conversation is pointless".[1] Indeed, we might not even be able to distinguish between successful and unsuccessful therapy: not only did Freud refer to therapy as "time-consuming and [...] laborious",[2] but also endless: he says, "[w]e do not regard an analysis as at an end until all the obscurities of the case are cleared up, the gaps in the patient's memory filled in, the precipitating causes of the repressions recovered".[3] In other words, it's not likely to end...

Freud tells us that between the analyst and the patient, "[n]othing takes place [...] except that they talk to each other. The analyst makes use of no instruments — not even for examining the patient — nor does he prescribe any medicines". The totality of what happens is this: the "analyst agrees upon a fixed

1   Benjamin Y. Fong, 'Freud's Radical Talking', *The New York Times* (18 March 2012), http://opinionator.blogs.nytimes.com/2012/03/18/freuds-radical-talking/.
2   Sigmund Freud, 'Transference', in *Introductory Lectures on Psychoanalysis* (Harmondsworth: Penguin, 1987), 1: 483.
3   Sigmund Freud, 'Analytic Therapy', in *Introductory Lectures*, 1: 506.

regular hour with the patient, gets him to talk, listens to him, talks to him in his turn and gets him to listen".[4]

Freud's imaginary interlocutor ("The Impartial Person") is amazed: "Nothing more than that? Words, words, words, as Prince Hamlet says".[5]

"So it is a kind of magic", the impartial yet contemptu-ous interlocutor comments: "you talk, and blow away his ailments".[6] Yes, Freud admits: "Quite true. It would be magic if it worked rather quicker. An essential attribute of a magician is speed — one might say suddenness — of success. But analytic treatments take months and even years: magic that is so slow loses its miraculous character".[7]

Eve Kosofsky Sedgwick's part haiku, part-prose memoir, *A Dialogue on Love* is a record of, and a re-enactment of, exactly this brand of aimless magical talking; the text reveals the details of her psychotherapy, her sessions with Shannon Van Wey, the therapist she started seeing to treat her depression after she was diagnosed with breast cancer. It is messy, aimless, genre-less (or, multi-genre), and endless — that is, while it does end, it ends (as perhaps most therapy does, if it does) arbitrarily.

While Stephen Barber and David Clark tell us that "while psy-choanalysis may have limited relevance to Sedgwick's work that same work has considerable consequence for psychoanalysis";[8] it may nevertheless be the case, under the circumstance of Sedg-wick's actual psychotherapy, that psychoanalysis has maybe a few things to tell us about *A Dialogue on Love*. Not least because this dialogue, this therapeutic exchange, maps the very structure and dynamic of the "talking cure", the frangible, yet remarkably durable, infrastructure of psychoanalysis. Although Sedgwick is not undergoing strict psychoanalysis, she does end up on the

---

4   Sigmund Freud, *Historical and Expository Works on Psychoanalysis* (Har-mondsworth: Penguin, 1986), Vol. 15: 287.

5   Freud, *Historical and Expository Works*, 15: 287.

6   Freud, *Historical and Expository Works*, 15: 287.

7   Freud, *Historical and Expository Works*, 15: 287.

8   Stephen Barber and David A. Clark, eds., *Regarding Sedgwick: Essays on Queer Culture and Critical Theory* (New York: Routledge, 2002), 34.

couch. And therapy of this kind — this talking cure — works by the same structures, methods, and results as more conventional and traditional psychoanalysis does.

One way to read this book is as a transcription of Sedgwick's therapy. Another is to think of it as poetry; it includes verse, and it can be elliptical and allusive in the way poetry is thought to be more than theory. The text is Sedgwick's creation, but not hers alone; it is written in conjunction with another, her therapist, in the vein of some of her published conversations and collaborations as essays, among them a conversation with Michael Moon,[9] a conversation with Barber and Clark,[10] a collaboration with Adam Frank,[11] and the occasional direct address ("Hi Michael!").[12] Elizabeth Stephens notes that *A Dialogue on Love* is "not an attempt to provide a direct or unmediated account of her experience in therapy; rather, it is a queer investigation of the terms in which such experiences can be inscribed, posing the question of how one might write about both sexuality and affective relationships".[13] It is also, therefore, an autobiography — or autobiographical, in that age old understanding that it is, mostly, in the first person and discusses personal (very personal) aspects of the author's life. Several critics modify the cat-

9 Eve Kosofsky Sedgwick and Michael Moon, 'Divinity: A Dossier, A Performance Piece, A Little Understood Emotion', *Tendencies* (Durham: Duke University Press, 1993), 215–251. See also Eve Kosofsky Sedgwick and Michael Moon, 'Confusion of Tongues', in Betsy Erkkila and Jay Grossman, eds., *Breaking Bounds: Whitman and American Cultural Studies* (Oxford: Oxford University Press, 1996), 23–29; Eve Kosofsky Sedgwick, Michael Moon, Benjamin Gianni, and Scott Weir, 'Queers in (Single Family) Space', *Assemblage* 24 (August 1994), 30–37.

10 Barber and Clark with Sedgwick, 'This Piercing Bouquet: An Interview with Eve Kosofsky Sedgwick', in Barber and Clark, *Regarding Sedgwick: Essays on Queer Culture and Critical Thinking*, 243–262.

11 Sedgwick and Adam Frank, 'Shame in the Cybernetic Fold: Reading Silvan Tomkins', in Eve Kosofsky Sedgwick, *Touching, Feeling: Affect, Pedagogy, Performativity* (Durham: Duke University Press, 2003), 93–121.

12 Eve Kosofsky Sedgwick, 'White Glasses', in *Tendencies*, 252–266, 266.

13 Elizabeth Stephens, 'Queer Memoir: Public Confession and/as Sexual Practice in Eve Kosofsky Sedgwick's *A Dialogue on Love*', *Australian Humanities Review* 8 (May 2010), n.p.

egory of this book: "intellectual autobiography".[14] But this text is messing around in every way with its likely genres — autobiography, experimental memoir, transcript, poetry, and queer manifesto.[15]

Even the first person does not belong to just one person. "Because of Sedgwick's and Van Wey's constant ventriloquizing of one another, the reader is confronted by a subtle vertigo when trying to distinguish between their uses of 'I'".[16] Although Sedgwick has been known to defend the first person — or rather than defend, query what is at stake in avoiding it (depersonalizing, clinging to sterility and anonymity, archness) — she nevertheless is here invested in a form that does not *avoid* the first person but also does not rely on it. For example, in *Tendencies* she suggests that "some people hate" the first-person singular in academic work, but she suggests that her use of it "represents neither the sense of a simple, settled congratulatory 'I', on the one hand, nor on the other a fragmented postmodernist postindividual — never mind an unreliable narrator". "No", she retorts, "'I' is a heuristic; maybe a powerful one".[17] However, as Jason Edwards observes: "Given that it is a memoir, there is [...] perhaps significantly less of Sedgwick's first person than readers might initially have anticipated".[18] Sedgwick becomes less and less invested in even this heuristic first person. By the end of *A Dialogue on Love,* she is tempted to abjure the first person altogether, but not in the direction of scholarly sobriety; rather in the direction of wordlessness: as she becomes more involved in crafting textiles rather than text, she reflects that a "texture book

14 Among them, Nancy K. Miller, 'Reviewing Eve', in Barber and Clark, *Regarding Sedgwick,* 219.

15 The Village Voice says about *A Dialogue on Love*: "Sedgwick has written the kind of book she has always been accused of. Queer Theory". David Kurnick, 'Queer Therapy', *The Village Voice* (3 August 1999), http://www.villagevoice.com/arts/queer-therapy-7155890. (The title of this Village Voice review: initially I admired it, then envied it, then stole it.)

16 Tyler Bradway, "'Permeable We!" Affect and the Ethics of Intersubjectivity in Eve Kosofsky Sedgwick's *A Dialogue on Love*', *GLQ* 19.1 (2012), 79–110; 82.

17 Sedgwick, *Tendencies,* xiv.

18 Jason Edwards, *Eve Kosofsky Sedgwick* (London: Routledge, 2009), 131.

wouldn't need to have a first person at all, any more than weaving itself does".[19] The book itself becomes more textured in the ways typography and space increasingly shape the book's pages.

Although an autobiographical text, this book becomes increasingly dialogic, in its presentation at least. The fonts of the text in *A Dialogue on Love* tells us not who is speaking — because sometimes they speak for or as each other — but whose notes are being presented. The standard serif-ed font is Sedgwick, and even this becomes irregular in form when it slips in and out of haiku, as part of its overall Japanese haibun form. This is contrasted with Van Wey's notes, which appear in small caps. But whose voice is inhabited in each person's text becomes harder to distinguish; Edwards describes it this way: "As *A Dialogue on Love* gets more collaborative and relaxed [… it] also gets harder to establish who is talking, since Sedgwick and Van Wey adopt a strange form of address in relation to one another: somewhere between talking to themselves, each other and another person".[20]

What often arises in discussions of genre in relation to this book is the use of the haibun form, which Sedgwick recognizes as apposite to her project of recording her therapy with Van Wey, upon rereading James Merrill after his death:

In New York for the weekend, I'm paused over Merrill's death with a friend. I've long been haunted by his piece about a trip to Japan, called 'Prose of Departure,' in an unfamiliar form: prose interspersed with haiku.

Spangled with haiku is more what it feels like, his very sentences fraying

into implosions
of starlike density or
radiance, then out

---

19 Eve Kosofsky Sedgwick, *A Dialogue on Love* (Boston: Beacon, 1999), 207.
20 Edwards, *Eve Kosofsky Sedgwick*, 132.

into a prose that's never quite not the poetry —.[21]

What also arises in genre discussions is whether and how the book is autobiographical, the typography and font on the page — and I shall return to address these things myself — but there is very little discussion of the genre of conversation. I did start out the essay suggesting that conversation — therapeutic conversation, particularly — is genre-less, but it is nevertheless a category of talk and transcription that is recognizable.

"In general", Lauren Berlant tells us, "conversation is a key genre of the present: when a conversation ends, its singular time ends, and then it becomes like all other episodes, something mainly forgotten, distorted, and half-remembered. [...] [C]onversation is a space of time that makes its own rules and boundaries".[22] Berlant is not speaking of Sedgwick when she writes "[h]er 'we' is both singular and general", but about Susan Sontag, whose "conversation piece", the short story 'The Way We Live Now', emerges out of a different illness, the AIDS epidemic. But the salience is the same when she writes that the "reader eavesdrops, participating as a lurker in the intimate public of the illness".[23] In the case of Sedgwick the illness might be her breast cancer; it could also be the AIDS illnesses that afflict her friends; it could also be her anxiety — the condition that brings her to therapy to begin with.

The story of the queer self cannot be told singly. We might say that under duress, in the realm of illness, for example, autobiography becomes community. Formalized queer conversation is often used to address debilitation and loss. I have suggested this in recent writing about AIDS, when I noticed that one emerging strand of AIDS literature was an increasing prevalence of transcribed conversations, including those of Sedgwick.[24] Ju-

21 Sedgwick, *A Dialogue on Love,* 193–194.
22 Lauren Berlant, *Cruel Optimism* (Durham: Duke University Press, 2011), 57.
23 Berlant, *Cruel Optimism,* 58.
24 Monica B. Pearl, AIDS *Literature and Gay Identity: The Literature of Loss* (New York: Routledge, 2013), esp.chapter 6.

dith Butler tells us that "loss has made a tenuous 'we' of us all".[25] And Berlant adds that it "was a matter of life and death to become, literally, conversant".[26]

Later, Berlant *is* talking about Sedgwick when she writes: "Reading is one place where the impersonality of intimacy can be transacted without harm to anyone; writing and paper-giving are others. There is no romance of the impersonal, no love plot for it. But there can be optimism, a space across which to move".[27]

Berlant is one of myriad readers who feel interpellated into Sedgwick's writing, who wish not just to be on the couch with her taking tea and talking, but are already doing it when they read her. Like Berlant, Wayne Koestenbaum actually did know Sedgwick; nevertheless he also imagines her, imagines being engaged with her:

> I'm drafting this essay on a green Hermes 3000 manual typewriter from the 1950s. A painting student gave it to me; he found it on the street. I imagine telling Eve about this typewriter.[28]

He confesses that "I became 'me' after reading *Between Men* and then more 'me' after reading *Epistemology of the Closet*. And it continued, this tidal process of becoming 'me', every time I read or encountered Eve. In no one else's eyes have I felt so recognized".[29] There are so many examples of readers who feel hailed by Sedgwick and who engage with her on the pages of her writing. One reader comments on reading 'Paranoid Reading and Reparative Reading', her first experience of reading Sedgwick: "I remember beginning by reading it on my computer,

25 Judith Butler, *Precarious Life: The Powers of Mourning and Violence* (New York: Verso, 2004), 20.

26 Berlant, *Cruel Optimism*, 57.

27 Berlant, *Cruel Optimism*, 126.

28 Wayne Koestenbaum, 'A Manual Approach to Mourning', in *My 1980s and Other Essays* (New York: Farrar, Straus and Giroux, 2013), 65.

29 Koestenbaum, 'A Manual Approach to Mourning', 69.

until partway through when printing it became a necessity because there was too much to annotate and underline. By the end", she comments, "I only had exclamation marks and hearts as marginalia".[30] Another reader has already capitulated to the transference of reading Sedgwick in the title of his essay: Jonathan A. Allan declares his experience of 'Falling in Love with Eve Kosofsky Sedgwick'.[31] And he is not the only one. In fact, according to James Kincaid, Allan's passion is textbook:

> Now I know why no one in love with Eve Sedgwick (all of us) can write about her. Consider that — 'write about her': We are all able to *write* and we all are inspired by *her*; it's the *about* we trip over. Who can find the distance or wants to? We all write *to* Eve or, more exactly, she writes to us. Better yet (I should have said this right off), we write with her. With Eve, it's always we. You'll be wondering why I haven't been saying 'I'. I haven't been saying 'I' because I don't have any 'I,' which is not modesty but something like the reverse. Eve is the we of me.[32]

Cindy Patton "bends[s] *A Dialogue on Love* to [her] own place and meaning".[33] ("There is so much in the text", worries Patton, "and, yet, so few hints about how to be a worthy reader").[34]

This "we", the community, is reflected pronouncedly in the ways that Sedgwick's readers want in. Sedgwick's book is queer therapy — *for the reader.* It describes and affects the ways that one wants transference with her — with her writing, her books, her words — all the time, nearly universally.

---

30 Jane Hu, 'I'm Nobody: Eve Sedgwick After Death' (2 May 2013), http://www. theawl.com/2013/05/eve-sedgwick-after-death.

31 Jonathan A. Allan, 'Falling in Love with Eve Kosofsky Sedgwick', *Mosaic* 48.1 (March 2015), 1–16.

32 James Kincaid, 'When Whippoorwills Call', in Barber and Clark, *Regarding Sedgwick,* 229.

33 Cindy Patton, 'Love Without the Obligation to Love', *Criticism* 52.2 (Spring 2010), 215–224; 217.

34 Patton, 'Love', 216

This kind of reading, or this way of being a reader — this interactive, interrogatory, enmeshed reading — is not particular to Sedgwick nor to queer discourse, for that matter, but there is something galvanic about this interaction here. If it is a banality to say of very enjoyable reading that it feels like the author knows me, or knows my life, or is speaking directly to me, it is less frequent that readers express a wish to be taken up, or in, by the author, to become not just engaged in conversation or discourse with the writer, with Sedgwick, but to be engaged with her in the writing or reading itself, a joint project, writing and reading together, not (just) an exchange, not (only) a back and forth. They want to be a "we" with Eve.[35]

Everybody wants to be in conversation with Sedgwick. And Sedgwick wants it, too. Not only does she interrogate and practically disavow the singular first person, but her "favorite pronoun" is "the dear/first person plural".[36] What she wants more than anything is not to be an "I", which she is rehearsing with Shannon but is also announcing: but to be a "we":

Promiscuous we!
Me, plus anybody else.
Permeable we![37]

---

35 And also to be in some extra-textual ideations of affiliations with Eve; see, for example, Katherine Bond Stockton imagining herself both as Eve's child and as siring a child with her in 'Eve's Queer Child', in Barber and Clark, *Regarding Sedgwick*, 181–199; Kevin Kopelson also imagines Sedgwick as his (and all gay men's) mother in 'The Mother of Us All?', *Substance* 43.1 (2014), 191–197; and earlier Kopelson, 'Fake it Like a Man', in David Bergman, ed., *Camp Grounds: Style and Homosexuality* (Amherst: University of Massachusetts Press, 1993), 265, who wants a pair of the very same white glasses that Sedgwick describes coveting of her friend Michael Lynch (in 'White Glasses', *Tendencies*, 252–266); and Lynch writes a paper in the voice of Sedgwick. For further disquisition on the second two examples, see my 'Eve Sedgwick's Melancholic 'White Glasses", *Textual Practice* 17.1 (2003), 61–80, further elaborated in my AIDS *Literature and Gay Identity*.

36 Sedgwick, *A Dialogue on Love*, 106.

37 Sedgwick, *A Dialogue on Love*, 106.

Sedgwick announces this wish in more than this pronounce-
ment, but in the very typography and space of her text. When
she realizes that haibun is the right genre for conveying her
therapy experience with Van Wey, she enacts and describes it
like this:

> To notate our strange
> melody, I have some use
> for all the white space.[38]

Edwards tells us that "*A Dialogue on Love* contains more white
space than any of Sedgwick's other books of prose, noticeable especially around her haikus and her therapist's non-justified (ragged right) text".[39] The unusual amount of white or blank space
on the page makes room for the reader; on one hand it invites
multiple layers of internal thinking and mulling — "Sweeping
into and through the arias, silent impasses, the fat, buttery condensations and inky dribbles of the mind's laden brush" — and
on the other, interaction with others.[40] Bradway suggests that
the white spaces and blank pages are precisely invitations to in-
terlocutions with others:

> We see each page's negative space anew as the haikus lin-
> guistically reference and graphically redraw the emptiness
> around them. In the absence of words, the page's materiality
> is highlighted as the condition of possibility [...] for its (re)
> emergence in the form of the reader's notes. There is no guar-
> antee that the reader will respond, but the space creates the
> possibility for readerly participation.[41]

Now, while I am suggesting that Sedgwick might be inviting us
in, her writing is also notoriously demanding to read. We may

---

38 Sedgwick, *A Dialogue on Love,* 194.
39 Edwards, *Eve Kosofsky Sedgwick,* 131.
40 Sedgwick, *A Dialogue on Love,* 194.
41 Bradway, "'Permeable We!'", 87.

recognize an open invitation to be in dialogue with Sedgwick, but this is not always easy to actually do. Her writing is famously recondite and forbidding. She might be issuing an invitation, but the routes in are not always evident.

Sedgwick invites and repels: her vocabulary and her syntax are difficult, sometimes invented, yet so welcoming because of how permissive, how expansive, how non-judgmental it is. Several refer to her writing as unusually "capacious".[42] "Even in her gnarliest sentences", Koestenbaum explains, "a reader could find a blessed phrase [...] on which to relax".[43]

We might understand this push and pull, this invitation that is irresistible but impossible to fully embrace, if we turn to another construction, besides the "we", that Sedgwick is inordinately fond of, and that is "enjambment". The notion of enjambment first arises in 'A Poem Is Being Written'. Enjambment is a poetic device whereby a line of poetry might end but the sense of the sentence carries on to the next. Sedgwick's point, in this essay, is to show that a childhood fascination with this technique in poetry echoed and in some ways recreated the experience of — and that is to say, an ambivalence towards — being spanked.

"The title of this essay", she writes, "obviously means to associate the shifty passive voice of a famous title of Freud's 'A Child Is Being Beaten' with the general question of poetry — with the scene of poetry writing, and with the tableau of the poem itself".[44] It is tempting here to consider Sedgwick's relationship to Freud, especially in an essay interrogating her experience in psychotherapy, but Sedgwick herself tells us:

> [T]he best strategy I can come up with for dealing with 'Freud' is not to try to go mano-y-mano with him as a gigantically singular, protean, transferential figure; that seems

---

42 See Barber and Clark, 'Queer Moments', who use this term, and note its use by both Berlant and Butler in the same volume (*Regarding Sedgwick*), 30.

43 Koestenbaum, 'A Manual Approach', 68.

44 Sedgwick, 'A Poem Is Being Written', *Tendencies*, 177–214; 177–178

like a mug's game, in the sense that the theorist's own propulsions lead circularly, inexorably to an endless reinstitution of Freud's terms and problematics.[45]

But let us stick with the literary term and think about how enjambment itself is ambivalent, or at least multivalent, doing two antithetical things at once: it invites, by leaving space, and repels, by letting there be no breath or aperture in that space. "[A]nd because I loved French", Sedgwick writes in that essay:

I knew *enjambment,* not just for a technical word in the introduction to my rhyming dictionary, but for a physical gesture of the limbs, of the flanks, the ham. [...] From all this I visualized *enjambment* very clearly as not only [...] the poetic gesture of *straddling* lines *together* syntactically, but also a pushing apart of lines.[46]

In *A Dialogue on Love,* this enjambment works poetically in the haibun that weaves through the prose — literally employing the technique of enjambment within the poems themselves and also between the prose and poems, as one leads recurringly into the other, but also within and between the dialogue between Shannon and Sedgwick, "producing a kind of enjambment", we might say — and Kent does, "at the level of genre".[47] As Patton explains,

'Eve' plays hide and seek with the reader, offering various angles on her body and feelings, and then veiling those with [...] Shannon's words, perpetually grafting fragments of her poems onto fragments of therapy notes, sometimes Shannon's official record, sometimes her therapy journals, in one moment her once estranged sister's childhood diary

---

45 Sedgwick, 'A Piercing Bouquet' in Barber and Clark, *Regarding Sedgwick* 260.

46 Sedgwick, 'A Poem Is Being Written', 185.

47 Kathryn R. Kent, '"Surprising Recognition": Genre, Poetic Form, and Erotics from Sedgwick's '1001 Seances' to *A Dialogue on Love'*, *GLQ: A Journal of Lesbian and Gay Studies* 17.4 (2011), 497–510; 508.

accounts of Eve, in other places e-mail exchanges with her friend Tim.[48]

Here is an example:

Oh, right, I keep forgetting, for lots and lots of people in the world, the notion of 'falling in love' has (of all things) sexual connotations. No, that's not what I think is happening. For me, what falling in love means is different. It's a matter of suddenly, globally, 'knowing' that another person represents your only access to some vitally

transmissible truth
or radiantly heightened
mode of perception,

and that if you lose the thread of this intimacy, both your soul and your whole world might subsist forever in some desert-like state of ontological impoverishment.[49]

As Koestenbaum puts it: "Enjambment — reaching toward the brim, and then exceeding it — came naturally to Eve: she liked containers, and she knew how to tease their limits".[50] Any reader of Sedgwick knows that rigid thinking is not her way; rather, as she puts it in a very late essay, she is invested in

a very thoroughgoing conceptual habit of nondualism. As soon as somebody posits 'concept X as opposed to concept Y,' I'm always the person who reflexively responds, 'But maybe X and Y aren't so distinct from each other after all'. Because of this nondualism, the methodological tools of deconstruction

48 Patton, 'Love Without the Obligation to Love', 216.
49 Sedgwick, *A Dialogue on Love*, 168.
50 Koestenbaum, 'A Manual Approach', 69.

have always been congenial to me. I'm also extremely interested in Buddhist thought for the same reason.[51]

Or, as she puts it more plainly in *A Dialogue on Love* (or, in the book's strange ventriloquism, Shannon puts it for her in his post-session notes): "Nondualism is mother's milk to me".[52]

Sedgwick's inspired notion of "reparative reading", an effort and gesture to supplant what she calls "paranoid reading", is part of this habit of thinking nondualistically. Reading Klein, Sedgwick came to understand that much scholarship is defensive, a way to catch other scholars in misapprehensions and malefactions, and to plant a flag on the little mound one has made atop the carcass communiques of one's colleague-competitors, only to be critiqued and interred by the next pettifogger. In her important essay, 'Paranoid Reading and Reparative Reading', Sedgwick suggests that instead we might aim to read reparatively, that is, with an effort to participate and understand rather than disparage:

> [T]o read from a reparative position is to surrender the knowing, anxious paranoid determination that no horror, however apparently unthinkable, shall ever come to the reader *as new*; to a reparatively positioned reader, it can seem realistic and necessary to experience surprise. Because there can be terrible surprises, however, there can also be good ones.[53]

Sedgwick's proposed theory of reading derives from Klein's observation that children feel guilty for the rage they feel towards their mothers when they develop violent resentment for not being able to control the imperative pleasures they sometimes and seemingly very arbitrarily receive. "Hatred and aggressive

---

51 Sedgwick, 'Thinking Through Queer Theory', *The Weather in Proust*, 190.

52 Sedgwick, *A Dialogue on Love*, 215.

53 Sedgwick, 'Paranoid Reading and Reparative Reading, Or, You're So Paranoid, You Probably Think this Essay Is About You', in *Touching Feeling: Affect, Pedagogy, Performativity* (Durham: Duke University Press, 2003), 146; emphasis in original.

feelings are aroused and [the baby] becomes dominated by the impulses to destroy the very person who is the object of all his desires and who in his mind is linked up with everything he experiences — good and bad alike".[54] Paranoia arises from our guilty certainty that we will be punished for our violent feelings and fantasies. Repair is the attempt not only to assuage the damage but to be open to the vicissitudes of the availability of these pleasures, namely, at this stage, the breast, but later other necessities and pleasures.

If Kleinian reparation is not exactly a version of enjambment, it nevertheless describes a paradoxical gesture of connection and deflection; as Janet Malcolm describes it, the baby is appalled to realize "what he is doing to his mother as he nurses at her breast — the 'hole' he is leaving as he sucks —" and wishes "to make reparation".[55]

It turns out that the difference between burying and accommodating the work and thinking of others — paranoia and reparation — can be seen as analogous to Freud's discovery of the talking cure and how he found it to be superior to his previous method: hypnosis. In the case of analysis, it is not the thinking of others that one is in battle with, but one's own repressed inclinations. The goal of therapy is to bring those repressed feelings and wishes into the light of day, but paradoxically, though we might believe we are invested in nearly every way in a cure, we nevertheless resist. Freud says, "[w]hen we undertake to restore a patient to health, to relieve him of the symptoms of his illness, he meets us with a violent and tenacious resistance, which persists throughout the whole length of treatment".[56]

Once more imagining his incredulous interlocutor, Freud explains:

---

54 Melanie Klein, 'Love, Guilt and Reparation', in Melanie Klein and Joan Riviere, *Love, Hate and Reparation* (1936; New York: W.W. Norton, 1964), 58.

55 Janet Malcolm, *Psychoanalysis: The Impossible Profession* (New York: Vintage, 1982), 34.

56 Sigmund Freud, 'Resistance and Repression', in *Introductory Lectures*, 327.

Only think of it! The patient, who is suffering so much from his symptoms and is causing those about him to share his sufferings, who is ready to undertake so many sacrifices in time, money, effort, and self-discipline in order to be freed from those symptoms — we are to believe that this same patient puts up a struggle in the interest of his illness against the person who is helping him. How improbable such an assertion must sound! Yet it is true.[57]

While in his initial attempts to cure patients of hysterical symptoms, hypnosis seemed to work to get right to the heart of the troubling symptoms and to stop them, Freud discovered that the symptoms were indeed stopped, but only because they were buried, not because they were unearthed or treated.

In the light of the knowledge we have gained from psychoanalysis we can describe the difference between hypnotic and psychoanalytic suggestion as follows. Hypnotic treatment seeks to cover up and gloss over something in mental life; analytic treatment seeks to expose and get rid of something. The former acts like a cosmetic, the latter like surgery. The former makes use of suggestion in order to forbid the symptoms; it strengthens the repressions, but, apart from that, leaves all the processes that have led to the formation of the symptoms unaltered. Analytic treatment makes its impact further back towards the roots, where the conflicts are which gave rise to the symptoms, and uses suggestion in order to alter the outcome of those conflicts.[58]

Queer therapy might include the ways that we can find to accommodate the uneasy attempt to reconcile the simultaneous experience of participation and resistance, of opening and foreclosing, of invitation and exclusion. One way it might be affected, as I have suggested, is through reading Sedgwick. It does

---

57   Freud, 'Resistance and Repression', 327.
58   Sigmund Freud, 'Analytic Therapy', in *Introductory Lectures*, 503–504.

not take much perspicacity to notice that anyone writing about Sedgwick is also ineluctably writing and thinking like Sedgwick.[59] In reading Sedgwick, we are all invited to write more experimentally.[60]

Koestenbaum explains it, while he is himself doing it: "Be complicated, she invites us; be obscure, oblique. Be odd. Especially if you can't help it. Like Henry James, be flush with innuendo, your clauses dependent, dilated, filthy, yet discreet".[61] In *A Dialogue on Love,* Sedgwick has "discover[ed ...] a queer genre that can accommodate all her complexity",[62] a platform to express "her feminist politics and queerish selfhood".[63] And in responding in our Sedgwickian ways, we enter that space of repair, permission, and queer possibility. "Above all", says Koestenbaum, "her writing gave license".[64]

We are not exactly cured reading Sedgwick (cured of what, she would ask? — "revel in your abjection", she would almost certainly say), but we are invited into a somewhat Socratic — yet hardly passionlessly platonic — dialogue, an endless aimless conversation, talking and talking with Sedgwick.

---

59 And in a nice oedipal genealogy, Sedgwick herself is said to write like those she writes about, Proust notably. See Barber and Clark, 'This Piercing Bouquet', 41. For more on the idea of experimental critical writing, see Eve Kosofsky Sedgwick, 'Teaching "Experimental Critical Writing"', in Jill Lane and Peggy Phelan, eds., *The Ends of Performance* (New York: New York University Press, 1998), 105–115.

60 See Sedgwick's own suggestion of this in 'A Poem Is Being Written', and also Barber and Clark, 'This Piercing Bouquet', 257.

61 Koestenbaum, 'A Manual Approach', 67.

62 Katherine Hawkins, 'Woven Spaces: Eve Kosofsky Sedgwick's *Dialogue on Love', Women and Performance: A Journal of Feminist Theory* 16.2 (July 2006), 251–67; 254.

63 Patton, 'Love Without the Obligation to Love', 219.

64 Koestenbaum, 'A Manual Approach', 67.

CHAPTER 6

Waiting in the Dark: Some Musings on Sedgwick's Performative(s)

Meg Boulton

This chapter was originally given as a paper at the *Fat Art, Thin Art* symposium held at the University of York on February 14, 2014, placed into the 'Autobiographies' section of the day. It is only now, only later, with the benefit of that oft-cited lens — hindsight — that the date seems a particularly apposite one, although I suspect it was anything but an arbitrary choice. So much of what was said that day was said with such emotion in the close quarters of a room full of people that seemed uncommonly close to each other and to the material they were presenting (although, in several instances, many had only just met) that it feels, now, improbably difficult to produce a written record of my part in that particularly lovely and particularly unusual academic event, and yet what follows is my effort to do just that.

As with the paper delivered on the day, it seems fitting to start with the barest of biographical outlines. In giving this paper, it felt, somewhat, like I was speaking from a mostly amateur place, spending my days researching things and themes that exist, mostly, far from Sedgwick's queer world and writings. My doctorate was awarded in Art History and my day-to-day research is concerned with space, with its conceptualisation and significance, and I should also confess that it quite frequently takes place in an Anglo-Saxon crypt in Northumberland.[1] However, in this case, at this time I am writing about two of the poems in *Fat Art, Thin Art*: 'Performative (Toronto)' and 'Performative (San Francisco)'.[2] While reading this, I hope you will forgive me the (inevitable) liberties taken, not least the conflation of these two poems, which doubtless deserve to have been considered individually, rather than as I have addressed them.

Now, given that I am currently talking at some remove from Hexham and the seventh century and that I was helpfully placed in the 'Autobiographies' session of this event, I thought, maybe, I would start by writing about how I first came to read Sedgwick[3] and, perhaps, how I read her now. As with many things, I have Jason Edwards to thank for an introduction to Eve, both in text and in person. My first encounter with Sedgwick, with reading Sedgwick, with struggling to think through the many complexities and intricacies, binds and double-binds, alley-ways and avenues, and openings her work presents was an immersive encounter more akin to an imagined group therapy than the usual module one expects and encounters in a post-graduate seminar.

For eight weeks, a group of six, then five, met in a small room, tiny really, for two hours and talked about one Sedgwick monograph or edited collection a week. Now, as I gave this paper I imagined, rightly or wrongly, that everyone in the room was familiar with trying to read that dizzying prose for the first time, and I imagine most readers of this, too, will share that experience — although, during these various imaginings, imagine, please, the amplified dizziness of moving from thesis to theory, to prose, to poetry, to art in such a condensed period. Today, six or so years later, I can only recall that module as an inti-

---

1   Meg Boulton, 'The Conceptualisation of Sacred Space in Anglo-Saxon Northumbria in the Sixth to Ninth Centuries', Ph.D. thesis, University of York, 2 vols.

2   Eve Kosofsky Sedgwick, *Fat Art, Thin Art* (Durham: Duke University Press, 1994), 17–18.

3   For a quasi-voyeuristic encounter with this period of Sedgwickian discovery, do read the acknowledgements in Edwards' introduction to her work in Jason Edwards, *Eve Kosofsky Sedgwick* (London: Routledge, 2009), xi.

mate blur of words, hers and ours, of terms, and thoughts, and fleeting ideas, of fragments and moments and bits and pieces. Of lists! More than remembering those days and texts in detail, I remember other things so clearly. I remember learning to read her. I remember learning *how* to read her. I remember it was easier to unpick her words, her thoughts on a bed or, more likely in a nest-like slump, piled in a soft heap on the floor. Surrounded by soft things it was somehow easier to find some space to think my thoughts, as well as hers. I remember that it was easier to read her in company, exclaiming in pleasure or pain, frustration or panic at particular words, or phrases, or books. Or, all of those.

Even today, *Tendencies* (1993) unnerves me.

Given this is how I have chosen to start, this may perhaps have been a more fitting part of the 'Memories' session, rather than strictly, precisely, autobiography. However, with the things I would remember about that time, that class, those people, there are also things I would forget. Six years ago, I learned how to begin reading Sedgwick. Six years ago, I also learned that things you think are permanent often aren't. People come, and they go. In every sense. Six years ago, I put her work aside to focus on other things, other places, other eras. Academically, I was seeing other people.

And then, this. An invitation to go back, to revisit, to rethink. To re-inhabit.

To reverse?

No, that last, impossible.

Still, Irresistible.

And so, here I am. And this is, I think, what I want to say...

I want to talk about Goodbye. Goodbye in our vocabulary.

Eve's Performative(s) in *Fat Art, Thin Art,* 'Performative (Toronto)' and 'Performative (San Francisco)', are the two poems that immediately called to me when Jason asked what I wanted to speak on, for reasons I still can't fully articulate. There are things here that I don't know. There are things here that I don't want to know. *Ever.*

Everyone who reads Sedgwick, everyone who reads Eve, struggles, I think, to define 'hers' and 'mine'.[4] Worse still than reading is writing (and by worse I might mean better). Impossible for writing on Eve to *not* be a derivation, a reclamation of sorts, of her words, that have come and gone before. But in these poems, these performatives, there is a common act, a repeated phrase, an implicit leitmotif that is shared socially and societally. Both, hers and ours. Mine.

So, Goodbye.

Goodbye in our vocabulary is impossible.

The shaved disyllable — Good. Bye. The flagrant implausibility of these two conjoined words existing to form one impossible utterance — except, it is all too possible, isn't it?

We say it. But we don't mean it.

Some of us don't say it.

The rest of us don't mean it. Can't mean it.

To borrow her questions here, as well as her words, as Sedgwick wrote with Andrew Parker in the *Introduction to Performativity and Performance* (1995): "When is saying something doing something? And how is saying something doing something?"[5] When all is said and done, Goodbye, for the most part, when said is not done, equating more to little lies, polite fictions, social contracts than to saying, to doing what is meant, than believing what is called into being by those words, that phrase.

Yet, although it is a polite, politic everyday ending: it is said, it is done and oh, how it wantonly highlights the fragility which lurks beneath the everyday; revealing the finite versus the infinite; the possible rather than the probable; the wolf in bed, in frilled cap, at Grandma's house, waiting just around the corner, through the woods, down the garden path. A day to walk through the woods, to find just one modest flower besides a modest road, less travelled.

---

4   For more, see Sedgwick's citation of C.P. Cavafy's 'Anna Dalassini' in Eve Kosofsky Sedgwick, *The Weather in Proust* (Durham: Duke University Press, 2011), 65.

5   Eve Kosofsky Sedgwick and Andrew Parker, eds., *Performativity and Performance* (London: Routledge, 1995), 1.

Enforced, policed, polite, pedestrian utterance.

Reading the 'Performative(s)' captures, fiercely, some of the difficulties of goodbyes — not least the difficulties of our goodbyes and of goodbyes that are not obviously ours. In writing this I had such a fear of appropriating the goodbyes of others. Of hers.

Her Good-byes, preserved on the page "flooding out, unstanchable", highlighting

The long moment
The long moment of no more
The long moment of no more Goodbye

Waiting in the dark morning

And later...
The horror in the taxi.

Hers. Ours. Hers? Ours?

And, to *this,* to these Goodbyes, Sedgwick attaches the idea of the Performative — and a specific geography in her presentation of them in *Fat Art, Thin Art,* which, taken together, may be read as mapping a personal, emotional topography, goodbyes stretching across cities, countries, oceans. Across time. This connecting in her titles of place and performativity highlights, for me, the fallacy of Goodbye. The presentation of a place, a confining encircling physical location as a background for this act, this utterance, is interesting. To go back to basics for a minute, and to revisit various definitions of the Performative:[6]

Performativity is the process by which semiotic expression produces results or real consequences in extra-semiotic reality, including the result of constructing reality itself.

6　See, for example, Catherine Soanes and Angus Stevenson, eds., *The Oxford Dictionary of English* (Oxford: Oxford University Press, 2005). See also Eve Kosofsky Sedgwick, 'Around the Peri-Performative: Periperformative Vicinities in Nineteenth-Century Narrative', in *Touching Feeling: Affect, Pedagogy, Performativity* (Durham: Duke University Press, 2004), 67–92.

Performatives are always already situated within larger social contexts.

Performativity problematizes notions of intention and agency.

Performative utterances (or performatives) are defined as sentences that are not only passively describing a given reality, but are changing the (social) reality they are describing.

Goodbye, then, to me, makes little sense as a performative. It is, I think, for most of us an utterance that we deny even as speak it; indeed, in speaking it, we negate its meaning rather than seek to enact it. Goodbye as a performance, maybe, but a performative?

Goodbye could be thought of as a performance we never want to happen.

Goodbye is a safety net uttered like a prayer, like a curse.

Goodbye, in most of its daily usage is made to mean, take care — I love you — be back soon.

We say goodbye, but we mean — see you soon, see you later, until next time, see you… again.

Au revoir, auf Wiedersehen, not Goodbye.

Constantly trying to make the word mean what we want it to mean, emboldened by each successive utterance that really embodies a future return, not a parting, as promised. As threatened?

If, then, the juxtaposition of this performative utterance described in 'Performative (Toronto)' and 'Performative (San Francisco)' is deliberate — that the Goodbyes here, are just that, a word that calls into being a state; the moment where meaning is truly meant;

"Does it feel to *you* like we are saying goodbye?"

But we were trying: we hugged each other, and for a while we cried…

then they are set against the physicality of place. They are not left to lie on the place/non-place of the page but realised in named cityscapes, in solid actualities, in darkened mornings and cars and taxis, set against personal geographies and lived contexts.

A performance generally involves an audience, and here these private goodbyes are preserved on the page, monumentalised and memorialised. They provide two brief encounters, her memories, our monuments, which perform and enact this utterance, driving its meaning home through her, to us; in our vocabulary.

The two *Performative* poems, located next to each other in the text, back to back, are presented separately, treated slightly differently, yet in my mind, even when keeping their individual natures clearly in mind, they are hard to separate. They pack a punch, these poems, excruciating in their proximity, highlighting and foregrounding the 'Goodbye' that for so many of the poems in the first half of the book is implicit, is subtext. Here it is direct, unavoidable; underlined by the double utterance of poems in proximity and our participatory, readerly performance of turned pages to encounter first one, then the other. Goodbye, goodbye.

Despite this proximity and their (inter)relationality, no two goodbyes are the same and some of the differences between the two are worth a closer look, separated, as they are, by no more and so much more than the turn of a page. In 'Performative (San Francisco)', for example, Goodbye is capitalized and this is a bloody parting; snapped off; broken; waxy; vengeful; flooding out, unstanchable; clotted gouts and gouts of blood, with horror, still to come in the taxi after that long moment; spaced out, separate, further down the page. The nuanced line break, too, of that long moment of no more Goodbye in our vocabulary speaks, perhaps, to the suggested disjunction of meaning and moment; the difference of words and meaning, and the impossibility of Goodbye meaning goodbye, either in its everyday usage in our vocabulary or of its meaning at all in that moment, that long moment of no more Goodbye, because here is the last, and here, it must mean what we say, what she says, what is said. 'Performative (Toronto)' also directly employs the word goodbye, but here, it is not capitalized and, instead of the horror, instead there is hugging and crying and giggling, absurdity, vitality, a decision, denial...

"Oh, honey, denial's gotten us this far".

But then, at the close, is one of the mysteries of *Fat Art, Thin Art* — and I can't go any further without thanking Jason for conversations about this, past and present — we arrive once again, here, in 'Performative (Toronto)' at the missing fourteenth line from the sonnet… present by its absence in 'Performative (San Francisco)', a sonnet forever incomplete, a facet found throughout Sedgwick's poetry, but that here, forcibly underlines the incompleteness offered by goodbye. Then, too, both poems leave with a sense of motion, of going on, of work, of locomotion, of movement, of a continuing. Life goes on. Until, of course, it doesn't and then we all must confront a wider loss, a more personal moment of goodbye.

Reading her today, these days, is, I suspect, for me, like for many, somewhat of a constant goodbye, an unending ending unfolding the beginning of an ending of a page, of a book, of an era, of a voice. Of Eve. As I implied at the outset of this paper, there were a lot of endings caught up in the beginnings of me discovering her work. And my relationship with her work, never simple, is nuanced with these endings. Reading her, now, feels uncertain, like a renegotiation of meanings. Yet the act of reading, too, is not a performance necessarily bound by endings. To open, to turn, to turn, to turn again, to close, only to reopen. But perhaps this is just a part of growing up; of keeping on… small endings of beginnings, beginnings of endings. Perhaps, in the space of these texts, in these poems, in these pages, in the papers so carefully and kindly delivered on the fourteenth of February, in a treehouse in a university in York we might find that there is room, there is breath for more than one type of goodbye. Performance, performative, utterance.

Does it feel to *you* like we're saying goodbye?

Goodbye in our vocabulary; it's gotten us this far.

PART II

SEDGWICK'S UNCOLLECTED POEMS

Someday We'll Look Back with Pleasure Even on This: Sedgwick's Uncollected Poems

Jason Edwards

On the Eve of the Past, or A Queer Young Woman is Being Remembered

In one of the final lyrics Sedgwick published in her lifetime, she offered a translation and recontextualisation of Virgil's phrase: "Forsan et haec olim meminisse juvabit": "Someday we'll look back with pleasure even on this". The poem documented how, even though "Things with us are actually very bad" at the time of writing, Sedgwick had a reparative sense of the future, masochistic pleasure she would experience recalling the sore scene; in a similar way to which, in the earlier 'A scar, just a scar', she knew that "someday soon" she would "feel more nostalgia" for the painful hospital experience she was immersed in "than for any school" she had fantasied about.[1]

As we learn from across Sedgwick's oeuvre, she suffered from depression, and her childhood, adolescence and early adulthood were often acutely painful. For example, 'Not' describes the youthful Eve Kosofsky's "wish not to be" and "not to

---

1   Eve Kosofsky Sedgwick, *Fat Art, Thin Art* (Durham: Duke University Press, 1994), 29.

reproduce".[2] In the summer of 1967, however, Sedgwick began her studies at Cornell University, where, amongst other courses, she took a year-long poetry writing class with A.R. Ammons, whose work she admired, and which generated a number of poems collected here.[3] It was also at Cornell where Sedgwick first met, and later married, her husband, Hal, aged 19, in the summer of 1969. Three poems in *Fat Art, Thin Art* return us to this moment of Sedgwick's life. 'Nicht Mehr Leben' (To No Longer Live) recalls the way her "old life abandoned her" at eighteen in favor of a "new life", where there was "abundance" and "always the kindest eyes / for her".[4] 'It seems that there are two kinds of marriage', returns us, a year later, to the

> coed on her honeymoon
> preregistered for 'George Eliot and Flaubert',
> reading *Daniel Deronda* in the frail airplane;
> learning to be pleased and to please,
> the silent corridors of marital exemption.[5]

'One of us falls asleep on the other's shoulder' again recalls Sedgwick as a "girl of nineteen", who otherwise "doesn't bear thinking about", but whose early marital experience with her patient young husband, provided an "inexhaustible […] motive" in the poem, and clearly inspired a number of poems in this collection.[6] Those poems fill out our understanding of Sedgwick's early life and poetic development and focus further our picture of the "performativity of the long unconventional marriage" Sedgwick began whilst still an undergraduate and that lasted throughout her life.[7]

---

2   Sedgwick, *Fat Art, Thin Art*, 36.

3   For a sense of Ammons' verse at the time, see A.R. Ammons, *Collected Poems, 1951–1971* (New York: Norton, 2001).

4   Sedgwick, *Fat Art, Thin Art*, 37.

5   Sedgwick, *Fat Art, Thin Art*, 34.

6   Sedgwick, *Fat Art, Thin Art*, 35.

7   The quotation is drawn from the inside cover blurb of *Fat Art, Thin Art*.

With her own adolescence in mind perhaps, *Tendencies* opens with haunting statistics documenting how queer teenagers were "two to three times likelier to attempt suicide, and to accomplish it, than others"; that "up to 30 percent of teen suicides" were "likely to be gay or lesbian"; that a "third of lesbian and gay teenagers say they have attempted suicide"; and that "minority queer adolescents" were "at even more risk" from the "despoiling" energies of a homophobic mainstream culture including numerous parents who would rather "their children were dead as gay".[8]

Sedgwick's major manifesto on the queerness of (her own) poetry, 'A Poem is Being Written', was composed with just such painful personal and political contexts in mind and represents a sustained "claim for respectful attention to the intellectual and artistic life of a nine-year-old child, Eve Kosofsky".[9] The poems I collect here represent a claim for respectful attention to the intellectual and artistic life of that same young poet in her mid-teens and early undergraduate and graduate days, at Cornell and Yale; as well as of that same poet, in the late stages of her life.

In choosing to bring together and to bring out Sedgwick's uncollected poems, and especially the ones that preceded and were not included in *Fat Art, Thin Art,* loyally ascetic, rather than greedy, readers might feel anxious about issues of consent and the cost to Sedgwick's reputation. But 'A Poem is Being Written' helps us think about what's at stake in what Sedgwick calls, there, the "fearful (*self*-fearful) and projective squeamishness that for successful adults churns around the seeing displayed of children in their ambition and thought and grievance, in their bodies, in their art".[10] And Sedgwick's Cavafy essay reveals a writer who was interested in the "youthfully melodramatic tone" of some of Cavafy's early verse that "made it ripe for later repudiation", differentiating such repressed poems from other, "very early"

---

8 Eve Kosofsky Sedgwick, *Tendencies* (Durham: Duke University Press, 1993), 2–3.

9 Sedgwick, *Tendencies,* 177.

10 Sedgwick, *Tendencies,* 177.

texts that Cavafy "allowed to remain in his canon" and that, she inferred, "had some kind of foundational importance for him", but not being interested in excluding those repudiated poems from either her essay or her artworks.[11]

Indeed, in the same essay, Sedgwick emphasized that she was not remotely averse to poems exemplifying the "shame of being small", even if such verse risked a "Disney cartoon" aesthetics of "funniness" or "cuteness".[12] Rather, she remained excited, as she had been across her career, by the idea of cross-generational self-relations in poets as they existed as a "person at different ages", and it would be a mistake to underestimate the "erotic warmth" of her, as much as Cavafy's, investment in such adult relations to a "younger self"; "an erotic ritual" in both of the poets' work, "seemingly […] attached to masturbation" and "central to the creation" of both of their poetry.[13]

In addition, in 'A Poem is Being Written', Sedgwick had earlier come out in favor of the "visibly chastised", which she described as her "favourite style", and as a person aesthetically and relationally concerned with apparently "spoiled" children, spoiled in the sense of food having gone off, having been left too long, rather than in the sense of having been given too much.[14] Indeed, in that essay, Sedgwick fretted that her own "sulky problem child" of a poem, 'The Warm Decembers', at that point "going on nine" destined never to be finished, would not "grow any *more*". Whilst not wanting to either "deform or abandon" Sedgwick's reputation, by a gauche editorial move, or by the inclusion of what she herself described as "juvenilia" and the "queasier", "charged-up work of a twenty-four year-old-graduate student", examples of whose work she was happy to skip or only

---

11 Eve Kosofsky Sedgwick, *The Weather in Proust* (Durham: Duke University Press, 2011), 56.

12 Sedgwick, *The Weather in Proust*, 44.

13 Sedgwick, *The Weather in Proust*, 50. For similar scenes of cross-genera-tional self-relation, in the case of Henry James, see Eve Kosofsky Sedgwick, *Touching Feeling: Affect, Pedagogy, Performativity* (Durham: Duke University Press, 2004), 35–66.

14 Sedgwick, *Tendencies*, 177–178.

partly cite; 'A Poem is Being Written' encouraged my desire for the shelf of available writings by, and about, Sedgwick, to just keep on getting fatter.[15]

In thinking about the fantasy book of Sedgwick's uncollected poems, and particularly her juvenilia, a book of poems that might, in readers' minds like Sedgwick's idea of reading Melanie Klein, "have a presence or exert a pressure" that "may have much or little to do" with the actual form or contents of those poems,[16] questions of the urbane and provincial, and of paranoid and reparative reading, are also crucial, since the paranoid fear is that Sedgwick's earlier writing might risk making her look less than cosmopolitan. However, as Sedgwick reminds us, in *Epistemology of the Closet*, "knowledge of the world" and ideas of the "worldly" or "urbane", whilst appearing to be "flatly descriptive" attributions "attached to one person", actually describe or create a "chain of perceptual angels", marking the "cognitive privilege" of a speaker "who through that attestation" to being cosmopolitan "lays claim in turn to an even more inclusive angle of cognitive distancing and privilege over both the 'urbane' character and the 'world'".[17]

But, even with that warning against cultural one-upmanship in mind, if there is still a risk of making Sedgwick seem potentially provincial by reprinting some of these poems, poems chock full of emphatically acquired *knowledge,* we can be again reassured that Sedgwick herself was in favor, as we learn in the 'Preface' to the second edition of *Between Men,* to coming out as manifestly and "irrepressibly *provincial*" as a "young[er] author", full of "passionate, queer, and fairly uncanny identification[s]", as she journeyed from her "provincial origins" and the "isolation" of her "queer childhood" to her, later, "metropolitan

---

15 Sedgwick, *Tendencies,* 178, 187, 191. In finding that my own introductory essay had gotten so large, I took comfort from the fact that the first 'proper' chapter of Eve Kosofsky Sedgwick, *Epistemology of the Closet* (Los Angeles: University of California Press, 1990), appears after 90 pages of 'introductory' material.

16 Sedgwick, *The Weather in Proust,* 123.

17 Sedgwick, *Epistemology of the Closet,* 97.

destiny".[18] And, as in many of her essays, Sedgwick herself provided the tools for readers to better understand the early poems that accompanied her on this journey.

Thus, in her famous 'Paranoid Reading' essay, Sedgwick suggested that her readers might want to consider more reparative forms of literary engagement, in which they would recognize, for queer authors, the fact that the "culture surrounding" them was "inadequate or inimical" to their nurture and survival and that queer authors might, as a result, tend towards "additive and accretive" aesthetics, involving "startling, juicy displays of excess erudition", "passionate, often hilarious antiquarianism, the prodigal production of alternative historiographies; the 'over'-attachment to fragmentary, waste, or leftover products"; a "rich, highly interruptive affective variety"; an "irrepressible fascination with ventriloquistic experimentation"; a "disorienting juxtaposition of present with past, and popular with high culture".[19] All of those descriptions resonate with Sedgwick's uncollected poems.

For example, those poems includes a number of examples that reveal, in Sedgwick's phrase from 'A Poem is Being Written', earlier and further examples of her youthful "exhibitionism" and "blissful new vocational pride", as a person just beginning to come out, to themselves and others, as that most potentially shameful of identities: a poet.[20] We find evidences of overt self-reference in 'Cain', whose mother is, of course, another Eve. 'Lawrence Reads *La Morte D'Arthur* in the Desert' alludes to the "Eternal spirochete of Eve" and a "fleshy Arab / as guilty as Eve". And the speaker of 'Epilogue: Teachers and Lovers' describes "my slight friend the snake", again suggesting the person speaking might be an Eve.

Evidence of vocational and educational pride, meanwhile, of "excess erudition", "ventriloquistic experimentation", "pas-

---

18 Sedgwick, *Between Men,* ix–x.

19 Sedgwick, *Touching Feeling,* 150.

20 Sedgwick, *Tendencies,* 194. I am grateful to Mary Baine Campbell for helping me to crystallise this idea of what is at stake in coming out as a poet, and for encouraging me to make that fraught journey myself.

sionate [...] antiquarianism", and the "prodigal production of alternative historiographies", occurs in the queerly-detailed, precocious Jewish-girl, Old-Testament theology that underpins both 'Cain' and 'Saul at Jeshimon', with its long epigraph from 1 Samuel 26 and in the repeated poems in which Sedgwick comes out, frankly, as a "vain virgin / Who has read the *Aeneid*" and the stories of Abelard and Heloise, as well as Richard Lovelace and *Romeo and Juliet,* with enough recentness and enthusiasm to want to write poems about them, to want to try out Middle- and early-Modern English, and to begin a poem with a direct quote from Shakespeare: "Thou Know'st the mask of night is on my face" ('Calling Overseas'); as well as to complete a famously unfinished poem by Shelley.[21]

Indeed, the uncollected poems rarely leave us in any doubt, as Sedgwick puts it in 'Epilogue: Teachers and Lovers', that we are reading "a poem after all". That is because, as we have just seen, and like Cavafy, she often employed literary quotations in her verse that became the "kernel of the poem". This meta- or para-literary-critical practice involved anything but "throwaway erudition". Instead, Sedgwick, like Cavafy, repeatedly set such, to her, novel, hard-won quotations "like gemstones, in a more or less elaborated periperformative surround"; a version of "over-learning whose taste is quite other than servility or abjection".[22] This is true to such an extent that, rather than daring to look or talk down to the youthful Eve Kosofsky, I frequently found myself embarrassed at my own lack of urbanity, as I tried to wrap my mind around Sedgwick's earlier work. There is, after all, learning coming out the wazoo in these poems that require a reader who is fluent in a millennium of English poetry, a reading knowledge of French, German and Latin poetry, as well an ability to recognize, and, if not, to internet search, unattributed quotations in those languages, with even the internet failing me

---

21 The tacit quotation is from *Romeo and Juliet,* 2.2:85. Compare Sedgwick's account of herself in similar terms, as a "vain virgin" whose passion is all *With Lawrence in Arabia* in 'Epilogue: Teachers and Lovers'.

22 Eve Kosofsky Sedgwick, *The Weather in Proust*, 45–47, 63, 65.

when it came to the German quotations, about which I had to seek the advice of a professor of German!

For example, if the affair de Monsieur O, as well as Sedgwick's discussion of Ronald Reagan's monolingual inability to address his French counterpart has understandably emphasized the "importance of French" to her poetic idiom, her uncollected poems also stress the importance of German literary and cultural history to her corpus. [23] This is apparent in the case of 'Siegfried Rex von Munthe, Soldier and Poet, Killed December, 1939, on the German Battleship *Graf Spee*' and in 'Die Sommernacht hat mir's angetan', with its tacit allusion to Joseph Victor von Scheffel's poem of the same name; a tendency that Sedgwick continued in 'The Warm Decembers', where Beatrix is haunted by various "short and violent bits of language" she learned from her father "for his plagiarisms". Passing through her mind on her midnight flit, for instance, is Andreas Gryphius' seventeenth-century grave inscription for his niece Marianne, "Geboren in der Fluct", "Des Vaters höchste / Furcht die an das Light gedrungen". The memory is apt: Beatrix is seeking to be re-"born in flight", and to escape her "Father's worst fear[s]", whilst Gryphius' poem itself — often associated, during Sedgwick's youth, with the flight of German children from Europe during World War II — must have been a key bid for cosmopolitanism in the case of a poet who described herself as a "secular Jew", who grew up in the immediate post-holocaust, Cold War era where identifications with German culture must have been especially fraught.[24]

In gathering together Sedgwick's collected poems, I thus hoped to do justice to a youthful Sedgwick who had, as a kid, committed to memory "one patch of dirt" in her "elementary school yard", having "stood staring at [it] and intensely willing" herself that "yes, *this,* I will remember, *this* I will project forward

---

23 Sedgwick, *Tendencies,* 23, 183.
24 Sedgwick, *Tendencies,* 206. Andreas Gryphius, 'Grabinshrift Marianae Gryphiae seines Bruders Pauli Töchterlein'. I am grateful to Stuart Taberner for helping me with these details.

into the future so that it's there as much as it is here, just *this*, not because it's exceptional but because it's ordinary, it's nothing, it's dirt; I will remember it".[25] I do not think, for a second, that the poems collected here are dirt, ordinary, or nothing. In fact I think they're really something exceptional and extraordinary, since they contain a fossil of the crucial "inner space" of the youthful, would-be-poet, Eve Kosofsky.[26]

As such, and especially if they remained uncollected, Sedgwick's poems risked representing something like, if not quite abandoned queer children, then otherwise neglected, queer adolescents and young women, whose inclusion here stands, in many ways, for Sedgwick's miraculous queer survival. And, in including them here, I look back at the teenage Eve Kosofsky and say, as Sedgwick would later say, in 1993, to a generation of queer teenagers and young adults, including myself: "farther along, the road widens and the air brightens", and I refuse the "profligate way this culture has of denying and despoiling queer energies and lives".[27]

In addition, like Van Wey at the end of *A Dialogue on Love*, I want to gather up, "with a low, graceful dip", the "clumps of" poetic "pine mulch" Sedgwick displaced from her canon, and to pat them "back into place", my hands smoothing them "in with the other [poetic] mulch".[28] And this seems particularly crucial, in terms of reparative aesthetics, because, rather than avoiding displays of excess erudition that might be potentially embarrassing, or genres that other poets and critics might find sentimental, morbid, cheesy or icky; insincere, manipulative, or

---

25 Eve Kosofsky Sedgwick, *A Dialogue on Love* (Boston: Beacon, 1999), 116.

26 Sedgwick, *A Dialogue on Love*, 116.

27 For more on queer children, see *Tendencies*, 1–2, 154–166, 177–214; Stephen Bruhm and Natasha Hurley, eds., *Curiouser: On the Queerness of Children* (Minnesota: University of Minnesota Press, 2004); Kathryn Bond Stockton, *The Queer Child, or Growing Sideways in the Twentieth Century* (Durham: Duke University Press, 2009); and Maggie Nelson, *The Argonauts* (London: Melville, 2015). For a queer refusal of the figure of "the child" and of reproductive futurism, see Lee Edelman, *No Future: Queer Theory and the Death Drive* (Durham: Duke University Press, 2004).

28 Sedgwick, *A Dialogue on Love*, 218.

vicarious; knowing, arch, or kitschy, Sedgwick seems, from the start of her writing life, to have repeatedly zoomed in on such "squeam-inducing" texts, which, in part, explains her passion for country songs and attraction to mournful aesthetics, as we shall now see.[29]

Walking Music for Your Feet, or Sedgwick's Country Songs

Sedgwick's corpus abounds, as we have seen, with allusions to the lyrics of standards and pop and country songs, and a number of her uncollected poems more than flirt with such genres. In addition to a 'Lullaby' that commences with lyrics from the Coventry Carol, and, specifically, the flight of the innocents from Herod; readers can find Sedgwick playfully exploring versions of the kind of shit-kicker country tunes that appear in part 4 of 'Trace at 46'. There, the respectable, contemporary, avant-garde composer Cissy overhears, playing on the radio of two dreamily absorbed young men in a pick-up truck, fragments of songs including "I go for baby eyes, I go for hair that's soft and curled", and "I could wear my heart / to rags, making you your pretty treats, giving / you (unintelligible) walking music for your feet".[30] In *Epistemology of the Closet,* Sedgwick also came out in favour of a related song, the homoerotic/romantic country classic 'In The Garden', by Willie Nelson, and documented the certainly related scene of herself weeping "in Ithaca in the mid-seventies", where she, disingenuously, "happened to tune into a country music station in the middle of the song".[31]

The three related poems in this volume are clearly lyrics of this kind. 'Hank Williams and a Cat' comes not only with a chorus, but references to country singers Loretta Lynn and Conway Twitty, and specifically to the lonesome whippoorwill of Williams' 'I'm So Lonesome I Could Die' and Lynn's 'Pill', her ode to the liberation provided by female contraception. The poem also

29 Sedgwick, *Epistemology of the Closet,* 148.

30 Sedgwick, *Fat Art, Thin Art,* 60.

31 Sedgwick, *Epistemology of the Closet,* 141–150.

tells, in the first person, the tale of an abandoned woman left with nothing for comfort but cold chicken, country music, and a feline pet, who, like the cat in Sedgwick's later 'Pedagogies of Buddhism' essay, has "brung" her a mouse.[32]

A prison lament, like Oscar Wilde's *Ballad of Reading Gaol* (1897), also discussed by Sedgwick in *Epistemology*,[33] 'Jimmy Lane' draws on the idiom of the blues — "I was blue as hell" — and evokes a queer homosocial triangle 'straight' out of *Between Men*. In the poem, the male speaker's friend, the eponymous Jimmy Lane, has taken seriously the speaker's wish that he "watch over" his female beloved whilst he is in the clink "wearing chains", with the result that his girlfriend seems to have abandoned him for Lane. The speaker, however, seems as excited by, as jealous of, the idea of Lane with his girlfriend as he is of his girlfriend with Lane, to the extent that he's wet "dreaming 'bout" Lane, because he knows that Lane's "got a tongue, sweet as honey dew".

The final poem in this trio, 'Jukebox', tells the equally lonesome tale of a previously hurt speaker, of an undetermined gender, who has failed to show up and meet a girl in a bar the night before, because the speaker "wasn't man enough to talk to her". Pondering the girl, the previous night, "sat an hour", watching the disks "go round and round in this old Wurlitzer", the speaker wishes and hopes his/her would-be girlfriend would return, and works hard at being brave and trusting again. Whilst Sedgwick leaves the grammatical gender of the speaker of the poem strategically unclear, if I had to express a preference, my own "skinny dime" would be on the speaker being a bar-room butch lesbian, *à la* k.d. lang, waiting on her femme. I make this claim because of the way in which the speaker keeps repeatedly "press[ing] the worn-down button" on, wait for it, her juke-box, as s/he waits,

32 Sedgwick, *Touching Feeling*, 153–154.
33 Sedgwick, *Epistemology of the Closet*, 147–148.

189

a masturbatory Gertrude-Steinian discourse of tender buttons that Sedgwick was far from averse to, as we have seen.[34]

Readers hearing the title of Sedgwick's 'Ring of Fire', meanwhile, should almost certainly have in their heads the Johnny Cash hit, co-penned by wife June Carter Cash, and, whilst the poem is not best placed in this 'country songs' section, since it in fact concerns an astronaut, as we have seen, the context of Sedgwick's broader anal poetics certainly encourages her readers to imagine the queer erotic possibilities of the man-in-black's hit where, lovers "bound by wild[/e] desire" not only go "down, down, down", to where "the taste of love is sweet", but end up with a "fiery ring" and a "ring of fire".

Between Men, and Between Women: (More) Homosocial Desire in Sedgwick's 'Juvenilia'

The writing and publication of *Between Men: English Literature and Male Homosocial Desire* in 1985 seemingly spelt the end of 'The Warm Decembers', which, Sedgwick documented, reached its final, incomplete state "between 1984 and 1986", and whose plot, especially around Chinese White, Humby, and Beatrix Protheroe, came into crisis as Sedgwick realized quite how much might be at stake, for the poem's contemporary queer readers, in the context of an AIDS crisis centrally scapegoating the figure of the "shadowy bisexual".[35] As a result of this over-determined plot crisis and the broader AIDS pandemic, Sedgwick's balance tipped, for about a decade after 1985, towards the literary critical, rather than the poetic.

---

34 For more on the discourse of female masculinity, see Jack Halberstam, *Female Masculinity* (Durham: Duke University Press, 1998), and Sedgwick's response to C. Jacob Hale's 'Leatherdyke Boys and Their Daddies: How to Have Sex without Women or Men', *Social Text* 52–3 (Autumn-Winter 1997), 237–239. For a discussion of Sedgwick's relation to Stein's *Tender Buttons* (1914), see Kathryn R. Kent, '"Surprising Recognition": Genre, Poetic Form, and Erotics from Sedgwick's '1001 Seances' to A Dialogue on Love', *GLQ* 17.4 (2011), 497–510.

35 Sedgwick, *Fat Art, Thin Art*, 153–154.

But triangular homosocial relations between men, and women's centrality to them, represented in many ways the origin of her poetic identity, as she revealed in 'A Poem is Being Written'. This is a claim confirmed by a specific sub-set of her uncollected poems that focus on three queer topics: Monsieur O; stories from the Old Testament; and related desert poems centering, mostly, on T.E. Lawrence.

In *Tendencies*, Sedgwick revealed much about the eleven-to-twelve-year-old Eve Kosofsky's French teacher, the "gorgeous" and "delectable Monsieur O", who got in "hot water", when he was entrapped in the "men's room of a down-town Y", and who was, Sedgwick thought, just "too pretty" in an affirmative sense. Sedgwick also described her mortification at not having been able to see what was right under her *petite nez* — Monsieur O's queerness — and she emphasized how quickly and deeply she was motivated to regain her "urbanity" through research beginning with what could only be described as "'wild' guesses" that, as she "got more experienced, turned out to be almost always right", when it came to, for example, the appropriately named Oscar Wilde.[36]

Sedgwick's homophonic juxtaposition, here, of her "wild" guesses with Wilde's surname provides a definite hint that, whatever else is going on in the difficult poem, 'Die Sommernacht hat mir's angetan', something queer certainly is, given the repetition of Keats' "wild surmise" in the first two stanzas of the poem, from 'On First Looking into Chapman's Homer' (1816), with its account of "some watcher of the skies / when a new planet", the suggestively named Uranus, "swims into his ken" and, given Sedgwick's own account in the poem, of how the summer night "came over" her.

But "wry, handsome", "pederast" Monsieur O, appears more explicitly "six years" on from Sedgwick's immediate pre-teens,

---

36 Sedgwick, *Tendencies*, 207–208. For more on the context of such 'wild/e' guesses, see Sedgwick, 'Writing the History of Homophobia', in Jason Potts and Daniel Stout, eds., *Theory Aside* (Durham: Duke University Press, 2014), 29–33.

in the delicious 'Epilogue: Teachers and Lovers' from *c*. 1967–1968, hanging, this time, for a newly filthy, fist-y Sedgwick, "bottom-upward like a sloth", from where he "takes with gravity the tendered limb". Having "eluded" a tearfully-frustrated Sedgwick at twelve, now that she "wish[es] desirously to be [a] bride", she can speak of Monsieur O more learnedly, as well as tacitly and emotionally, in the repeated, romantic ejaculation "O" commencing no fewer than four lines. In addition to its use of a Shakespearean "womanish" that brings to mind the homoerotic and androgynous poetics of sonnet 20, and inclusion of a Shakespeare-like figure who "goes down from Belmont into Venice", the poem incorporates an unattributed quotation from Baudelaire's 'Au Lecteur' (1857), "O mon semblable", and encouragement to let our "ears flap wide". Baudelaire's poem had earlier chided its readers that if the "drab canvas" they "accept[ed] as life" contained no "rape, or arson, or the knife", it was because they were "not bold enough". Sedgwick's similar poem "about poetry" encourages its readers into a "turbulent speculation / with the stroke of eyes" and into "inappropriate" and "curious questions". Sedgwick identifies herself, meanwhile, as she does in more than one poem, as a "vain virgin",[37] as we have seen, an acknowledgement both of her youthful, provincial, virginal lack of sexual experience and her increased masturbatory pleasure: the vanity referring both her misplaced adolescent self-regard and to a now highly sexual body that delights, vainly, in itself, just as the later 'When in Minute Script' describes a speaker turning to themselves "like a hermaphrodite".

But, the still-frustrated poem anticipates nothing so much, perhaps, as *Between Men* in its recognition that "Men are for men, and poems / For poetry" and that whilst the snake / Monsieur O / a later tutor might brush from her cheek a "puzzled tear", he does not love the female poet as he does the "Silken hair of a grave and pickle-faced freshman", even if she would be

---

37 For example, in 'Calling Overseas', Sedgwick describes herself as singing "with the sluttishness of a vain virgin / Who has read the Aeneid".

Socrates' Athens or God's Jerusalem.[38] The poem ends with the speaker expressing her desire to "make you read" further, and admits a second, homoerotic youthful passion, this time *With Lawrence in Arabia,* the title of Lowell Thomas' 1924 biography of T.E. Lawrence, the subject of no fewer than three uncollected poems.[39]

With Lawrence in Arabia: Poems from the Sotadic Zone

In 'A Poem is Being Written', Sedgwick had included parts of the opening of 'Lawrence Reads *La Morte D'Arthur* in the Desert' as an example of the way in which, for her teenaged self, "narrative poetry" was "coextensive with, was the same as, one or another plot of male homosexual revelation", in a list also including David and Jonathan, *The Man from U.N.C.L.E.,* Roger Casement, the Round Table, and an "avant-Girardian reading of *Jules et Jim*".[40] In the same year in which she started work on the essay, 1985, Lawrence was also popping in in *Between Men,* which was preoccupied with the scene of his rape in *The Seven Pillars of Wisdom* (1926).[41] But the queer juxtaposition of Law-

---

38 This "pickle-faced Estupinan" returns in 'The City and The Man', haunting the "warmest dreams" Sedgwick has, always capturing and consigning her to the "asylum or prison", and in which she tacitly follows Richard Lovelace's 'To Althea, From Prison' (1642), in declaring that "Stone walls do not a prison make".

39 For more, see Lowell Thomas, *With Lawrence in Arabia* (London: Hutchison, 1924).

40 Sedgwick, *Tendencies,* 208.

41 For more, see Eve Kosofsky Sedgwick, *Between Men: English Literature and Male Homosocial Desire* (New York: Columbia University Press, 1985), 106, 173, 193–196, 198; Lawrence carried Mallory's text with him, in the desert. According to Angus Calder, however, "we now know that the most dramatic single episode" in Lawrence's *Seven Pillars of Wisdom* (1926) — "our hero's flogging and sodomisation in Deraa — simply cannot have happened" since "the dates given do not square with Lawrence's known movements" and the "Turkish governor who allegedly desired him was in real life, it seems, a notorious womanizer". For more on Mallory, the rape, other highly queer moments, and "gay talk about the war", see, T.E. Lawrence, *The Seven Pillars of Wisdom* (1926; Ware: Wordsworth, 1987), x, xvi, xix, 1, 82, 96, 150, 228, 316, 380, 384, 398, 402, 423, 428–429, 432–438, 476, and 545.

rence and the Round Table had occurred earlier in 'Lawrence Reads', which informs its readers that

> It was not Honour
> That made Launcelot
> Love Guinevere,

nor mottoes, nor morals, but, the poem suggests, his triangulated love for Arthur, a figure that Lawrence explicitly identifies himself with, leaving a scene of battle, "frank as Arthur". Towards the end of the poem, Lawrence's rape and Sedgwick's own complicity in imagining it so frequently may also figure in the admission that

> I have a body,
> And the fleshy Arab
> Is guilty as Eve
> And twice as shoddy.
>
> It's good to know
> I couldn't help it.

'Falling in Love over *The Seven Pillars*', meanwhile, begins with an extract from 'To S.A.', the poem Lawrence wrote to an Arab boy that Sedgwick also cites in *Between Men,* where she suggests that the young man provided the "motive of [Lawrence's] entire commitment to the fate of the Arabs as a race": "I loved you, so I drew these tides of men into my hands / and wrote my will across the sky in stars", although the *Between Men* version enjambs the sentence differently and breaks the line after "my".[42]

In the poem, Sedgwick acknowledged that, when she was fourteen, she was engaged in a self-set, post-Monsieur-O homework, in which she was "partly seduced" by the "queer soldier", gazing often at "all [the] portraits and photographs" in *With Lawrence in Arabia.* The poem stages the scene of Sedgwick

---

42 Lawrence, *Seven Pillars*, 1; Sedgwick, *Between Men*, 193.

reopening the volume, years later, "its binding falling off", and seeing, for the first time, the "flyspecks pressed obediently / Like flowers, but in passive files"; the equally passive book lying "open". Again, the rape seems quietly figured in Sedgwick's account of Lawrence's "backward grimaces" and "muffled iambs", an early account of the s/m dynamics of meter that anticipated 'A Poem is Being Written' by decades, as well as her description of the book's anal appearance as "brown and profound, with a little gilt". The poem ends with a prayer to God to grant her poetry "greater love and equal chastity", but since she had earlier described, with relish, Lawrence's "perversions" that prayer is a pretty queer one.

Sedgwick's Old Testament poems are equally preoccupied with the homoerotism of the Biblical desert. In *Epistemology of the Closet,* Sedgwick would subsequently write about the story of Esther, particularly as mediated by Jean Racine and Marcel Proust, as a "model for certain simplified but highly potent imaginings of coming out and its transformative potential". She would also offer up a snapshot of herself, in this context, aged about five, probably taken by her father, "barefoot in the pretty 'Queen Esther' dress" her grandmother made for her, "making a careful eyes-down toe-pointed curtsy".[43] But this later braid of herself, Jewishness, and queerness was already present in her juvenilia.

There, in the two versions of 'Saul at Jeshimon', we encounter David and Jonathan. They are seen from the triangulated perspective of Jonathan's father, Saul, "through shadows" and "over the seductive sand". Jonathan "dreams sweetly of his friend", the "loose and muscled" David, who "comes with such grace"; whilst the speaker, who "know[s] them better than sleep" and who has "listened, as well, wakeful", also documents how two dreamy, "lovestruck" men "lie with an ancient tome beneath their hands", a deeply "desired" book, whilst he "smooths the distended skin" of a water bottle. Sedgwick's Cain and Abel, meanwhile, in 'Cain', represent another peculiarly homoerotic,

---

43 Sedgwick, *Epistemology of the Closet,* 75, 82.

Old Testament couple, with the Cain-identified poet admiring Abel's "golden head" and remembering him "winding with deliberation / through his indifferent fingers / my sleeky hair".[44] In spite of its cross-gender pairing, and probable location in American cattle country, given the presence of the "cowgirl", we might also locate 'The Prince of Love in the Desert Night' in this company, if only by virtue of its title and eroticized sandy locale.

As Sedgwick acknowledged in 'A Poem is Being Written' and as Kent's essay in this volume explores, Sedgwick survived the "depression" of her teens through "passionate and loving relationships" with women, although she remained baffled, "during that time" and after, as to why she failed "to make the obvious swerve that would have connected [her] homosexual desire and identification with [her] need and love, as a woman, of women".[45] As a result, Sedgwick has been better known for her explorations of male than female homoeroticism. But the uncollected poems, especially in the form of Sedgwick's third great narrative poem and queer bedtime story, 'Pandas in Trees', written by the adult female poet for a girl, challenges that trend with its sustained exploration of the triumph of the finally sublime, cosmopolitan, and passionately panda-loving female friendship of Carrie and Louise, in spite of their culture's cold-war homo-

---

44 If we can read Sedgwick's Cavafy essay as a guide to some of the themes of her earlier poems, the loving attention paid by the crop farmer Cain to his brother-lover's "artichoke heart"-like head, in Sedgwick's 'Cain', and the vegetables that, "lately / named", grew about him — "cabbage", "lettuce", and "green grape" — in turn, perhaps, explains why Sedgwick was drawn, in the Cavafy essay, to the first-century CE poem by Philippus of Thessalonica she cited from the Greek Anthology, with its similarly homoerotic description of "A yellow-coated pomegranate, figs like lizards' necks, / A handful of half-rosy part-ripe grapes, / A quince all delicate-downed and fragrant-fleeced, / A walnut winking out from its green shell, / A cucumber with the bloom on it pouting from its half leaf-bed, / And a ripe gold-coated olive" all "dedicated to Priapus" by "Lamon the gardener" (*The Weather in Proust*, 64).

45 Sedgwick, *Tendencies*, 209.

phobia and xenophobia. The poem is surely meant as a rich lesbian resource in the project of how to bring up your kids gay.[46]

Equally Explicit

In 'A Poem is Being Written', Sedgwick encouraged her readers to differentiate between the absorption and theatricality of
masturbatory fantasy, as it appeared in her poetry, and the "visibly rendered plural possibilities of sadism, voyeurism, horror,
Schadenfreude, disgust or even compassion" in the pornographic verse she included in the essay.[47] In the second part of *Fat
Art, Thin Art,* she collected together four poems from the mid-
1970s — 'An Essay on the Picture Plane', 'Everything Always Distracts', 'Sexual Hum', and 'Sestina Lente' — that resonated in that
sadomasochistic context. Three previously uncollected poems
further round out our picture of Sedgwick's s/m poetry: 'When
in Minute Script', 'Explicit', and 'Lost Letter'. 'When in Minute
Script', which appears here in two variants, tells of a man waking
up to find himself castrated "with even the fever of torture not to
be regained", but within the narrative frame of a warm, childlike,
masturbatory fantasy that is pleasurable enough to make the pillow blush and that recalls, again, Lawrence's rape "in the lethal
desert", who awoke similarly from an unmanning "liquefying
sleep" "in terror" to "find it done".

The similarly dream-like 'Explicit' imagines the scene of a
"dark downtown office building" where the narrator is "half-
fainting [...] with pain and humiliation", before waking up,

---

46 For more, see *Tendencies,* 134–166. The queer eroticism of 'Pandas in Trees'
also benefits from knowing something about the "PANDA RITUALS" Sedgwick and her husband Hal had, which, "AMONG OTHER THINGS", "ALLOWED
HER TO FEEL MAGNETIC, RARE", "happier", and "VALUED EVEN WHILE
GAUCHE AND UNSEXUAL" (*A Dialogue on Love,* 215–216).

47 For Sedgwick's relation to Michael Fried's account of these two terms, see
Tendencies, 182–183. Fried's *Absorption and Theatricality: Painting and Beholder in the Age of Diderot* (Berkeley: University of California Press, 1980)
is also relevant to 'An Essay on the Picture Plane'. For more on the way in
which lyric poems "thrust [...] up out of the picture plane", see *Tendencies,*
185.

coming out from the warm, dark, dream, like emerging from a cinema or Plato's cave, into the "light and innocence" of a nearby "parking lot". 'Lost Letter' returns to the dark erotic goings on in that downtown office building, this time in the context of a relationship between a tenure-track writing teacher and her former mentor, within the James Merillian frame of a novel-within-in-the-poem. As such, the poems are kissing cousins, who beat off, in some curious ways, to the "hidden treasure" of the scene that ends *A Dialogue on Love,* where, in a similar "parking lot", Van Wey, as we have seen, "gather[s] up from the pavement the clumps of pine mulch" she "kicked down" as she was "teetering on the brink", before patting it "back into place"; a "condensation of sweetness", an "enigmatic pebble" of meaning to be "secretly finger[ed]" that might "in the past" have made Sedgwick "fall in love".[48]

Other poems also resonate in this masturbatory register. 'Another Poem from the Creaking Bed' is already alive to eroticism of language — "we desire certain words" — and to the feelings of shame and embarrassment that preoccupied Sedgwick in the mid-to-late 1990s. The poem also suggests the already close relationship, for the youthful Sedgwick, of poetry, sadomasochism, and anality. Written from a "Creaking bed", the poem is focused on the erotic possibilities of "five hot fingers" upon the "bottom" amongst other areas, whilst the young lovers' hearts are "creaking in mysterious leather straps". We also find this anal eroticism in the "stunning hamstrings" and "backside round as apples" in 'Movie Party', whilst urinary aesthetics are present in 'Once There was a Way to Get Back Homeward' with its account of how "He knew she was there because she / peed on trees". 'Ribs of Steel', finally, begins with an account of how "The skin is discrete, / red and hot" and "stretches to / your remotest tender, elastic parts // spreading listless fever", whilst lovers are compared to "white whales heaving in play" and "red lobsters boil[ing] in passion".

---

48 Sedgwick, *A Dialogue on Love,* 218–220.

Sedgwick's later poetic preoccupation with the symptoms of both cancer and HIV–AIDS, meanwhile, are prefigured in the references, in 'Lawrence Reads *La Morte d'Arthur*', to what "Cancers the hale / Tanned body" and "spirochete[s]" — the bacteria that cause syphilis.[49] Sedgwick's later meditation, in 'Mobility, speech, sight', on the comparative losses of a bowel, genital, hand to grasp, and breast, is anticipated by 'Phantom Limb's earlier reflection on the different losses of our "senses", "reason", "love", and "limbs".[50] 'What the Poet Thought' considers the Proustian scene of overhearing the "*knock,* / *Knock* of exhausted asthma" from a thin bed[51] and begins in the epistolary vein Sedgwick would explore again in 'Lost Letter', Chapter 7 of 'The Warm Decembers', and in her 1998–2003 *Mamm* column.[52] And, finally, and this list might have been considerable longer, what Sedgwick would call the absorbing, "force-field creating power" of reading, in *Touching Feeling*, resonates with the "extreme quietness" of 'Lawrence Reads *La Morte d'Arthur*',[53] a poem whose focus on military victories being "Neither vital nor / Particularly sullying" suggests Sedgwick's early interest in "the middle ranges of agency".[54]

---

49 For more, see *Fat Art, Thin Art,* 9–18, 28–30.

50 Sedgwick, *Fat Art, Thin Art,* 28.

51 For more on Sedgwick's relation to Proust, see *Epistemology of the Closet,* 213–252; *The Weather in Proust,* 1–69, 144–165.

52 Sedgwick, *Fat Art, Thin Art,* 139–146. For examples of Sedgwick's self-penned and replied-to agony aunt letters in *Mamm,* see February–March, April–May, and August–September 1998; April, June, and October–November 1999; January, April, June, and September 2000; May and June, 2001; November 2002; and January 2003. Compare specifically the June–July 1998 column, 'A Scar is Just a Scar: Approaching the First Mastectomy Tryst', and the earlier poem 'A Scar is Just a Scar', both employing the same pun on Freud's supposed, but apocryphal remark: "Sometimes a cigar is just a cigar" (*Fat Art, Thin Art,* 29).

53 For more, see *Touching Feeling,* 114–115.

54 Sedgwick, *The Weather in Proust,* 48.

Ars Longa, Vita Brevis, or Last Poems

In *Epistemology of the Closet,* Sedgwick had encouraged her readers to think again, in more positive terms, about the overlapping characteristics of the sentimental and the morbid, drawing particular attention to the "uncanny shifting first person after death".[55] In *Touching, Feeling,* she later encouraged her readers to think about the Buddhist idea of 'the bardo', the space between life and death, or between lives.[56] But death, and the various adjacent positions readers might find themselves in relation to it, as well as what Sedgwick would describe as Cavafy's "writing about and 'around' epitaphs",[57] had evidently been a subject long close to Sedgwick's heart, as a number of her uncollected poems reveal.

'A Death by Water' focuses on the effects on the speaker of a "real death on a real summer night". 'Two P.O.W. Suicides' admits to taking "from the dead what I get", and struggles "to keep in charity" with the "happy endings" of other war stories than the poem's own, even with the returning "men with no legs" who still owe the poet "a friend". 'Ring of Fire' deals, as we have seen, with the death of one of the three astronauts in the Apollo I fire of January, 1967, as its subtitle makes clear; whilst 'Siegfried Rex von Munthe' addresses the death of a fictional World War II soldier-poet from the perspective of his child; and 'Yellow Toes' seems to imagine the last moments of a mariner drowning in freezing water, a subject Sedgwick was fond of, as she acknowledged in the case of Cowper's 'The Castaway' (1799)[58] and Shakespeare's *The Tempest* (1610–1611).[59]

In 2006, Sedgwick published her final three lyrics: 'Death', 'Forsan et haec olim meminisse juvabit', and 'Bathroom Song'. We have already had cause to talk about her late take on Virgil, and all that remains for this final, melancholy section is to intro-

---

55 Sedgwick, *Epistemology of the Closet,* 148.

56 Sedgwick, *Touching Feeling,* 177.

57 Sedgwick, *The Weather in Proust,* 63.

58 Sedgwick, *Epistemology of the Closet,* 147–148.

59 Sedgwick, *Tendencies,* 99; *Touching Feeling,* 48.

duce further the remaining two poems. 'Death' follows Audre Lorde in encouraging survivors of breast cancer to not "grab that prosthesis",[60] and readers to embrace "what's you" rather than "what becomes you", whilst 'Bathroom Song' represents, as we have seen, Sedgwick's last great urinary/anal poem. In this, she compares her future death to the scene of her toilet training, a parallel that suggests, as she put it in a still unpublished essay, 'Come As You Are', that toilet training, like the task of dying, is about "learning, forcibly, to change the process of one's person into a residual product — into something that instead exemplifies the impersonal in its lumpishly ultimate and taboo form".[61]

Sedgwick may be "gone, gone, forever gone", as 'Bathroom Song' suggests, a fate she bravely and passionately embraced with all the curiosity and relish the poem can muster, but for some of us left behind in "the ravening flush" of fate, who have not achieved "enlightenment", coming to terms with the fact that Sedgwick has "utterly gone" remains a tall order. For that reason, her uncollected poems, across the following pages, begin with her 'Death' and return her to poetic life, being arranged in reverse chronological order.

The poems are drawn from five main periods of Sedgwick's life. The first two periods occur in the decade after the publication of *Fat Art, Thin Art* and focus on the time around 2006, when she published her three last poems, and the period between 1988–1997, when she had finished the abandoned 'The Warm Decembers', was working on *A Dialogue on Love,* and when she was simultaneously at work upon 'Pandas in Trees', some untitled Panda poems after Blake, and a number of other lyrics, including a 'Valentine' to Van Wey.

The third key period of Sedgwick's production is the early to mid-1970s, when she was a graduate student at Yale and working towards what she hoped would be her first collection of

---

60 For more, see Audre Lorde, *The Cancer Journals* (San Francisco: Spinsters Ink, 1988) and *A Burst of Light: Essays* (Ithaca: Firebrand, 1988). Sedgwick briefly discusses Lorde in *Tendencies*, xii, 13.

61 Sedgwick, 'Come as You Are', manuscript, 21. I am grateful to Hal A. Sedgwick for making this script available to me.

poems, before she started work on 'The Warm Decembers' and 'Trace at 46'. Belonging to the period *c.* 1974–1976 are a number of the most pornographic and sadomasochistic poems — 'The Palimpsest' (1974), 'Lost Letter' (1974), and 'Explicit', as well as Sedgwick's three country songs. To the years 1971–1973, we owe the poems 'Die Sommernacht hat mir's angetan', 'Phantom Limb', and 'Two P.O.W. Suicides'.

The vast majority of the poems stem from the late 1960s, however, when Sedgwick was an undergraduate student at Cornell. We can securely date 'Once There Was a Way to Get Back Homeward' to 1969–1971, and, to the *annus mirabilis* 1968–1969, some sixteen poems, written partly for the year-long, poetry-writing class that Sedgwick took with Ammons: 'The Ring of Fire', 'The Prince of Love in the Desert Night', 'Artery', 'Death by Water', 'Yellow Toes', 'Soutine', 'Another Poem from the Creaking Bed', 'Cain', 'City and Man', 'Lullaby', 'No More Dusk', 'Ribs of Steel', 'To a Friend /When in Minute Script', 'To a Swimmer', 'Untitled ("Wonder no more upon the mysteries")', and the ending Sedgwick provided for *The Triumph of Life.*

Seven poems date from the year before, 1967–1968, the year in which Sedgwick was at Cornell's Telluride House. These are 'T.E. Lawrence and the Old Man', 'Movie Party, Telluride House, Ithaca, New York', 'Falling in Love over The Seven Pillars', 'Calling Overseas', 'What the Poet Thought', 'Epilogue: Teachers and Lovers', and 'The Last Poem of Yv*r W*nt*rs'. Finally, there are three poems that date from the mid-1960s, when Sedgwick was at High School in Bethesda, Maryland, on the outskirts of Washington, DC. These are 'Siegfried Rex von Munthe', 'Saul at Jeshimon' (1965–1967), and the earliest poem in the collection, dated by Sedgwick herself to 1964, 'Lawrence Reads *La Morte D'Arthur* in the Desert'. Sedgwick certainly wrote poetry earlier than that, which may yet emerge, but it is likely that she herself destroyed most of it, consigning it to a category beyond her canonical juvenilia.[62] But much more remained to be seen, known,

---

62 I am grateful to Hal A. Sedgwick for helping me to date the poems.

and enjoyed of Sedgwick's "winged and beaked" "Greater Aesthetic".

The Uncollected Poems

2006
Death
Bathroom Song
Forsan et haec olim meminisse juvabit

1988–1997
Pandas in Trees
Untitled (Blake panda poems)
Tru-Cut
Valentine

1981
2/81

1974–1976
Lost Letter [1974]
The Palimpsest [1974]
Explicit
Hank Williams and a Cat
Jimmy Lane
Jukebox

1971–1973
Die Sommernacht hat mir's angetan
Phantom Limb
Two P.O.W. Suicides [1972]

1969–1971
Once There Was a Way to Get Back Homeward

1968–1969
The Ring of Fire
The Prince of Love in the Desert Night
Artery
Death by Water
Yellow Toes
Soutine
Another Poem from the Creaking Bed
Cain
City and Man
Lullaby
No More Dusk
Ribs of Steel
To a Friend/"When in Minute Script"
To a Swimmer
Untitled ("Wonder no more upon the mysteries")
From an Ending for "The Triumph of Life"

1967–1968
T.E. Lawrence and the Old Man
Movie Party, Telluride House, Ithaca, New York
Falling in Love over *The Seven Pillars*
Calling Overseas
What the Poet Thought
Epilogue: Teachers and Lovers
The Last Poem of Yv*r W*nt*rs

1965–1967
Saul at Jeshimon (1967) [First Variant]
Saul at Jeshimon (1967) [Second Variant]
Siegfried Rex von Munthe

1964
Lawrence reads *La Morte D'Arthur* in the Desert

Forsan et haec olim meminisse juvabit (2006)

Someday we'll look back with pleasure even on this.
In fact I can feel it encroaching on me already, the
future pleasure — which is disconcerting.
Things with us are actually very bad.

Death (2006)

isn't a party you dress up for, man,
it's strictly come-as-you-are, so don't get too
formal, it's useless. *Don't grab* that prosthesis,
those elevator shoes, or girdle to jam your tummy
in, for your interview with Jesus or
forty-nine days in the bardo of Becoming.
The point's not what becomes you, but what's you.
Why did I buy those silk PJs with feathers
so long before the big affair began?
I've always slept in the nude. Now I sleep in the nude forever.

Bathroom Song (2006)

I was only one year old;
I could tinkle in the loo,
such was my precocity.
Letting go of Number Two
in my potty, not pyjama
was a wee bit more forbidding
 — and I feared the ravening flush.
So my clever folks appealed
to my generosity:
"What a masterpiece, Evita!
Look! We'll send it off to Grandma!"

Under the river, under the woods,
off to Brooklyn and the breathing
cavern of Mnemosyne
from the fleshpotties of Dayton —
what could be more kind or lucky?

From the issue of my bowels
straight to God's ear — or to Frieda's,
to the presence of my Grandma,
to the anxious chuckling
of her flushed and handsome face
that was so much like my daddy's,
to her agitated jowls,
Off! Away! To Grandma's place!

As, in Sanskrit, who should say
of the clinging scenes of karma,
"Gaté, gaté, paragaté"
(gone, gone, forever gone),
"paramsgaté; bodhi; svaha!"
(utterly gone — enlightenment —
svaha! Whatever svaha means),
Send the sucker off to Grandma.

Gaté, gate, paragaté;
paramsagaté; bodhi; svaha!

Pandas in Trees (*c.* 1996)

Carrie was fond of hieroglyphics.
Also, she didn't mind dining out.
She thought her friend Louise was terrific.
But what she was insane about
was pandas. When her gang, for fun,
impersonated the National Zoo,
Carrie was always the goofy one
munching thoughtfully on bamboo.
She knew just how to do it, too:
she knew that pandas have a thumb
(sort of) for holding bamboo shoots
so they can nibble with aplomb
the leaves off. It was very cute.
"But isn't it," her friends who were
lions or monkeys or buffalo,
"isn't it, ah — dull?" they'd murmur.
"Well," she explained, sighing patiently, "no.
Somebody else might find it so,
but I don't. I feel most at ease
looking serene and answering
to some double-barreled Chinese
name like Hsing-Hsing or Ling-Ling.
Don't' ask me why. I've heard it said
that when I was a tiny pup
my parents hung above my bed
a panda picture postcard up
and that might, I suppose, explain
why I was even as a child
so meditative and urbane
and extra large and extra mild."

Her friends respected this, as well
they might. Her best friend Louise
considered pandas thoroughly swell
though she cared more for climbing trees,

herself. But you should see her leap
to the defense of pandahood
and fire up at any creep
who found the species not so good.
For instance, Emma claimed that *she'd*
hid in the panda house one night
and watched to see the keepers feed
the pandas, and turn out the light,
and then (still hidden) she had heard,
from either cage, a ripping noise,
like Velcro. And without a word
three small blue-suited Chinese boys
who looked like spies, had one by one
crawled out of a Velcro opening
in each of the panda suits! and run
into the night, abandoning
the panda house and leaving in it
two crumpled black-and-white fur coats.

This stumped Louise for about a minute.
Then she started feeling her oats
as usual. "It isn't true,
I know it isn't," she announced.
"I know pandas, Emma, and I know you,
and I know your story doesn't bounce."
"Yes,, said Carrie. "It would have been
in all the papers, if they'd found
a couple of hollow panda skins
balled up one morning on the ground."
(Still, she was shaken, you could hear.)
"And," said Louise, "I don't see why
the spies should impersonate a *bear*.
To get into the zoo and spy?
But anyone can go to the zoo."
Carrie bucked up and said, "You whopping
liar, Emmie. Plus, the bamboo —
boys couldn't turn it into *panda droppings,*

even if they could really eat it.
Panda droppings are different from ours.
But plus" (she was unusually heated)
"don't you think it would be bizarre
that with millions of enterprising children,
the biggest country in the world
would choose, if it wanted spies, to send
six small boys and not one girl?"

Emma had to agree with that.
In fact, she dropped her story flat.

But how did Carrie come to know
all about panda droppings? Well, in
a book that was edited by Zhu
Jing, together with Li Yangwen,
The Giant Panda, she'd found out
from Chinese scientists practically
all that there is to know about
her favourite beast, the Giant P—
how long its tail is when it's born;
whether it hibernates (no); what
it eats (bamboo); how it keeps warm;
whether it is sublime (you bet);
and other useful facts like these
with lots of and lots of pictures.
"Wow,"
Carrie whispered to Louise,
"I wish, I wish that I knew how
I could have a round black nose
and small black cookie-cutter ears
like all the pandas this book shows."
Louise smiled happily. "My dear,
I hope you appreciate that I do
already and by nature have
a round black little nose, and two
small round black ears. I call that suave,

don't you?"
"Aha," said Carrie. "True."
And when she'd thought about it some
she let on to Louise that, well,
she did have a fluffy round white tum.
"That", said Louise, "is also swell."

"But speaking," said Carrie, "of mysteries
(not that we were), give this some thought:
Do you think pandas really climb trees?"
"Sure," said Louise. "I mean, why not?
Or maybe not. Why should they? Must
I have a firm opinion?" "Look,
you muffinhead," said Carrie, "just
look at the strange thing in this book.
Now, take this picture. What do you see?"
"Only," Louise said matter-of-factly,
"only a panda in a tree."
"Yes. You are right. That's its exactly.
Now look at this page for a minute.
What do you see before your eyes?
Only a tree with a panda in it."
"Right," said Carrie. "Very wise.
And this page? and the next?" Louise
said, as if it seemed ordinary,
"Couple of pandas, couple of trees."
"Yes, that's what I thought, too," said Carrie.
"Now tell me this: How many shots
of pandas in trees are there between
the covers of this book?" "Oh, lots.
Wait a sec. Let me see. Fourteen?"
"I think that's right," said Carrie. "But
Now, read this caption, if you please."
"This caption here? Okay, why not.
'Pandas seldom climb trees'.
What? 'Pandas seldom climb trees?'
"That's what it says. Peculiar, no?"

("Yes! Peculiar!" breathed Louise).
"I thought so. Look at this one, though.
'Pandas do not usually climb trees'.
What are we to make of that?"
"Well don't ask me," Louise said. "I'm
beefaloed. Really. Tumbled flat."
"Pandas are unable to climb,
this caption says," Carrie went on.
"Honestly, something is amiss.
We should investigate. We'll want
to do some thinking about this."

And meanwhile in the dusty yard
among the sandbox and the swings
chattering in the airy hard
tea-colored evening of the spring
the gang of friends scattered and wheeled
like noisy atoms glittering
to sudden halts, and spun, and squealed.
Pandas, among other things,
formed a subject of debate —
How do they figure (asked Yvonne)
out with whom they're meant to mate,
up in the wilds of Szechuan,
since boys and girls look just the same?
(It's true! It's true! You're right! They do!
"*What* a life!" Marsha Lou exclaimed.
"Lively times in the bamboo. …")
Joe said they look like the Abomi-
nable Snowman. Paul thinks, Maybe.
Hal perceives them all as mommies.
David thinks they look like babies.
"I'd like to be," remarks Rosemary,
"A panda's pet, and learn Chinese."

Oh. By the way. Where is Carrie?
Come to think of it: Where's Louise?

And meanwhile from the dusky yard
the children yo-yo home to bed.
The eastern sky is tarred and starred.
The heavens to the west are spread
with ochre bars of peanut butter,
which the sunset barely jellies,
and the wind drops the dust. And utter
silence drops. The two-horned snail is
snailing up a shadowed hill
where the shadow overtook her —
she stops. It is so still.
Up the pines that overlook her
shadow has climbed. Shadow is high.
Shadow is very near the top.
Only a keen and distant eye
could see to where the shadows stop —
very near the pinetrees' heads.
Only two piney spindles push
their winking tops above the ledge
of dark.
It's odd. The thickening hush
that's dropped around the playground swings
is troubled.
It's almost as if
the pines themselves were whispering.

One of them seems to give a sniff.

"Pandas," it murmurs acidly,
"may do whatever else they please,
for anything I care. But surely
they never — almost never — climb trees?"

"Surely," the other one agrees.
"Naturally. Not hardly never.
Imagine pandas climbing trees!
Virtually not whatsoever."

It is distinctly odd. A breeze
is making both the pine-tips wiggle.
Down, down from the peaky trees
floats something like a breezy giggle.

"Nonono," one of the trees declares.
"Other beasties climb aloft —
but surely not the panda bear,
so lovably inept and soft.
It's true they're wise. They're strong and massive.
And they're resourceful. And they're clever.
But they are (how to put it?) — passive.
And that is why the panda never —"

"Never, never," sang the tree
beside it, "o no never never
(or at least not frequently)"

"Well I should *say* not. Really *bearly*
(you should pardon the expression)
ever. Quite remarkably rarely."

"And if at all, with much discretion —"

"Not to say timidity."

"(As we know from scientific
works of great validity) —"

"Not that pandas aren't *terrific* —"

"Natch. But do they. ...? No, they *don't*."

"I didn't think they did. Did you?
It is *not* the panda's wont —"

"Left to its own devices —"

"— to."

"To what?"

"You know as well as I."

"… up trees."

"Ever at all."

"Oh my."

"(Perhaps it's just a wayward breeze
that drops the pandas into trees?)"

"O yes. I think that must be so.
For otherwise they can't, you know —)"

"(They can't?)"

"(Well, only *very seldom,*
unless necessity compelled 'em)."

"Pandas are not Amazons.
They do not do such things for fun —"

"Fond as they are of mild diversion
they are *not* given to exertion —"

"So it would be distinctly queer —"

"Unheard-of!"

"— If a panda could
climb up a tree, Louise, my dear."

(I told you something was afoot,

didn't I, now? Not just the trees
giggling and whispering, but, oy vey!
One of the trees is called Louise!
Don't ask *me*. Why can I say?)

"Of *course* they don't climb trees. Because
climbing is very very scary …"

"And *not* a treat that would amuse
a fuzzy kind of mammal, Carrie."

"O no, not fun at *all*. How true."

(Here's a pretty how-d'ye-do.
The other tree's named Carrie, too!
O, *I* don't understand. Do you?)

"And that must be why people so
infrequently see nose or ear
or little panda furbelow
(ahem) — up trees. Isn't that clear?"

"O yes indeed. Imagine — hiding
up in the barest treetops — waiting
to see the whole horizon sliding
off into night —"

"Exhilerating?
No ho ho ho! O no, no way."

"And *that* is why I always say
the normal panda"

"— would not dream
of doing something so extreme —"

"and will not, will not climb a tree".

"Pass the bamboo."

"Good night."

"Tee hee."

Untitled (Blake Panda Poems) (c. 1988–1997)

The road of excess leads to the Panda of wisdom.

The Panda, wandering here and there,
Keeps the human soul from care.

A fool sees not the same Panda that a wise man sees.

One Panda fills immensity.

The blackness of a Panda's paw
Brands the statesman's brow with awe.

Eat bamboo in the morning. Ponder in the noon. Eat bamboo in
the evening. Sleep in the night.

The Pandas of intolerance are wiser than the starfish of instruction.

No Panda wanders too far, if he travels with his own paws.

To create a little Panda is the labor of ages.

The head Sublime, the heart Pathos, the genitals Beauty, the
paws and ears Proportion.

The Panda of sweet delight can never be defiled.

Everything possible to be believ'd is an image of Panda.

God appears, and God is light,
To those poor souls who dwell in Night;
But does a Panda form display
To those who dwell in realms of Day.

Tru-Cut

He says he wants to do a Tru-Cut biopsy, which will
yield a cross-section of tissue to send to Pathology.
I say, "But what's the point of that? Even if
it turns out negative
you'll still have to excise the lump
to ascertain the whole thing is negative.
He says, that's true. But I
don't expect it to be negative.

Valentine

Said, "It's a good thing Shannon doesn't spank."
Said, "That felt fine, but does he think I'm stinko
or don't know how to act right with a shrink?
I love the way he's patient and not cranky;
never accuses me of *intellect-*
u-al-izing when in fact I'm *thinking*;
I dig the feel of it when things get funky,
adore that he won't blink
no matter how inquisitive or kinky
a girl might get who likes to put things frankly;
and 'HEART' the sudden way in which my rankest
fantasy scenes will make his face go blank—
and how, when *I* get cheeky, *he* gets pink.

And always has a hanky for my panky;
seems not to mind a bit the way I think
I'm *so-o-o* smart; stays loose when I act yukky
cause he himself's so beautifully shrunk—
otherwise, God almighty! I'd be sunk!
It *is* a good thing Shannon doesn't spank."

Course, that's assuming Shannon doesn't spank...

2/81 (1981)

The other day I had occasion to retype
'Lost Letter'. More than incredulous,
I would keep hopping up, or grinding teeth,
sampling a terrible grin from my own lips,
and then when I looked out,
around the buoyant houses colored straw, I saw
a brown stain spreading under the snow.
Now I forget how we arrived
from there, at this insistent apollonian glee
that's now almost the only usage of my heart.

Lost Letter (1974)

1.
My letter cools its heels in a suburb
of Paris — there's a mail strike now —
or is lost in some confusion. And rightly:

it was a confused letter anyhow.
I thanked you (in it) for a recommendation
(you've been writing them since I was a freshman).

"I'm teaching writing now," I said, "isn't it
uncanny the authoritativeness
of puppy genius, and so distant."

No wonder we're uncomfortable, I meant.
The pain of teaching being so akin
the pain of studenting, of envy and arousal

at language barely meant for our proper eyes and ears.
Both shy, we nowadays wolf down
our letters as greedily as if

2.
they might shift everything. And they might, but not toward us.
The time I spend writing lost letters!
    Weeks, sometimes, for yours, or witness

in pages of minute pornographic script
a novel in letters, about a man
hurrying to the dentist, doctor, or, it may be, shrink,

past an open door in a downtown medical building
who glimpses in a waiting room a naked girl
submitting to something evidently

jazzy and frightening in the way of punishment.

He's appalled, he can't watch it,
But he's recognized her, a student he's fond of,

and, once home, writes her a hesitant note.
"If you ever feel it would help to talk,
please consider me at your disposal. ...

If, though, I've completely misunderstood
the fleeting scene, forgive me, Eve, it just
seemed you might need something as obvious as this:

nobody, human, would turn from you for your
having suffered some sickening discipline. ...
How long do you expect it to continue?"

3.
What kind of novelistic world is this
where college women, on their own,
find their way to offices in downtown medical buildings

for jazzy, frightening punishment? What crimes
do college women know how to commit,
and where, in a college town, is such an authority

as could force the firm, unspeakably reluctant feet
up sloping flights of dingy stairs, and in?
What keeps the face, under punishment, impassive,

the nude body motionless as ordered
though trembling? Not, for sure, the individual
volition, nor yet the school. A shadowy arm

maybe of Parenthood, mysterious and known to all,
ramifying in every city
with conspiratory potency. Of course

in the real pornography these questions are

— *comment dit-on* — extratextual, moot;
mute, taken obscenely for granted, or part of the *frisson*:

so much so, the mention of them even here is recklessness.
The compulsion in the story's real;
"There is real violence being done right now,"

4.
he writes back later, "and it's not to my sensibilities.
Please don't write nonsense, no outside infliction on you,
I don't care how messy it is (for it's messiness you're talking about,

reading about someone else's pain isn't nearly
as assaultive as reading about their mess) could even threaten
my 'sympathy and identification' with you now.

I don't much care about being told these things.
Or more accurately, my reaction to being told
is just what you might guess, in a more lit-critical mood:

i.e, a not unfamiliar mix of pain of anger
and disgust, yes, and furtive arousal, also yes, but so
what? Shit, Eve, we can't

let our friends withdraw from us, or ourselves withdraw from them,
just because we've complicated reasons
for caring about each other," I'm embarrassed too

at the wishfulness of this, but please remember
the wash of helplessness that's bringing them together,
everything outside the letters spelling shame and terror.

5.
"The details you've mentioned are almost incredibly cruel:
so I can guess I should be understanding 'every
conceivable indignity' quite literally, and almost

as much so, 'unspeakable consequences'. But they
are speakable, no? some genital assault?
   I'm not sure how to feel

about having precipitated a crisis in the room
by appearing there at the doorway shattering
your enforced composure — aside from sorry:

it's almost a relief, though this is being selfish,
to find my part in the savaging was that direct,
acknowledged by you at the time, not just a voyeuristic

complicity with the tortures and audience.
I guess I thought you hadn't seen me, I guess
I thought the rigid, sightless gaze was your defense

against the nakedness below, the pain to come: I didn't know
they could wipe expression off your face. I didn't guess
you were in pain already, there, and struggling.

   Oh yes, I heard someone gossip about 'a whipping'
over the weekend. Was it of you? I trust not;
incidentally it will be hard to stay in school

if any of this gets too well known. I can try
to muffle it when I hear of it; it would help
for you to come to classes again, if you can.

Also, are you really more comfortable
writing than talking about this? I don't mind
writing but would just as soon talk if you would.

6.
Try and bear up, anyway." Unexpectedly,
this letter angers her. "'A whipping,'" she repeats,
"'some genital assult' — 'voyeuristic complicity' —

you express yourself with admirable suaveness. But
that's me — that naked trunk that's bent and tied
over the abdomen-high table, waiting for stripes.

Those are my real ankles hobbled by my own panties.
'Some genital assault', that will mean my real thighs
with something rough between them. That's me, all these weary nights

waking to my own screams five and six times before dawn
afraid to fall asleep, afraid to wake and find
a note of summons slipped under the door

to climb the steps again in sober winter daylight
arriving, shaking, at the right floor, for more.
Sorry about the voyeuristic complicity. Of

course there are rumors: there were people there
and cameras, very close." But later, sorry and frightened,
"Please don't think I'm angry at you, in fact

I don't know what I'd do without you. That's literally true.
My sense of the world is broken and past fixing.
Don't think I'm angry, either, that you saw me shamed —

the truth is yesterday, under the whip,
it came to me in a thud of longing — or nostalgia —
how much I'd give to see once more that my

naked parts could still embarrass and appall.
It's a tricky situation. It takes patience
and magnanimity. And I'm astonished

at finding them ready — for me — and in you.
　　As for talking instead of writing, I'm not sure,
but I mean to be in class tomorrow so we'll see.

Please, by the way, don't call on me in class.
I'll volunteer if I can talk, but may be struggling
Just to sit still. I'll see you soon.

7.
P.S. Forgive the way I began the letter."
The next letter, from him, next afternoon:
"I meant to stop you after class but it was clear

it wasn't going well for you. Every time
one of the boys in class moved or spoke you flinched
and went white. It was awful. I guess

it hadn't been so present to me, before,
how much you've been abused just lately at the hands
of men specifically. It makes me look down at my own"

which he really does, long hairy ones, "terrified.
You don't seem to mind much when I write,
but I was afraid you'd wince away from me too,

and you shouldn't have to do that, so let's write.
If you mean to stay in school though you'll have to come to class.
And for your good, you need to work

on overcoming the horror of men. And I don't think
I say that just because I'm a man, certainly not
from not knowing what horrors it's a response to.

I'm especially sorry if I sounded flippant
about some of your fears; it wasn't
that I'm not frightened myself at what may happen

but (1) because — that's language — 'genital assault'
is words, while parted thighs, ruptured membranes,
pain and rage, and not moving, these things are real;

but also (2) because I wanted you to realize
that you are — if I can put it this way — allowed to talk
about a punishment directed at your parts

as much as about a flogging. My impression is
your style with these words is modest: maybe especially now.
That childish blur makes your state too vivid.

I wanted you to know, these things, if done
might embarrass on paper but could hardly alienate
me. I hope now I haven't alienated you.

Please, Eve, don't imagine me unable
to envision the violence being done you.
Partly it's just the vertigo of language:

say I learn, unexpectedly, you've had a flogging,
I don't receive that very bad news without emotion,
without my mind, my impotence, racing to the aid

of an image of you publicly shamed and in pain:
I could guess from what I'd seen from the door
that you'd have been stripped naked, or nearly so —

the details you mention, the bending, the shivering buttocks, even
the longing, the stripes themselves, it was all there,
but when I write it turns into 'a whipping'

and you think I'm being casual or debonair
at your expense. But no, I'm not.
Your letter can bring fresh shocks of impotence,

urgency, vicarious humiliation, but even
without a word from you further, I remain yours truly:
the fixed slave of your continuing punishment."

8.

It's hard overcoming the horror of men
when almost daily, for a long time, she'll have to seek out
and penetrate the blank ugly downtown building

to discover subtle and blindingly new
accesses to her of pain, of dread, of
weariness, new forms of nakedness,

and old impassivity fresh and fresh imposed.
They never — the pair of them — learn
to talk it over, so the shrewd

punishing repetitious letters shuttle back and forth
with all the comfort there is;
the shy obsession grows, but never turns,

for them, toward bed. Besides
every orifice in her is so fatigued!
Just twice more, headed for his therapist,

the man takes the slow stairs past the open door,
the first time seeing a boy in a corset
and with stripes, being baited to impermissible tears.

That night the man himself is waked by his own screams
but smothers them to lie in silent tears
trying not to wake his wife with the sheer terror.

The second time his dreadful expectation is rebuked
for there she is. This time he isn't noticed
since the girl is positioned to front the wall, away from the door,

her face not being, this time, the focus of attention.
He never tells her what he's seen
nor the therapist, though the therapist is observant

of a particular stiff tenderness as the man sits down
and some semaphore in the brow, and is savvy enough
to be grateful there are things he genuinely can't interpret.

9.
Like the detective's gift, or shrink's, the poet's gift
is blank fatuity and no hint of anger.
As if this resourceful immobility

could, for more than the riveted instant, assuage
the storms of anger that travel around poets!
I've been reading an anthology of recent poets

so as to sound, in conversation, like a poet
so as to get a job teaching young poets
the scopophilic and exhibitionistic transports

that are — no kidding — what makes it beautiful.
I haven't found any other poems like this one,
neither as risky nor as unnecessary.

In fact the fierceness of my love for these pages,
all these pages, is the least oblique thing going, here.
I haven't overheard them or hurried past them

or hidden my hand from them for fear
of their flinching from it. Nothing's without
obliquity, pain itself is not, language

about pain least of all, but the shame itself
of privacy should give place with a thud
of longing to this much, this good, attention.

The Palimpsest (1974)

You must have dropped off on top of the covers
after only a couple of brief throes, for when I
found you in the morning you were just treading

up toward consciousness — still in the costume of your obsession.
Under a latex body suit — rubber corsets.
Then chalk and crayon hieroglyphs to the flesh.

These showed, on the front of the thigh, marks of claws
and bits of leopard fur; at the back,
uneven horizontal stripes in red.

How different if I had found you in a whipping orgy for real.
How different if some biography had told as a true fact
how puckered, long-healed, horizontal scars

were seen in that place by the impassive coroner;
the biographer mentioning, what were really unpublishable,
some corresponding documents: your life in the family, your school.

In fact the scars don't answer to the wounds.
You surface, hence, in the narrow warmth of meaning,
being peeled and washed on the coverlet where found.

Explicit (1974–1976)

In these fantasies, "half-fainting," as the books say,
"with pain and humiliation," and punishingly harrowed,
stiff and empty now I button my clothing
and climb slowly out of the dark downtown office building.

By now it is almost seems like home
so warm with terror it is, the life around it so estranged
with light and innocence. I loiter in the parking lot,
the flesh in too much pain to sit, marked and dazzled.

This masquerade, here, is what's delirious, for
in the thin sweet air of the street you happen by.
My blood and immobility are short on discretion:
"Can I ask," asks your compassion, struggling, "what did they—?"

If I were free to talk, and could form the words, you'd know.
This dizzy way, I think, is better, though,
when faint of courage and from loss of blood
and shrinking, still, with pain, I reel at delicate words.

Mornings I've shuffled from the intimate cave
knocked hot with just this fantasy, or another worse,
to stitch and heel along the thin sweet thoroughfare
steadying as I can against sheer nerve

the delicious formal tongue of mental pain; when, facing you,
the doors fly open and the windows fall.
Then the world takes on its own mobility,
and the whole nerve, untransfixed, breathes in at every cell.

Hank Williams and a Cat (1974–1976)

Tonight I came home from work, found an empty house.
Little gift outside the door, cat brung me a mouse.
I turn on my radio to where the music's at.
Hello, Hank Williams! Hello, cat!

CHORUS:
My man ain't coming home tonight, he found another girl.
Loretta says I'll be all right if I take the Pill.
Pill ain't what I need cause any fool can tell you that
A woman don't get pregnant from Hank Williams or a cat.

I eat my lonely dinner, Conway's singing out his soul.
Nothing cold as ashes, 'cept chicken two days old.
Cat comes by and helps me out, I know I won't get fat
Sharing dinner with Hank Williams and a cat.

You hear that lonesome whippoorwill, he's not as blue as I
The cat's upon my pillow, radio close by.
I wish your cheating heart was here, I'd give you tit for tat
A bed can be so lonely with Hank Williams and a cat.

Jimmy Lane (1974–1976)

Two cells down, a small-time burglar had an awful cough,
The corridor outside my cell, the lights were never off.
I couldn't draw upon the wall, so in my mind I drew
A cozy room that had a bed, and in the bed was you.

Two months after I went in, I was blue as hell
The warden gave out letters but I didn't get no mail.
I felt like no one wanted me, but when the days were through
I dreamed about our crazy quilt, and under it was you.

No mail from you and none from my old buddy Jimmy Lane.
He said he would watch over you while I was wearing chains.
He said he'd try to do for you the things that I can't do.
Last night I dreamed 'bout Jimmy Lane, and in that dream was you.

I wanted things to be okay for you while I was gone,
I know a woman needs a man's shoulder to cry on.
Now Jimmy Lane he's got a tongue, sweet as honey dew.
Talked me out of my whole life, for in my life was you.

When I get out of prison I'll hunt down Jimmy Lane.
Come back behind these bars, and take up my heavy chains.
If things go bad with you I hope you'll lie alone and see
A pallet on the cold hard floor, and on it they'll be me.

Jukebox (1974–1976)

The brightly-lighted jukebox seems to be
A different world that's full of melody.
A skinny dime will make it all begin
And go through the whole thing once again.

    D-5, that's the one we heard last summer.
    Push 7-C and hear the violin.
    I wish I knew the button I could push to make
    The front door open and my girl walk in.

I had a date to meet her here last night.
I wasn't man enough to talk to her.
They say she sat an hour and watched the discs
Go round and round in this old Wurlitzer.

    B-2's a song to make your sad heart break
    About a soft green love that might have been.
    I wish I knew the button I could push to make
    The front door open and my girl walk in.

I hate to think of her waiting alone
In this dark bar with just the jukebox light.
She'll probably never want to try again
But just in case she does, I'll wait all night.

    G-4, that's our song, for her and me.
    It says be brave and try to trust again.
    I press the worn-down button, I look up and think I see
    The front door open and my girl walk in.

The brightly-lighted jukebox seems to be
A different world that's full of melody.
A skinny dime will make it all begin
And go through the whole thing once again…

Die Sommernacht hat mir's angetan (1971–1973)

It was the summer night that came over me,
walked through me, in my permeable condition,
as if I were a wild surmise, and perhaps
thought me windy: "It's windy," the summer night
said about me.

All over New England tonight people are wild surmises,
for the possible is too anxious, the night is too sweet,
the parenthesis of skin and air, the parenthesis which
we live, is too unstable, and the night takes us.
The night takes and reimagines us.
It has no estrangement:

Tim, so much is speakable
and is not what we fear
or have lost, but lies open to us, when we wake to work
which also imagines us.

Phantom Limb (1971–1973)

No, of course not; *no one* can bear
the bad losses, of what was never ours,
our reason, our love — say, our limbs themselves.
And our senses, what keeps turning from us.

Someday you like Nietzsche will be heard upstairs
to cross and recross, swarming like adrenalin
always on the same spot,
will be heard, heavy and hollow above, by unstrung women

all over the house: like Nietzsche to Nazis
ours would have been one of the great
overdetermined loves, had it been ours.
Now nothing will mitigate the sickness of loss

but, say, a rage of self-amputation
that sets our limbs, our loves, parading against us
as the stomach refusing its nourishment,
so the wrist its hand, the groin its thigh, nothing will save.

There, under the groin, the nerves, inundated
and corroded, drown and are undone,
for obscure reasons of desire, in blood.
Thus the phantoms are sent to the outskirts of the self

impersonating our limbs, but here begins the uncertainty.
Or if it would. Of course — of *course* it hurts.
Move here these, the bad, the deepened and stagy
limbs, whose life is loss —[1]

---

1   Some drafts end the final line with a period rather than a dash.

Two P.O.W. Suicides (1972)

"A program of foreign aid: we camped in the airfield,
wore khaki, and walked around with shovels.
It was a farce. I kept getting promoted"
　　the dream said, in the voice of a friend
young a couple of years back when he died
from a landmine in a program of foreign aid.

That was the closest to truth in the dream,
not verisimilar, not intimate, but
I take from the dead what I get,
and like it — similarly, I hope,
some little of what's ours might grow available.
So I struggle to keep in charity

with happy endings, returning prisoners
having now to work on their marriages. Each
one owes, to about a hundred American
families, a son: the wrong ending:
men with no legs, even, owe me a friend
and so does every thing that demands to be asked

whether it wasn't better to die. Nothing will make
this interrogation possible, not torture or maiming,
only, maybe, the black confusion of survival
the shrinks say must grow worse. Just old depression.
Just old death, soldiers, just your own old
resources, what repeats, distorts, coming through.

Once There Was a Way to Get Back Homeward (1969–1971)

It had been in the sinking swamps
                           the 3-toed scaly horse
who saw in the egg his oval sun,
                           the fragmentary mate.
He knew she was there because she
                           peed on trees.
Confusion died, the wolf
                           her child cut away
would dash her breasts on things
                           to make the trees accept
until she found and fed
                           the infant men.
Later the only way to get back
                           home was through confusion.
Sight, sleep, the fragmentary world
                           were there —
not there enough for the functioning and
                           functioning mind where
I was the voyage no one could permit.

The Ring of Fire (1968–1969)

Apollo I fire, January, 1967

Inside the capsule rolled up in a babyish ball
he had started to emerge by the escape-hatch
into the natural world of natural accident
because the whole thing happened rather slowly.
It took him several seconds to realize
what harm his desire to see the moon had done him,
and even seeing how he was going to die
he didn't see at once that it was a tragedy,
only that it was as high as he would get;
and something pressed upon him quickly and brightly

and now he sees the fire and being inside it
is like a dentist who has crushed a tooth
that lies along the gum in rosy shards,
but must to the gagged child whisper from the height
of a taught fatherly vision, firmly, "You're all right."

The Prince of Love in the Desert Night (1968–1969)

The prince of love in the desert night
and the golden cowgirl wallward flew.
They hurtled in the little room
and danced a dance I never knew

as if the mad and the crippled old
has risen with a wild accord
and ruptured in a sudden dance
the sordid loins we had ignored.

Artery (1969–1971)

Like Plath, it began with a finger sliced.
But knowingly. Blood was to be let.
Not even fasting had subdued the metabolic
return, again, of daring freaks of the blood:
it thought it wanted out, then, to fall out

deep into loss. That was understood,
that was the edge she needed
and so far we went with her; she took then
though, her wrists, which were her own,
no one took them from her, in short she died.

Planets may bear life; not she, her delicate continent
held rock and supported nothing
that moved from within itself; much was extinct.
Rock has its own behavior and behaves in beauty:

its demeanors are stress and craze:
it crawls: it buckles and can only refuse.
It quivers on its bed
in stony ways, it withholds
itself, susceptible to robbery and rape.

Pain is constitutive all right, always believe it.
That pain is not precisely constitutive
is only the space we have for excitement and the bad
surprises — compact into the melten core —
On this earth now too much space by one more.

A Death by Water (1969–1971)

There was a real death on a real summer night.
I rocked and rocked, to offer the death, room and time,
but it had taken its own time and contracted its own room
and was really gone.

I was so adequate on that chair,
so naked, compact, inexorable, and rich.
I worked. I was all there.
Not dead in struggle like a fish.

It will not be borne — I want to say — we are lost.
I want to rock this death out, but it's already
out: it *is* bearable. But at the usual cost.
This world has rocked me badly.

Yellow Toes (1969–1971)

Yellow toes will not move from
superficial ice in the soul;
the ice is blind that tears itself
and screams in stupidity

"For shit! I will kill myself!";
life supports this pain of
feet, freezing to the spot.
Then goes out the head of the mariner

up and down the wave.
He sees horizon all around.
The horizon is a wave.
The blind submarine of his body

pushes, and resists, and extends
its soft periscope, its eye.
In the hostile medium
the pressure and twist of cold

support him, almost.
"If I could only talk to the fishes," but no,
for the fishes make love on his broad feet,
so he dreams of the desert.

Desire dies,
childhood we cannot want,
vanity brushes dust from the shoulder
of our deepest failure.

Soutine (1969–1971)

I want to be a blown-up photograph:
when you're far away
I'm there,

if you touch me there's
nothing behind me,
just the feeling grains;

there's a cat that I think I am,
too — pink and brown,
white-throated, white-legged,

compact, but a great mother!
It's Soutine, and she has a crumpled ear.
I pick her up for

some stroking,
she purrs in long grains
slips down my hands like sand

in grains
doesn't like me much:
I'm a pool of rice leaked from a grocery bag

a pool at the bottom of the bed
I'm a dry weight in my hand
rolling balls…. No, I'm on a city corner;

suburban girls who want to belong
suck in both cheeks
over their hard and hollow mouths.

You get tired,
Can't spit it out
the dusty pea of chewing gum

can't swallow it
make you sick....
When I blow up....

Another Poem from the Creaking Bed (1969–1971)

When the first white man rolled into Owens Valley
before Los Angeles needed the water, it was very green;
and even within memory you drove by yourself
in a truck over Westguard Pass from Bishop
back to Deep Springs.
We can never, in the future, enter the valleys like that.
Although we are certainly a godly image,
it is only when we cross to the window like giraffes
in the dark
that the absent curtain will not rustle sexually
between
what we are and what we want.

    And so shiver together your massy brow
    and make your five hot fingers be five cities
    across my chin, shoulders, bottom,
    and the bay area.
    So if you cannot wake me, hold me, and surround
    my quaking, hollow dreams:
    networks of communication and transportation stringing
    along the suburbs carrying a senseless voice
    from my head, motion without muscle
    tone — trying, like the molten, magnetic earth,
    to waken and go on.

Between what we are and
what we want, runs like electricity
poetry.
We are more than this. But we desire certain
words; we love shame, and need the embarrassment
of a nerveless, unlovely communication:
we hear our hearts creaking in
mysterious leather straps.

So let us take the wanderlust and go
to Ames, Bliss, Provo, Olmstead:
names from a bitterer, firmer age.
Forget to me both what
we are, and what we want, and come
to me bundling passion, with a giraffe's legs.

Cain (1969–1971)

Like the Persian prophet I look down
as Abel breathes asleep
swaddled in green, his golden head
enclosed like an artichoke heart.
About him grow the vegetables lately
named, cabbage and lettuce,

broad leaves under my cheek, while above
hangs the green grape, the only tree in the valley.
Such memories occupy my mind
as Abel, remembered in his chair,
or winding with deliberation
through his indifferent fingers my sleeky hair.

He is sleeping on the center of the world:
the flat earth grinding circles under the flat sky,
the center still, while the periphery
rends it, running or skulking like drooling dogs.
Yammer ahead like a smooth-backed, willful bitch;
or in the desert night, drag our hearts with memory.

The City and Man (1969–1971)

Pickle-faced Estupinan, it is always you
Who in the warmest dreams that later people my days
Capture me and consign me to the asylum or prison
As if, pleasingly, you were a stranger.
I can almost remember a crime against this city
But prison and your holding me thus by the wrists
Redeem it satisfactorily, as I vision
Into the intimate city more marked, in these dreams,
By our friendships. City beside city spread
Across the countryside I draw toward me like an afghan:
In San Francisco you imitate me under the menacing strobe
Or we walk through Ithaca's gorges under floating fairy palaces
While an arsonist is somewhere, and Washington in flames.
This will be a prison without riots or escape
And I shall write on all the walls:
"Stone walls do not a prison make." Waking from that dream I cried
To see the unfiltered sun at my free window
As in St. Augustine and Ithaca and San Francisco
And country and city, all that lay between.

Lullaby (1969–1971)

Lullay, lullay, like a child,
Shiver in sleep, thou art beguiled.

Pity the sensuous caravan
That shuffles in thy body's sleep;
I have thee bounded in my arms
And will thy safety silent keep,
Will turn to seek thy gaze awake,
Thine open eyes curved and wild
As turneth earth to the waning moon.
Lullay, my darling, like a child,
Shiver in sleep, thou art beguiled.

We shelter in the waning eaves
Over the night, beneath the rain,
In autumn's middle, and where the year
Slants to the earth and back again.
Beguile thee, love, from slivering time
And I shall guard thee yet awhile
From the nakedness that children fear;
And so besleep thee like a child
While as in sleep thou art beguiled.

No More Dusk (1969–1971)

No more dusk, on the porch,
where girlfriends in sleeping bags try to tell secrets
and cry over Walt Whitman

and no more nights, in bed where I
turn away under him, breathing calmly
and trying to cry —

the future has stopped sweating.
It lies pink and unwilling
since months ago I acquiesced to

do what I could
and shut up like a dormouse, so to write now
is a choice I won't make until —

Sleepy, unwilling, I always turn
to lie on him lightly, but
enough;

Renoir says, "I paint with my penis;" it must
be gorgeous, limp, taken day by day
as I'll go now, through a world of colors.

Ribs of Steel (1969–1971)

This skin is discrete,
red, and hot, that stretches to
your remotest tender, elastic parts

spreading listless fever.
Our memory stills with fear
secreted in your own mother's dreams

as dry as a mouth: your rasp of fever;
my rasp, rasp of love.
It is even in your shrinking eye

and I move to remember
the wheeled bed where my mother
looks like a boy, legs akimbo with

hospital apparatus,
irises sliding in a crescent
over wallpaper eyes, drawling gibberish;

I wait for them all to leave, so she will
stop it and speak to me,
but the doctor is leaving directions with

my father, who is, however, surreptitiously
peeking down at the pages of an
absorbing modern novel.

So in childhood and youth, sleeping alone,
we see what the truth is worth,
but still it is sometimes gratifying to

say it anyway. This skin is discrete,
waterproof, and impervious to fever.
Even moving in tender silence

like white whales heaving in play
imitating the lofty Klein bottle
and inside outside, we would be

just here
as the world is a white cave
in which

the red lobsters boil in passion
and grapple slantways, to find
their own remarkable parts.

To a Friend (1969–1971)

I
To make the turning of the day
more like the turning over of sleep
I have turned again to Wyatt
just as the agitation of the journey,
heart spinning on its heels and not speaking,
makes us lie down in the road. O make my bed
both long and narrow, a good dirt road
with the rain falling in our eyes, and the worms will
crawl half across, and maybe a green snake.
But what you said, is why I'm lying here
knowing I have to think — my heart is floating away —
and perhaps, run over by a bicycle,
soon to crawl away in both directions.[2]

II
When, in minute script, the children write of torture
that must always end with castration, their blank cheeks
and brows will darken only at the after dream:
to wake in terror and find it done,
in a white bed, without desire, surrounded
by loving friends, empty, inconsolable:
with even the fever of torture not to be regained.
Warm children give up, when they sleep,
to the tight blanket and the pillow that makes them blush
the warmth of their dreams and bodies. So that when they rise
they surrender it entirely, the shell of warmth, and go
out trembling. And you, when you collapsed
in the lethal desert, may also have wondered
what would remain after the liquefying sleep.
The years in which Abelard had awakened in your brain
from sudden sounds on the stair, to find it done,
stood over you in a feminine intuition.

---

2   This stanza is crossed out in the manuscript version.

You turn to yourself like a hermaphrodite
and black out in dry-bubbling speculation.

III
Aristotle, tell me please
how is a very small *polis*
different from a very large
hermaphrodite?
Well, you see, it's partly
a matter of ends. The hermaphrodite has two,
which is hardly natural.

IV
Ah, friend, this fuzzy cactus tongue
must be a joke, a joke about a dream
of the desert: this incongruous, broad flower
a trivial metamorphosis of a traveller
who died in the valley at noon, lacking water
turning and turning in black dreams, as a child
lies still, with all his warm diffusive strength
intending to get up and go to the bathroom.
But no. It is not a flower, not an idle gaping;
it is a manly city that awakes
discrete upon its hill. But on the roofs
wry blackbirds turn and turn inexplicably,
whether we wake or sleep, upon themselves.

When In Minute Script (1969–1971)

1.

When, in minute script, small children write of torture
that must always end with castration, their blank cheeks
and brows will darken only at the after dream:
to wake in terror and find it done,
in a white bed, without desire, surrounded
by loving friends, empty, inconsolable:
with even the fever of torture not to be regained.
Warm children give up, when they sleep,
to the tight blanket and the pillow that makes them blush
the warmth of their dreams and bodies. So that when they rise
they surrender it entirely, the shell of warmth, and go
out trembling. And you, when you collapsed
in the lethal desert, may also have wondered
what would remain after the liquefying sleep.
The years in which Abelard had awakened in your brain
from sudden sounds on the stair, to find it done,
stood over you in a feminine intuition.
You turn to yourself like a hermaphrodite
and blackout in dry-bubbling speculation.

2.

Aristotle, tell me please
how is a very small *polis*
different from a very large
hermaphrodite?

To a Swimmer (1969–1971)

The day you won your school the race
just such must have been the stirless
eyes within your speculative face
out of the water, just as when
looking up from a violent grappling
on my shivering breast you stare
under your wet forehead straggling defiant hair.

Surety, desire, doubt, hurt, in your
curved eye who would think:
I've imagined you the huddled poolside
shivering schoolboy, but the act
proves triumph, triumph. And so silent
are we, broad faces, that the truth
will stir between us, treading the shining water, fact.

Untitled ('Wonder no more upon the mysteries') (1969–1971)

Wonder no more upon the mysteries:
The silent man has tempted the lean cat
From its wild refuge behind the radiator
By means of wiry nerves and a saucer of milk.
From under the puritanic sweater of his wrists,
Which are rather childish, and his round long hands
Submit it to a civilizing caress.
Then silently turns round the silent man
And from the kitchen door the earth unrolls
With stars and orchards like a painted parchment;
The silent orbs uncurl, with the silent man
Stroking their furry bellies and knotted nipples.
"Wild cat, beware the terrible cooing of women."

From an Ending for 'The Triumph of Life' (1969–1971)

Rousseau has disappeared. The narrator fervently vows to know himself, and mercifully falls asleep. In his sleep, he sees two beautiful women, Asia and Ashtar, approaching. He has a frightening hallucination concerning them, and awakens.

When I awoke, it was as it had been.
Ashtar and Asia still approached the spot
Where I upon the flat and brightening plain

Lay still. At last they reached my grassy plot
And stretched to me their white and open hands
Which I accepted. Words they uttered not,

But drew me to my feet to see me stand
A head above them, and then drew me on
With fleet, mysterious steps across the land.

I felt a curious clarity at the run
As if to move beside these dark-haired women
Were moving through a tortuous maze headlong:

Or seeingly interfolded in the dimming
Maze of Astarte's soul, in its turning;
Or musically lucid, to be skimming

Asia's heart, while in her breast sojourning.
So was my heart by motion intertwined
In the purest light, with the acutest burning,

Nor has it ever since been still — or blind.
And then we stopped. I saw a barren place
Without a trace of other humankind,

A mountainous rock, with others at its base
Carelessly strewn. I felt unwilling awe:
Such God-abandoned barrenness of space!

And then I felt the speechless sisters draw
My body to the ground, and lay my head
Gently upon a boulder — hot and raw,

A companionable, if an ungentle bed,
But I could not be still, and so Ashtar
Bent over me, and quiet-voiced she said:

"Stranger, we have travelled very far,
And this is a hallowed place. Be still therefore.
We cannot say what mysteries these are,

But here the earth to heaven has a door,
and wisdom here rewards the vigilant."
Then by a name I cannot speak she swore,

And round the mountain, through the boulders slant
In the desert afternoon whereon the sun
Shone without mercy, they began to chant

And chanting, round the landscape wild to run:
Their song was strange and soft. When they began
I feared to die beneath the heavy noon,

But through my agitation soon there ran
A visionary grace from their wild song;
And soon my mazèd eyes beheld a span

Running from earth to heaven all along!
It was a ladder reaching from the sky,
And down the ladder multitudes did throng:

An army in its triumph walking by;
Without a marching order or parade
They passed and passed in natural array,

Both up and down, with quiet promenade,
Each on his own implicit purpose bent.
Then Ashtar drew me from where I was laid

And took me to the place of the descent.
Modestly hid, we watched the men progress
Flushed on by a continual increment:

They swelled and passed in numbers limitless,
The floodgates of the sky being flung wide,
As if a race mighty and numerous,

Impelled into an onward-rushing tide,
Were yet moved on each by his energies:
For though the human torrent had no guide,

It came upon the rocks with purposeful ease
And seemed, in sort, to moderate the scene,
Creating from the barrenness surcease,

And swarming the vast boulders in between
Making them seem familiar and sweet:
As on a map of an unknown demesne

Names that we know we may with pleasure greet.
No, this was not the blind, anonymous mass
That shows its vain desires in every street:

I marked in every face as in a glass
Such well-known, individual lineaments
As when our dearest friend we overpass

Upon the road; but never had I met
A man of these! Yet were their faces clear
And intimate, although magnificent

And in a mass they moved in their career.
I turned to Ashtar's beauty with a cry:
"Who are the men that pass before me here

And sweetly scale a ladder from the sky?
The stately progress of the human wave
Strikes godlike my all-too-unsteady eye:

Are these the gods or ancient heroes brave?
What is the lasting certainty they follow
That makes their faces confident and grave:

Is it some mystery of long-ago,
Philosophy or religion, or are these
The envy of my blinded guide Rousseau,

Who by their introspection have found peace
And knowledge? –Surely these are men who *know
Themselves* — and thus the hungry fates appease —

Say 'yea!'" Ashtar turned slowly to me. "No,"
And sate me down with strange serenity.
"I will detail to you this human flow,

Then will my sister guide you to the quay
Whence to embark a voyage semblable;
But now relax; observe; listen to me."

But sorely was my nerve irritable,
And agitation kept me from repose:
I heard with vast astonishment her fable

And fear lest it my soul should discompose:
But she was calm and secret. She began,
Taking me in her long arms to inclose:

"Here is the truth unfathomable of man:
Take all your little words of what and why
And fit your little knowledge in their span

And thus explore the world until you die:
Define, propose, corroborate, and prove;
And only death will teach you that you lie.

You have beheld Rousseau, whose words reprove
Like murderous acts the impulse of his soul,
For with his body died the springs of love

Because he would his love as fact enroll
Down to its various parts, which namèd are:
As if a million names could make it whole!

And this is where philosophers must err:
Not that they don't but that they think they can
Begin to *know themselves,* as if they were

A list of parts and passions, not a man:
As if the word were not a mere invention
Of human thought, but rationed out its ken.

The greatest mystery is not definition:
In naming out our parts, we name our chains:
The mystery awaits the comprehension

Of those who see that wholeness is humane:
To be themselves must comprehend the world:
To name ineffable mysteries is vain.

And now before you, multitudes unfurl
Who seem to walk in peaceful certainty:
But it is only mysteries encurled

The deeper into their humanity.
The incredible void is deeply intervolved,
And at its center there is poetry.

Shakespeare is there, in whom the void resolves
At last upon the world like heavenly dew:
He encompasses but does not name his love —

Fantastically, knowing that nothing is true
But what transpires on us beyond expression
In the dark night when every old is new.

And so the metaphors in sweet succession
Radiate from a center of unknowing:
Murder, senility, and dispossession

From mystery to poetry outgrowing:
Love moves within, but love unnamed, unknown:
Its immemorial agitation slowing.

Shakespeare proceeds with gravity, alone.
Behind him Wyatt moves who sought a stay
In poetry between the dark and dawn:

He turns with us again the winding way
To make us know eternally the fleet
Point before we emerge into the day —

Embodying the mystery of conceit
As if it could be borne like England's crown.
And there beside him is the cockney Keats

Of whom I cannot speak."
She stopped. I, in an unspeakable fear,
For some more certain matter cast around.

At last: "And what of Plato? Is he here,
Or all that is not mortal of him?" "Yes,
Plato, invisible, is very near,

But is not as the rest, for bodiless
And comfortless he wanders; he assumed
The mystery, but did not acquiesce

At last to bear it freely, and is doomed
In part therefore to suffer ignorance."
Suddenly Ashtar was in tears, and dumb.

I brooded until Asia's advance;
And then we could not speak, but hand in hand
Began to walk across the world of trance.

The vision disappeared as it began,
And then we walked in tears a little way
Till Asia stopped and said: "You are a man."

And then she kissed my brooding tears away
And took me in an intimate embrace
And stirred within my heart such disarray

As nothing from my memory could erase.
And then she rose and quickly turned away
Nor let me see the corner of her face
And left me in the desert where I lay.

***

I waken here, but do not arise
For every motion is within me rolled
As by the sea; I am devitalized

And comprehend vitality untold
Around me, like the still dreams of the brave.
Our words are acts, but the truth interfolds

Motionless in the center of the wave,
In metaphor and the mystery of love.
For Shelley turning in his watery grave,
All human agitation stillness proves.

T.E. Lawrence and the Old Man, His Imagined Tormentor
(1967–1968)

As if Arabia were a broad-leaved book
and the rest of his life had been the merest tenets
of its philosophies, he cocked his head
like a child in bed, and curiously invented
a logical machine of storybook torture
that ran on lies to friends and ended with
the physical rod, on certain anniversaries.
But when he took the book in his dry hand
it became cold and curved, a scimitar
in the hand of the Old Man; it ought to have cut
his husk of manhood. What a machine! He was left
without the book he turned to in his sleep.
Suicide is a machine. Arabia
unfurls her terms like an absurd equation;
the silent Wailing Wall; or a Buddha's palms.

Movie Party,
    Telluride House, Ithaca, New York (1967–1968)

I.

O stunning hamstrings, her back-pointed legs
Stand brightly by him, him whose childish arm
Rests on his backside round as apples. Here
The smartest of a smarting generation
Gather for learning, strength, and luxury.
All come in presently to join the party.

II.

The mad projector once subdued, they sit
Perching in conscious clusters on cocked legs
Triangulate the screen, the moving shadows
Shielding the false decades wherefrom this spring
Is winding. And presently, being so ruled,
They are sisters and brothers touched with intimacy:

Passing at breakfast; morning anger; or now,
Watching together, or coffee: unknown to courtship
Intimacy beyond philosophy, watching
As they grow in one another's days. Or watch
For they see in the great red House's crumbling moods
A haven for the examined life; or watch

For all the shadowed corners of generations
To spy upon each other, decades outrolling.
Some are the sons of dead men or of madmen
And quarrelling women; one like Prospero
Creates his magician's state in lettered studies,
One in the chambered love of remembered names;

And one, most loved, is like the honey of bees
Spooned upon bread and let sit — or waking after
Crying in dreams, for he sits upon the eyes
In confident sweet crustiness, as grainy

As an old movie. One father is a spy.
The whirring decades coil upon the screen.

There are movies, too, in Ward 3-East sometimes
At the clinic in Bethesda, where the adult
Manic-depressives shucking off their families
And own volition are gathered, watching themselves
Crabwise upon the sands of 'Thirties shadows
Like a thing of their own generation. Although mind moves them

Slantways across the course of human love.
Who that is born and has not given birth
Can crumple up his heart in judgment? — Caught
Like a lone balloonist in a contracting skin
They soon enough will bear and judge, who watch
The Oak Ridge suicide, and the drugged mother,

Paul Aebersold who is incontinent.
The young topple remorseful generations,
Learn and grow strong, they exercise their minds
Rending and comforting. In this gymnasium
They strip for battle with the naked elders
Whose bodies droop with patience coarse as grain.

III.
O stunning hamstrings, her back-pointed legs
Stand brightly by him, him whose childish arm
Rests on his backside round as apples. Here
With brightness slanting upward from the valley
She takes his elbow between her finger and thumb,
In oblique shadows turning to join the party.

Falling in Love over The Seven Pillars (1967–1968)

"I loved you, so I drew these tides of men into my hands
And wrote my will across the sky in stars."
When I was fourteen this was my only study,
Leaned, after school, over the grandiose
Pipings of the queer soldier, partly seduced
By the uncandor of his pennyworth glory.
At twenty you loved him because he was a stoic.
The decade-weary margins now unfold
Again, the flyspecks pressed obediently
Like flowers, but in passive files, lie open:
All his perversions are dead, and all his deaths
And backward grimaces, the muffled iambs,
Smother like mummies into eternity:
His passion too, and his sincerity
Pocked like a shield by all his tragedy.
How much he tricks us! yet we see by now
What he at last regards: only himself
And truth; where Sophocles had time and age,
Shakespeare senility and transparency.
Gaze, love, upon this volume with secretive eyes:
I will lid it again and again, and turn to your stoic charms.
It is heavy and full. Its binding is falling off;
I used to gaze so much at the much-too-elfin
Secrets of all its portraits and photographs:
The book is brown and profound, with a little gilt;
Your face is closed and fine, and watches me
Like a brave comrade. As for my poetry,
God grant it greater love and equal chastity.

Calling Overseas (1967–1968)

Thou know'st the mask of night is on my face;
And the hours thrash their legs across the Atlantic
Like drowning sailors from some piggybank;
Or else naked, like the women painted
As queens of hearts on packs of dirty cards.
The queen of my heart is reclining in excitement

And quite, quite naked; her Carthaginian court
Humming and scurrying like my anthill body.
I sing with the sluttishness of a vain virgin
Who has read the *Aeneid*; I sing of Heloise
For whom was first unmanned and then ordained
Pierre Abelard of Saint-Denis; or of you,

Just such a scholar as he, so quick and hurt,
O nothing ill come near thee! and of your tender
Fraternal friends who loved you, and the man who taught
The passions and beauty, and loved you till you left him.
And lastly the vain virgin sings of herself
Speaking persuasively into the humming box.

What the Poet Thought
And What She Found in the Telluride Files: (1967–1968)

          — The image of a drowned four-year-old
child is sufficiently horrible, but it is the memory of his weight
on my arm and the sun-bleached baby down on his back as last
summer I waded with him into deep water that makes the fact
of his death real and painful.

All year I've been so brave and mummy, writing
"O don't be lonely — I love you" to you far away;
And how our children are to be fat and red
Piglets. And April creeps on the ocean, as soft
As a comforter. And I lean upon your arm
As we pace out along the shoals of the dead

I lean upon your arm and like a child
With a firm and palpable round neck and chin
Toe-pointing tread the blanching sand; thin back
Bleached and curved like a wave on the earth; for it drowned,
Fingers, shoulders, insteps, and the bright trunk.
And did your father listen to the knock,

Knock of exhausted asthma from your thin bed,
The rebellion of the terrifying ribs?
And did we hear the scissoring of your throat
Gasping and sobbing? — yet we now step forth
Weeping invisibly as children, until
We have roamed the bank and are tired; then we shall wait.

Epilogue: Teachers and Lovers (1967–1968)

It is, of course, a poem after all.
O after I am tired of the game
Of images of images, O I would
Move you into a turbulent speculation
With the stroke of eyes, the inappropriate question.
O mon semblable, let your ears flap wide;

I wish desirously to be the bride
Of one. I seeingly trust, as all about him
Lap wormwood tongues of friends. O womanish
He vanished; he is ill; and they say still
He loved them, with his equivocating mind
And bitterly. Such passions are not nice,

I shiver at their tenderest disguise:
The coverlet tendered as he sorely wept
For a baby's death; or his own severed breath
Locking his teeth into a furious friend.
They are fast foes; he worries like a woman;
His heart hangs bottom-upward like a sloth

And takes with gravity the tendered limb.
Some of these images are courtesy of
A palsied teacher with tragic olive jowls
Mocking his students into filial tears.
"I think he only loves the world for him."
Shakespeare goes down from Belmont into Venice

As pederast teachers file into the past.
My mind has circled, these six years, upon
The men's room of a Y in Washington
Where the wry image of a handsome Frenchman
Eluded me at last. O tears of eleven,
This was the poetry of a vain virgin,

Her passion all *With Lawrence in Arabia*;
Will you not weep; no no not weep, but ask
Curious questions? My slight friend the snake
Who rattles like an insincere magician
Has currant eyes and mocks me as he ropes
Around and round, like poems about poetry.

He brushes from my cheek a puzzled tear
But will not love me as he does the corn
Silken hair of a grave and pickle-faced freshman.
O Socrates, I would be your Athens now,
Or God's Jerusalem! Men are for men, and poems
For poetry. She stopped, and shook her hair,

Having moved her mind to verses to make you read.

*The Last Poem of Yv*r W*nt*rs* (1967–1968)

Wife, though the vulgar madmen call us old,
Atrophied in our coffins, we still stand
Foremost among the wisdom of the bold,
And take grand Aristotle by the hand,
Sweet Plato, and others of olden times
Whose names are sweet to hear, and limp apart
With dignity through venerable rhymes,
To find at last the marshmallow-soft heart.

Saul at Jeshimon [First Variant] (1967)

And Saul lay in his tent, and the people pitched round about him... then said Abishai to David, God hath delivered thine ene-my into thine hand this day... and David said to Abishai, Destroy him not... but I pray thee, take now the spear that is at his bolster, and the cruse of water, and let us go...

1 Samuel 26: 5–11

Through shadows over the seductive sand
And across shapes I know better than sleep
Comes David, where we lie upon the slope;
As Jonathan dreams sweetly of his friend
Not knowing I am wakeful without end.
The lion child that I have hunted creeps
Into the tent for water
                              which now drops
Forever, into the terrifying sand.

Spilled water. Two men in my dream, lovestruck,
Lie with an ancient tome between their hands,
Passion an animal, haughty and fierce —
But turn again to the desired book;
And all our vain desires fall like tears
Upon the dumb and multitudinous sand.

Saul at Jeshimon [Second Variant] (1967)

1 Samuel 26

Over the seductive sand
from the lid of a curving hill
David drops on the plain
traverses the furrowed valley
thinking himself unseen.
David thinks that I sleep

couched in the savage camp
among the unmoving shadows;
but I know them better than sleep
and have listened, as well, wakeful
to every ranting infusion
between frail well and wall

of the dim aortic river.
David comes with such grace
I would think him a she-lion;
asleep in the tent beside
lies Jonathan who dreams
that David has come from the mountain

among the guardian shadows.
The loose and muscled boy
having killed his tens of thousands
comes within my curtains
troubled by my slack power.
He is a hunted lion child

and looking for water here,
but caught like a lone balloonist
in a contracting skin
the desert drawing around him
David forbears to kill.

I lie. I watch him.

He takes the water bottle
and smoothes the distended skin,
and pumps the water from it
upon the patient sand.
Sweet Jonathan beside me
dreams that it plumbs the sand.

***

Spilled water. Two men in my dream, lovestruck,
lie with an ancient tome between their hands,
passion an animal, haughty and fierce —
but turn again to the desired book,
and all our vain desires fall like tears
upon the dumb and multitudinous sand.

Siegfried Rex von Munthe, Soldier and Poet, Killed December,
1939, on the German Battleship Graf Spee (1965–1967)

If a man is no more
than a creaky fishnet
around some sea,
what is the power
of my father's death
so to stun me?

Heartbeaten tides
have washed him over;
yet here am I still
in the teeming medium
older only,
the struggling last

plasmic mortal
in his death's vast
and voided realm;
only remembering
twenty years
after his storm

the new-coined blindness
of an afternoon
in the spangled nursery;
copying in
fourfold precision
his glittering every

poem and letter.
What death then was
felt of the sunflecked
morsels alighting
within the dappling
nursery checks

of the son's heart,
or after the sun fell,
quilt-covert fantasies:
the trifling poet
of the deft and sordid
parcels despair

for the sun to steal
in quantum digestibles.
    You, father,
being a poet,
would understand
the fractioned thought,

of mankind blinded
but for the magician —
poet at the window
of the floodlit nursery,
seeing light conjoined
or discrete as dew

bubbling and falling
on vestigial fragments
of paternal bones.
Deceitful atoms beam
piecemeal on the seafloor.
    Eyeless fool, know

that that same poetry —
all we know of mercy —
kept for you Germany,
brought you to
this last filtering ocean
defending tyranny

and into vastness
humanly, flimsily.

That was our poetry, too,
and all our beauty
ephemeral necessity
stunned to virtue.

Lawrence reads La Morte D'Arthur *in the Desert* (1964)

Having killed
Six Turks
Personally, in style,
I will enjoy
Extreme quietness
For a while.

They shot
(Briefly) at our last
Flag. It sighed
And exhaled around
The wound, and died
As the wind died

And fell. Six
Hundred camels
Tramped its bellying.
This incident,
Neither vital nor
Particularly sullying,

Ended a certain
Revolution
Of colours. From
That battle, we
Without the shame-rag
Of Chivalry come

As frank as Arthur
After the fall
And free as Adam.
So are we all
The plainest equations
Reduced to Latin.

For man shall know
It was not Honour
That made Launcelot
Love Guenever.
It was not
   The mottoes, not

The morals, "Might
For Right," that brought
This gentle knight
To Camelot.
Each corruption,
Every night

That sows the seed
— Eternal spirochete of Eve —
Is of guilt
A dark haven
In the great house
My father built.

In one shadow
My stern mother
Still unmarried
Scolds the silence.
Here Elaine
The Rosy tarried,

Beckoning
To Launcelot.
Here is Prometheus,
Still surprised
By his fire,
Still curious.

Beneath the extinguished
Chandelier

Stands another
Of greater portent:
Young King Oedipus
Married his mother

Killed his father
Knowing nothing
Of Chivalry,
Only the divine
Architecture
Of, "to be,"

The celled house
Of human fate
Prometheus saw
That dazzled him;
The broken window
Of causal law;

The celled house
Of human knowledge
Of which the builder
Is the precious
Fire Prometheus
Grasped and flung.

Fair Arabia,
Pride abandoned
On some fouled desert,
Plain as Man,
Has only to watch
As the single hurt

Where she caught the fire
And knew the end
Cancers the hale
Tanned body.

Knowing as well
That I will fail,

I and Arabia
Sit and watch
Naked of pretense
As Prometheus.
We can laugh
From crumbling tents

At the great joke
We could not stop.
I have a body,
And the fleshy Arab
Is guilty as Eve
And twice as shoddy.

It's good to know
I couldn't help it.
Not with Honour
(It came to Launcelot)
Not with religion
(My mother a Puritan!)

It's good to know
So I can enjoy
So I can see
The Greater Aesthetic,
Winged and beaked,
Devour me.

Bibliography

Adams, Carol J. *The Sexual Politics of Meat: A Feminist-Vegetarian Critical Theory*. London: Continuum, 1990.

Allan, Jonathan A. 'Falling in Love with Eve Kosofsky Sedgwick'. *Mosaic: A Journal for the Interdisciplinary Study of Literature* 48.1 (March 2015), 1–16.

Ammons, A.R. *Collected Poems, 1951–1971*. New York: Norton, 2001.

Ariwara no Narihara. *Tales of Ise,* trans. Henry Harris. Boston: Tuttle, 1972.

Barber, Stephen and Clark, David A., eds. *Regarding Sedgwick: Essays on Queer Culture and Critical Theory*. New York: Routledge, 2002.

Bashō, Matsuo. *The Narrow Road to the Deep North and Other Travel Sketches*, trans. and ed. Nobuyuki Yuasa. London: Penguin, 1966.

Bennett, Paula. *My Life a Loaded Gun: Female Creativity and Feminist Poetics*. Boston: Beacon, 1986.

———. *Emily Dickinson: Woman Poet*. London: Harvester Wheatsheaf, 1990.

Bergman, David, ed. *Camp Grounds: Style and Homosexuality*. Amherst: University of Massachusetts Press, 1993.

Berlant, Lauren. *Cruel Optimism*. Durham: Duke University Press, 2011.

Bishop, Elizabeth. *Poems: The Centenary Edition*. New York: Farrar, Strauss, and Giroux, 1987.

Bohm, David. *Thought as a System*. London: Routledge, 1994.

Bond Stockton, Kathryn. *The Queer Child, or Growing Side-ways in the Twentieth Century*. Durham: Duke University Press, 2009.

Boulton, Meg. T*he Conceptualisation of Sacred Space in Anglo-Saxon Northumbria in the Sixth to Ninth Centuries*. Ph.D. thesis, University of York.

Bradway, Tyler. "'Permeable We!" Affect and the Ethics of Intersubjectivity in Eve Kosofsky Sedgwick's A Dialogue on Love'. *GLQ: A Journal of Lesbian and Gay Studies* 19.1 (2012), 79–110.

Brown, Angus. *Between Lines: Close Reading, Quotation, and Critical Style from Practical Criticism to Queer Theory*. Ph.D. thesis, Oxford University.

Bruhm, Stephen, and Hurley, Natasha, eds. *Curiouser: On the Queerness of Children*. Minnesota: University of Minnesota Press, 2004.

Bundtzen, Lynda. *Plath's Incarnations: Woman and the Creative Process*. Ann Arbor: University of Michigan Press, 1983.

Butler, Judith. *Precarious Life: The Powers of Mourning and Violence*. New York: Verso, 2004.

Campbell, Mary Baine. *The World, The Flesh, and Angels*. Boston: Beacon, 1989.

———. *Trouble*. Carnegie Mellon University Press, 2003.

Castle, Terry. *The Apparitional Lesbian: Female Homosexuality and Modern Culture*. New York: Columbia University Press, 1993.

Connor, Steven. *Beyond Words: Sobs, Hums, Stutters, and Other Vocalizations*. London: Reaktion, 2014.

Denman, Kamilla. 'Emily Dickinson's Volcanic Punctuation'. *The Emily Dickinson Journal* 2.1 (Spring 1993), 22–46.

Derrida, Jacques. "'Eating Well", or the Calculation of the Sub-ject: An Interview with Jacques Derrida'. In Elizabeth Weber, ed., *Who Comes After the Subject?*, trans. Peggy Kamuf et al., 255–87. Stanford: Stanford University Press, 1995.

———. *The Animal That Therefore I Am*, trans. David Wills. New York: Fordham University Press, 2008.

―――. *The Beast and the Sovereign,* vols. 1–2, trans. Geoffrey Bennington, eds. Marie-Louise Mallet et al. Chicago: University of Chicago Press, 2009–2010.

Desprets, Vinciane. 'From Secret Agents to Interagency'. *History and Theory: Studies in the Philosophy of History* 52 (2013), 29–44.

D'Silva, Joyce. 'The Welfare of Cows'. In Andrew Linzey, ed., *The Global Guide to Animal Protection,* 173–175. Urbana, Chicago: University of Illinois Press, 2013.

Edelman, Lee. *No Future: Queer Theory and the Death Drive.* Durham: Duke University Press, 2004.

Edwards, Jason. *Eve Kosofsky Sedgwick.* London: Routledge, 2009.

Ferenczi, Sándor. 'Confusion of Tongues Between Adults and the Child' (1933). In Michael Balint, ed., *The Language of Tenderness and of Passion,* 156–167. London: Karnac, 1994.

―――. *Thalassa: A Theory of Genitality.* 1938; London: Karnac, 1989.

Foer, Jonathan Safran. *Eating Animals.* London: Penguin, 2009.

Fong, Benjamin Y. 'Freud's Radical Talking'. *The New York Times.* 18 March 2012. http://opinionator.blogs.nytimes.com/2012/03/18/freuds-radical-talking/.

Forster, E.M. *A Room with a View.* 1908; London: Penguin, 2000.

Franklin, R.W. ed., *The Poems of Emily Dickinson: Reader's Edition.* Cambridge: Harvard University Press, 1999.

Fried, Michael. *Absorption and Theatricality: Painting and Beholder in the Age of Diderot.* Berkeley: University of California Press, 1980.

Freud, Sigmund. *Introductory Lectures on Psychoanalysis.* Harmondsworth: Penguin, 1987.

―――. *Historical and Expository Works on Psychoanalysis.* Harmondsworth: Penguin, 1986.

Fuss, Diana. *Human, All Too Human.* London: Routledge, 1996.

Gill, Jo. *The Cambridge Introduction to Sylvia Plath.* Cambridge: Cambridge University Press, 2008.

Glaser, Linda B. 'The College Years of Eve Kosofsky Sedgwick, A Founder of Queer Theory'. http://as.cornell.edu/college-years-eve-kosofsky-sedgwick-founder-queer-theory.

Gallop, Jane. 'Sedgwick's Twisted Temporalities, "or Even Just Reading and Writing"'. In E.L. McCallum and Mikko Tuhkanen, eds., *Queer Times, Queer Becomings*, 47–75. Albany: State University of New York Press, 2011.

Gunn, Thom. *The Man with the Night Sweats*. London: Faber, 1992.

Halberstam, Judith. *Female Masculinity*. Durham: Duke University Press, 1998.

Hanson, Ellis. 'The Future's Eve: Reparative Readings After Sedgwick'. *South Atlantic Quarterly* 110.1 (2011), 101–119.

Haraway, Donna J. *The Companion Species Manifesto: Dogs, People, and Significant Otherness*. Chicago: Prickly Paradigm Press, 2003.

———. *When Species Meet*. Minneapolis: University of Minnesota Press, 2007.

Hardy, Thomas. *Jude the Obscure*. London: Harper and Brothers, 1895.

Hawkins, Katherine. 'Woven Spaces: Eve Kosofsky Sedgwick's Dialogue on Love'. *Women and Performance: A Journal of Feminist Theory* 16.2 (July 2006), 251–267.

Herman, David. 'Storyworld/Umwelt: Nonhuman Experience in Graphic Narratives'. *SubStance* 40.1 (2011), 56–181.

———. 'Modernist Life Writing and Nonhuman Lives: Ecologies of Experience in Virginia Woolf's Flush'. *Modernist Fiction Studies* 59.3 (2013), 547–568.

Hiley, Basil. 'Process and the Implicate Order: Their Relevance to Quantum Theory and Mind'. Unpublished conference paper. 1 October 2005. https://www.ctr4process.org/sites/default/files/pdfs/lsi/Hiley%20paper.pdf.

Hoffmann, Yoel. ed., *Japanese Death Poems: Written by Zen Monks and Haiku Poets on the Verge of Death*. Boston: Tuttle, 1986.

Hu, Jane. 'I'm Nobody: Eve Sedgwick After Death'. 2 May 2013. http://www.theawl.com/2013/05/eve-sedgwick-after-death.

ID450 Collective, 'Writing the Plural: Sexual Fantasies'. *Criticism: A Quarterly for Literature and the Arts* 52.2 (Spring 2010), 293–307.

Irigaray, Luce and Burke, Carolyn. 'When Our Lips Speak Together'. *Signs* 6.1 (Autumn 1980), 69–79.

Irigaray, Luce. *This Sex Which Is Not One*. New York: Cornell University Press, 1985.

Jarrell, Randall. *The Lost World*. 1948; New York: Macmillan, 1966.

Kent, Kathryn R. *Making Girls into Women: American Women Writers and the Rise of Lesbian Identity*. Durham: Duke University Press, 2003.

———. '"No Trespassing": Girl Scout Camp and the Limits of the Counterpublic Sphere'. *Women and Performance: A Journal of Feminist Theory* 8.2 (1996), 183–203; and reprinted in Steven Bruhm and Natahsa Hurley, eds., *Curiouser: On the Queerness of Children*, 173–191. Minneapolis: University of Minnesota Press, 2004.

Klein, Melanie and Riviere, Joan, *Love, Hate and Reparation*. 1936; New York: W.W. Norton, 1964.

Koestenbaum, Wayne. 'A Manual Approach to Mourning'. In *My 1980s and Other Essays*, 65–70. New York: Farrar, Straus and Giroux, 2013.

Kopelson, Kevin. 'The Mother of Us All?'. *Substance* 43.1 (2014), 191–197.

Kosofsky, Leon and El-Baz, Farouk, *The Moon as Viewed by Lunar Orbiter*. Washington, DC: NASA, 1970.

Kristeva, Julia. *The Powers of Horror: An Essay on Abjection*, trans. Leon Roudiez. New York: Columbia University Press, 1982.

Kurnick, David. 'Queer Therapy'. *The Village Voice*. 3 August 1999. http://www.villagevoice.com/arts/queer-therapy-7155890.

Laquer, Thomas. *Solitary Sex: A Cultural History of Masturbation*. New York: Zone Books, 2003.

Lawrence, T.E. *The Seven Pillars of Wisdom*. 1926; Ware: Wordsworth, 1987.

Lorde, Audre. *The Cancer Journals*. San Francisco: Spinsters Ink, 1988.

———. *A Burst of Light*. Ithaca: Firebrand, 1988.

Love, Heather. *Feeling Backward: Loss and the Politics of Queer History*. Cambridge: Harvard University Press, 2009.

Lynch, Michael. *These Waves of Dying Friends: Poems*. New York: Contact, 1989.

Lytton, Edward Bulwer. *The Last Days of Pompeii*. London: Marshall Cavendish, 1976, with illustrations by Felix Gluck Press.

Malcolm, Janet. *Psychoanalysis: The Impossible Profession*. New York: Vintage, 1982.

Marcus, Sharon. *Between Women: Friendship, Desire, and Marriage in Victorian England*. Princeton: Princeton University Press, 2007.

Marvin, Garry 'Unspeakability, Inedibility, and the Structures of Pursuit in the English Foxhunt'. In Nigel Rothfels, ed., *Representing Animals*, 139–158. Indiana: Indiana University Press, 2002.

Merrill, James. *The Changing Light at Sandover*. New York: Athenaeum, 1982.

———. *Collected Poems*. New York: Knopf, 2002.

———. 'A Different Person: A Memoir' (1993). In J.D. McClatchy and Stephen Yenser, eds., *Collected Prose*. New York: Knopf, 2004, 457–683.

Munoz, Jose Esteban. 'Race, Sex and the Incommensurate: Gary Fisher with Eve Kosofsky Sedgwick'. In Elahe Yekani, Eveline Killian, and Beatrice Michaelis, eds., *Queer Futures: Reconsidering Ethics, Activism, and the Political*, 103–115. Aldershot: Ashgate, 2013.

Nelson, Maggie. *The Argonauts*. London: Melville, 2015.

Quinn, Emelia J. '"Is He a Martyr Or Is He a Fucking Jalfrezi?" Reading Islamophobia Through a Vegan Lens'. MA dissertation, University of York, 2014.

Patton, Cindy. 'Love Without the Obligation to Love'. *Criticism* 52.2 (Spring 2010), 215–224.

Payne, Mark. *The Animal Part: Human and Other Animals in the Poetic Imagination*. Chicago: Chicago University Press, 2010.

Pearl, Monica. 'Eve Kosofsky Sedgwick's Melancholic "White Glasses"'. *Textual Practice* 17.1 (2003), 61–80.

———. AIDS *Literature and Gay Identity: The Literature of Loss.* New York: Routledge, 2013.

Plath, Sylvia. *The Collected Poems*. New York: Harper Perennial, 2008.

Poitier, Sydney. dir, *A Warm December* (1973).

Rich, Adrienne. 'Compulsory Heterosexuality and Lesbian Existence'. In Henry Abelove, Michele Aina Barale, and David M. Halperin, eds. *The Lesbian and Gay Studies Reader*, 227–254. New York: Routledge, 1993.

Sedgwick, Eve Kosofsky. 'A Death by Water'. *Epoch* 23.3 (Fall 1973), 78–79.

———. 'Explicit' and 'The Palimpsest'. *Epoch* 24.2 (Winter 1975), 112–113.

———. 'Ring of Fire', 'An Essay on the Picture Plane', and 'When in Minute Script'. *Poetry Miscellany* 5 (1975), 42–44.

———. 'Sexual Hum'. *Salmagundi* (Winter 1979).

———. 'Trace at 46'. *Diacritics* 10.1 (March 1980), 3–20.

———. 'Sestina Lente'. *Massachusetts Review* 25.4 (Winter 1984).

———. *The Coherence of Gothic Conventions*. New York: Arno, 1985.

———. 'Whitman's Transatlantic Context: Class, Gender and Male Homosexual Style'. *Delta* 16 (1984), 111–124.

———. *Between Men: English Literature and Male Homosocial Desire*. New York: Columbia University Press, 1985.

———.

———. 'Selections from *The Warm Decembers*'. *Raritan* 6.2 (Fall 1986).

———. 'A Poem is Being Written'. *Representations* 17 (Winter 1987), 110–143; reprinted in *Tendencies*. Durham: Duke University Press, 1993, 177–214.

————. *Epistemology of the Closet*. Berkeley: University of California Press, 1990.

————. 'Writing, Gay Studies and Affection'. *Lesbian and Gay Studies Newsletter* 18 (November 1991), 8–13.

————. 'White Glasses'. *Yale Journal of Criticism* 5.3 (Fall 1992), 193–208, reprinted in *Tendencies*. Durham: Duke University Press, 1993, 252–266.

————. *Tendencies*. Durham: Duke University Press, 1993.

————. *Fat Art, Thin Art*. Durham: Duke University Press, 1994.

————. 'Our'. *Raleigh News and Observer*. September 25, 1994. and 'Penn Central: New Haven Line'. *Los Angeles Times Book Review*. October 2, 1994.

————. and Moon, Michael, Benjamin Gianni and Scott Weir, 'Queers in Single Family Space'. *Assemblage* 24 (August 1994), 30–37.

————. and Parker, Andrew, eds., *Performativity and Performance*. London: Routledge, 1995.

————. 'Pandas in Trees'. *Women and Performance: A Journal of Feminist Theory* 8.2 (January 1996), 175–183.

————, and Frank, Adam, eds., *Shame and its Sisters: A Silvan Tomkins Reader*. Durham: Duke University Press, 1996.

————. 'Afterword' to ed., *Gary in Your Pocket: Stories and Notebooks of Gary Fisher*, 273–291. Durham: Duke University Press, 1996.

————. and Moon, Michael, 'Confusion of Tongues'. In B. Erkkila and J. Grossman, eds., *Breaking Bounds: Whitman and American Cultural Studies*, 23–29. Oxford: Oxford University Press, 1996.

————, ed. *Novel Gazing: Queer Readings in Fiction*. Durham: Duke University Press, 1997.

————. Response to C. Jacob Hale, 'Leatherdyke Boys and Their Daddies'. *Social Text* 52–53 (Autumn–Winter 1997), 237–239.

————. 'Teaching "Experimental" Critical Writing'. In Jill Lane and Peggy Phelan, eds., *The Ends of Performance*, 105–115. New York: New York University Press, 1998.

———. *A Dialogue on Love*. Boston: Beacon, 1999.

———. *Touching Feeling: Affect, Pedagogy, Performativity*. Durham: Duke University Press, 2003.

———. 'Three Poems'. *Women and Performance* 16.2 (July 2006), 327–328.

———. 'Teaching/Depression'. *The Scholar and Feminist Online* 4.2 (Spring 2006). http://sfonline.barnard.edu/heilbrun/sedgwick_01.htm.

———. *The Weather in Proust*, ed. Jonathan Goldberg. Durham: Duke University Press, 2011.

———. 'The 1001 Seances'. *GLQ* 17.4 (2011), 451–516.

———. 'Writing the History of Homophobia'. In Jason Potts and Daniel Stout, eds., *Theory Aside*, 29–33. Durham: Duke University Press, 2014.

Sedgwick, Hal. A. 'A Note on "The 1001 Séances"'. *GLQ* 17.4 (2011), 452–453.

Sianne, Ngai. *Ugly Feelings*. Cambridge: Harvard University Press, 2007.

Solomon, Melissa. 'Flaming Iguanas, Dalai Pandas, and Other Lesbian Bardos'. In Stephen M. Barber and David L. Clark, eds., *Regarding Sedgwick: Essays on Queer Culture and Critical Theory*, 201–216. New York: Routledge, 2002.

Spivak, Gayatri Chakravorty. 'Translater's Preface' to Jacques Derrida, *Of Grammatology*, trans. Gayatri Chakravorty Spivak. Baltimore: Johns Hopkins, 1976.

Stein, Gertrude. *Tender Buttons: Objects, Food, Rooms*. 1914; New York: Dover, 1997.

Stephens, Elizabeth. 'Queer Memoir: Public Confession and/as Sexual Practice in Eve Kosofsky Sedgwick's *A Dialogue on Love*'. *Australian Humanities Review* 8 (May 2010).

Thomas, Lowell. *With Lawrence in Arabia*. London: Hutchison, 1924.

Turner, Lynn, ed. *The Animal Question in Deconstruction*. Edinburgh: Edinburgh University Press, 2013.

Ueda, Makoto, ed. *Bashō and his Interpreters: Selected Hokku with Commentary*. Stanford: Stanford University Press, 1992.

Vemeule, Blakey. 'Is There A Sedgwick School for Girls?'. *Qui Parle* 5.1 (1991), 53–72.

Vendler, Helen. *Part of Nature, Part of Us*. Cambridge: Harvard University Press, 1980.

Vincent, John. 'Flogging is Fundamental: Applications of Birch in Swinburne's Lesbia Brandon'. In Eve Kosofsky Sedgwick, ed., *Novel Gazing: Queer Readings in Fiction,* 269–298. Durham: Duke University Press, 1997.

Wada, Yoshiko Iwamoto. *Memory on Cloth: Shibori Now*. Tokyo: Kodansha, 2002.

———, Rice, Mary Kellogg, and Barton, Jane, *Shibori: the Inventive Art of Japanese Shaped Resist Dyeing*. 1983; Tokyo: Kodansha, 1999.

Wittig, Monique. *The Lesbian Body*. Boston: Beacon, 1986.

Wolfe, Cary. *Animal Rites: American Culture, the Discourse of Species, and Posthumanist Theory*. Chicago: Chicago University Press, 2003.

Wood, Sarah. 'Swans of Life (External Provocations and Autobiographical Flights that Teach Us How to Read'. In Lynn Turner, ed., *The Animal Question in Deconstruction,* 13–33. Edinburgh: Edinburgh University Press, 2013.

List of Contributors

Mary Baine Campbell is a poet and Professor of English and Comparative Literature at Brandeis University. Her books include *Wonder and Science: Imagining Worlds in Early Modern Europe* (winner of the MLA's Lowell Prize for best book), *The Witness and the Other World: European Travel Writing 400-1600*, and two poetry collections: *The World, the Flesh, and Angels* (winner of the Barnard New Women Poets Award) and *Trouble*. She is currently working on 16th- and 17th-century dreams and dream theories on both sides of the Atlantic.

Meg Boulton is a freelance lecturer in Art History teaching between Oxford and London. Her research interests centre on the conceptualization of space from the Medieval to the post-modern. Meg has published several articles on a range of material including the spatial and material aspects of early Anglo-Saxon Art and Architecture and the spatial implications of cabinets in the televization of *Agatha Christie's Poirot*. She is engaged in a longer-term research project on curiosity cabinets and Joseph Cornell boxes and is currently preparing a monograph on *Visualising Jerusalem in Anglo-Saxon England*.

Angus Connell Brown is a Leverhulme Early Career Research Fellow at the University of Birmingham. He is the author of articles on Henry James and Alan Hollinghurst. Angus is currently completing a monograph on the style of close reading in twentieth-century literary culture. His next project is focused on affect and the history of the book.

Jason Edwards is a Professor of Art History at the University of York and is the author of more than twenty articles, as well as *Eve Kosofsky Sedgwick* (2009) and *Alfred Gilbert's Aestheticism,* and the co-editor of collections on the Aesthetic interior, Joseph Cornell, British sculpture 1760–1830, and Victorian sculpture. Jason is currently completing a monograph on Sedgwick's work as a queer craftsperson.

Kathryn R. Kent is a Professor of English and Women's Studies and Gender and Sexuality Studies at Williams College. She is the author of *Making Girls into Women: American Women's Writing and the Rise of Identity* (2003), as well as numerous articles. She is currently working on an experimental biography of Eve Kosofsky Sedgwick, of which this piece is a small part. Katie is also working on a book on gender and sexuality in the Girl Scouts.

Monica B. Pearl is Lecturer in Twentieth-Century American Literature at the University of Manchester. She is the author of *AIDS Literature and Gay Identity: The Literature of Loss* and essays on *Fun Home, Angels in America,* Audre Lorde, Janet Flanner, Sedgwick's essay 'White Glasses', W.G. Sebald, and opera.

Ben Westwood is an AHRC-funded Wadham scholar reading for a doctorate in English at the University of Oxford. He also currently holds a fixed-term lectureship in English at Keble College, Oxford. His thesis focuses on intersections of animal figure and literary form in nineteenth-century British literature, while other interests include queer theory and the new field of vegan theory. Ben is the co-editor, with Emelia Quinn, of *Thinking Veganism in Literature and Culture: Towards a Vegan Theory.*